# COLLECTED
# LITERARY   ESSAYS

T0381932

A. W. Vendh

# COLLECTED
# LITERARY ESSAYS

## CLASSICAL AND MODERN

BY

## A. W. VERRALL, Litt.D.

KING EDWARD VII PROFESSOR OF ENGLISH LITERATURE
AND FELLOW OF TRINITY COLLEGE, CAMBRIDGE
HON. LITT.D., DUBLIN

EDITED BY

## M. A. BAYFIELD, M.A.

AND

## J. D. DUFF, M.A.

## WITH A MEMOIR

## Cambridge:

at the University Press

1913

CAMBRIDGE UNIVERSITY PRESS
Cambridge, New York, Melbourne, Madrid, Cape Town,
Singapore,  São Paulo, Delhi, Tokyo, Mexico City

Cambridge University Press
The Edinburgh Building, Cambridge CB2 8RU, UK

Published in the United States of America by Cambridge University Press, New York

www.cambridge.org
Information on this title: www.cambridge.org/9780521238083

First published 1913
First paperback edition 2011

*A catalogue record for this publication is available from the British Library*

ISBN 978-0-521-23808-3 Paperback

# PREFACE

THE essays contained in this volume have been collected from various periodicals, some of which are now difficult of access. The selection was made by the author a few months before his death, at a time when there was every expectation that he would live to see the republication. The names and dates of issue of the periodicals in which the essays originally appeared are given in the Table of Contents.

For permission to republish, our thanks are due to the editors of the *Quarterly Review*, the *New Quarterly*, the *Oxford and Cambridge Review*, the *Independent* (and *Albany*) *Review*, to Mrs M°Nalty, executrix and literary legatee of the late editor of the *Universal Review*, and to the Executive Committee of the National Home-Reading Union.

The Commemorative Address by Dr Mackail, which is appended to the Memoir, was delivered at a meeting of the Academic Committee of the

Royal Society of Literature on November 28, 1912. We are much indebted to him for his kindness in allowing us to include this valuable appreciation, and we have to thank the Society for permission to reprint it.

We have also to thank Mrs Verrall for valuable assistance.

M. A. B.
J. D. D.

*May* 1913.

# CONTENTS

*a* 5

# MEMOIR

Whatever way my days decline,
  I felt and feel, tho' left alone,
  His being working in mine own,
The footsteps of his life in mine.

*In Memoriam.*

ARTHUR WOOLLGAR VERRALL was born at
Brighton on February 5, 1851, and was the eldest
of a family of three brothers and two sisters. His
father, Henry Verrall, was a well-known solicitor
who held for many years the office of Clerk to the
Magistrates of the town. Since it is always interesting to trace the influences of heredity, some
characteristics may be mentioned here which seem
to have been part of the boy's natural debt to his
parents. From his father he would appear to have
derived his remarkable inductive powers, his simple
tastes and dislike of ostentation, and the patient
endurance with which he bore the sufferings and
disabilities of his later years. His mother's gift
embraced a rare conscientiousness, the aptitude for
languages and teaching, the delight in music and the
ear for rhythm. The tie of affection between mother
and son was unusually strong.

At the age of nine, his health being thought too fragile even for the conditions of a preparatory school, he was sent as a private pupil to the Rev. R. Blaker, Vicar of Ifield. Mr Blaker soon discovered the boy's genius for languages, and Greek was immediately begun. Progress was exceptionally rapid, and two years later Mr Blaker wrote:

> He certainly gives promise of more than ordinary scholarship, and if his health is good, I augur an honourable future for him....He evinces a quickness of comprehension which is remarkable for so young a boy. His memory is excellent, and he is able to retain facts and draw inferences from matters connected with his reading with wonderful clearness.

An amusing little story of nursery days perhaps gives an even earlier indication of his bent in this direction. The child was looking at some pictures of red-legged partridges, and was overheard saying to himself, 'Arthur is a good boy; he doesn't say *them's grouses*, he says *them's grice.*'

In 1863 he went to Twyford, the well-known preparatory school for Winchester, where he stayed a year and a half. His health during this time was, however, much broken. In 1864 he competed for a Winchester scholarship, and failed. No doubt the failure was a disappointment at the time, but in after years he would refer to it as really a piece of good luck, since if he had gone to Winchester, he would have been sure to go to Oxford! In this judgement we may concur, for we can see that Oxford would hardly have helped him to 'find himself.' The Greats course would have led him into fields of study foreign to his intellectual temperament, and for metaphysics he had a whole-hearted dislike, as he had for all speculation that promised to lead to no definite conclusion. Nevertheless, he had a great respect for Oxford and a special affection for Winchester, where he was a frequent visitor. The defeat was almost immediately retrieved. In October of the same year, at the suggestion of Dr Beard, a friend of his father, he was hurried off at a few hours' notice to compete for a scholarship at Wellington College. Though his name had not been previously entered, his candidature was accepted, and he gained the second scholarship, being just beaten by E. Heriz Smith, afterwards Fellow of Pembroke College, Cambridge. In a letter now before me, Dr Benson wrote that the boy 'was nearly though not quite equal to the first candidate....I like very much the boy's clear and unassuming manner, and am very glad nothing prevented him standing.' It was like Benson to add that he hoped he had 'been comfortable under the odd and hurried circumstances of his competition.' While at Wellington, Verrall must have experienced and observed many such instances of thoughtful courtesy, and as we know, they bore abundant fruit.

Mr Wickham of Twyford, in a letter written when the boy was leaving the school, repeats Mr Blaker's impression of his character and augury for his future. An earlier letter of Mr Wickham's contains one significant remark : ' I must try to get him to read a little Ovid next half year, to get him into more

style in his verses.' The boy, then, was capable of
independent reading at the age of thirteen, had
learned to dislike Ovid, and needed persuasion
before he would read him. This dislike Verrall
never lost, and I can recall the tone of real sadness
with which he once referred to the essential trivi-
ality of Ovid's art; it actually distressed him that
a man who could have done better things 'should
have left only piffle.' One can well believe that
the boy dimly felt the same disappointment, that
he was even at that early age seeking in his
author something more than the 'topmost froth of
thought.'

He entered Wellington at the end of his
thirteenth year. Naturally reserved, of a temperament unusually refined, and with enthusiasms pre-
dominantly intellectual, he was not one of those
best fitted for the rough and tumble of public school
life. 'Something of home-life,' he wrote in his
contribution to the Archbishop's *Life*, 'something
like the sympathetic and intelligent circle from
which I came, was almost as necessary to me as
bread and butter.' When he got into the Sixth, as
he very soon did, Benson's keen observation detected
this want, and he and Mrs Benson supplied it in the
best of ways, by treating the boy as one of the family.
He was continually in and out of the house, and
whenever he liked, which was two or three times
a week, he used to join the 'nursery tea,' at which
Dr and Mrs Benson were habitually present. The
value to him of this happy modification of the

ordinary conditions of school life, and the incalculable gain from these closer relations with two such natures, he always felt he could not overestimate. He would say, referring to those days, 'the Bensons made Wellington possible for me'; and he has written, 'He [Dr Benson] saved my health and my sense; I believe that he saved my life.'

If Verrall had written an autobiography (a thing incredible), not the least interesting period of it would have been that of his later school years. Unfortunately even recollections of him as he appeared to others are disappointingly meagre. One school-fellow writes, 'As soon as Verrall was in the Upper Sixth we were aware that his mind was of a different order from ours,' and mentions 'the width of his reading.' In an obituary notice in the *Wellingtonian*, Mr E. K. Purnell, also a school-fellow, gives a little *vignette* of unmistakable fidelity :

A contemporary, who knew him first as a clever boy of 18, described him as in those days a most talkative vivacious youth, his eyes kindling with life and enthusiasm as he talked, his voice running up into a kind of falsetto. He observed and was interested in everything and everybody, and his personality, with its many-sided sympathies, impressed itself on all with whom it came in contact. The same person, meeting him when he was examining for the Benson a few years ago, was drawn irresistibly by the charm of his intense vitality, and the unconquerable courage which still helped him to keep up his part in the scheme of life—in a Bath chair.

These two brief scraps are all that can now be obtained. One episode, however, Verrall has himself related with curious but characteristic detachment and candour in the contribution to the *Life* of the Archbishop referred to above.

> I saw that after the approaching holidays I should... almost certainly be 'Head of the School,' a really laborious and responsible change. I was then a rapacious student and (except perhaps an infamous player of football) nothing else. My perturbation may be measured by my helpless impertinence. Without any intimation of the Headmaster's purposes, I actually went and told him that I could not be 'Head,' and that I should leave! I ought, I dare say, to have been snubbed. What I know is that a harsh or light word then would have ruined my best chance in life, and (as I make bold to say) would have lost a good year to the school....He discussed the matter with me almost daily, always from my point of view....In a fortnight I was a very little ashamed and exceedingly sanguine. And during my year I was to the Headmaster like a third hand.

In the spring of 1869 he obtained a Minor Scholarship at Trinity College, Cambridge, and a Foundation Scholarship in the following year. He was bracketed with Henry Butcher from Marlborough and Walter Leaf from Harrow—a remarkable trio to have entered for the same examination. When the result was known, Dr Benson wrote to Mr Henry Verrall:

> He has done beautifully, and he deserves success. For his heart is wholly in his work, and that with so much modesty and so much affectionateness, that no one can rejoice too much at his success or fear that it may spoil him. His two co-equals are respectively thought the best of their two

schools for several years past. And one of the examiners has written to tell me that if it had been possible to make a difference it would have been in Arthur's favour.

We may congratulate each other most sincerely—only on one point you must not congratulate me, for it is hard to part with him, I assure you.

Of the undergraduate period available information is scanty, and no letters have been preserved. In the time at which he went up to the University he was not a little fortunate, for among his contemporaries and friends were such men as Walter Leaf, Henry Butcher, F. W. Maitland, J. G. Butcher, Frank and Gerald Balfour, A. J. Mason, A. T. Myers (a younger brother of F. W. H. Myers), T. O. Harding, Edmund Gurney, G. H. Rendall, W. Cunningham, and F. J. H. Jenkinson. With all these, and the first three especially, he maintained a life-long friendship, and the deaths of F. W. Maitland in 1906 and of Henry Butcher in 1910 were blows little less than overwhelming. Among his older contemporaries were Henry Sidgwick, R. C. Jebb, Henry Jackson, and Frederick Pollock. One event, which occurred early in his University career, he spoke of at the time as 'the best thing that ever happened to me in my life.' This was his admission to a private but not obscure society, consisting of graduates and undergraduates, which met, and still meets, for intimate discussion of any and every subject. Dating at least as far back as the time of Tennyson, it counts among its numbers, I believe, many of Cambridge's most distinguished men, and Verrall always considered that he owed more to his membership of this 'glorious company' than to any other influence of Cambridge life. Another surviving incident of the undergraduate life is sufficiently characteristic to deserve record. It fell to him to have to read in the College chapel the lesson about the feast of Belshazzar from the Book of Daniel. Those who were present declare that the solemnity and dramatic power with which he delivered it, combined with the rare quality of the voice, were astonishingly impressive and made the occasion quite unforgettable.

To *The Tatler in Cambridge*, an unusually good example of those short-lived periodicals with which the undergraduate genius from time to time promotes the gaiety of University life, he contributed four clever papers. The most amusing of these is perhaps one on Bain's *Mental and Moral Science.* The book, he discovers, has running through it a vein of subtle humour, and he gently warns the author that this is a talent which in such a work should be exercised with philosophic discretion. The criticism of satire is perhaps all that the work deserves, and an admirable piece of fooling closes with the following poetical summary of Mr Bain's views.

> There was a Professor called *Bain*
> Who taught, in the Land of the Rain,
>    That the ultimate Fact
>    Which induced you to act
> Was an Inkling of Pleasure or Pain.

He proved that Volitional Force
Depended entirely on Sauce,
    Inasmuch as the Question
    Was one of Digestion,
And Morals would follow of course.

Your Head was impressible Batter
Compounded of White and Grey Matter,
    So your Measure of Reason
    Would flow from 'Adhesion'
To a tender and merciful Hatter.

He laid the Foundations of Virtue
In finding by Trial what hurt you;
    And spite of your Terror
    Would stick to his Error,
And at last, and at best, would desert you.

Religion and Duty he made
A Manner of feeling afraid;
    And Tact, on his showing,
    Consisted in knowing
The Feel of the Tongs from the Spade.

Faith, Charity, Hope were reducible
To Phosphate or Salt in a Crucible,
    Dissent and Dysentery
    Both 'Alimentary,'
Manners and Mammon both fusible.

If Flesh can be sane or insane,
And Meat the sole Factor of Brain,
    Then hey! for the Cooks,
    Since the Moral of Books
Is 'Leave Writing for Eating,' O *Bain*.

In 1872 he obtained the Pitt University Scholarship, and in the next year passed out in the Classical Tripos, being bracketed second with T. E. Page; Henry Butcher was Senior Classic. In the examination for the Chancellor's Medals, which immediately followed, the three were bracketed equal, and a third medal was awarded,—a thing never done before or since.

In connexion with his Tripos Verrall used to tell an amusing story, which he always regarded as illustrating in a remarkable manner the perverse vagaries of the human mind. He had to translate a passage from Tacitus in which Tiberius is described as doing something *Rhodo regressus*. These words he rendered by 'on his return to Rhodes,' and added two marginal notes, the first explaining and endeavouring to justify the use of *Rhodo* for *Rhodum*, and the second explaining how Tacitus came to speak of Tiberius as having done after his return *to* Rhodes what it was common knowledge that he did after his return *from* Rhodes. Not till he got back to his rooms did it occur to him that it would have been simpler to write *from* in his translation!

In the same year he was elected Fellow of Trinity College, and resided in Cambridge until the summer of 1874, taking private pupils. I was myself an undergraduate at this time, and knew him by sight, but alas! did not know what I was losing by not asking to be allowed to join those lucky youths.

In July Benson, who had now left Wellington, wrote to him that there was a vacancy on the staff of the School :—

> I need scarcely say to you that the idea present to all men's minds is what would have been present with me, viz.

whether it would be compatible with your arrangements that you should give them any help....I need scarcely put into words the fact that you would be more useful to Wellington College than any man living. What they want is *enthusiasm* —high-couraged work—with *scholarship*. And of course they want a feeling, understanding soul.

Happily he resisted this earnest appeal.

For the next three years he lived in London, reading for the Bar and doing a certain amount of teaching work. From 1875 to 1877 he was 'Supernumerary Instructor in composition and extra reading' at S. Paul's School. He gained the Whewell Scholarship for International Law in 1875, was called in 1877, and held one brief, if not two. A legal career, however, had no attraction for him : in October he returned to Cambridge, and was soon afterwards placed on the teaching staff at Trinity. From that time onwards Cambridge was his home. For the next five years he combined with his work at the University some teaching at Wren's well-known coaching establishment in London. He also taught at Newnham College, and in connexion with his work there Miss Jane Harrison tells a delightful story.

I have sometimes wondered if a brilliant dramatist was not lost in the finding and making of a subtle classical scholar. One day, as quite a young man, he was looking over my composition in the then library of Old Hall. Coals were wanted and no coal-scuttle in sight. After a longish hunt I remembered that the library coal-scuttle always lay *perdu* between the double doors that led to Miss Clough's sitting-room. The arrangement, owing to its ingenious economy in coal-scuttles, used to cause Miss Clough a quite peculiar and intimate joy. No less though a slightly different joy did it cause Mr Verrall. On catching sight of the coal-scuttle and the double doors he stood transfigured and transfixed. ' What a scene for a play ! ' he exclaimed, and coal scuttle in hand, me and my composition utterly forgotten, the plot of that play he then and there constructed and enacted.

In 1881 he published his first book, an edition of the *Medea* of Euripides. He had been asked by Messrs Macmillan & Co. to prepare a school edition of the play, but on getting to work he found that the limits of a school-book, even if that were the proper medium, would be far too narrow for what needed to be done for the *Medea*, and what he felt he could do. The book was remarkable not only as the production of a young man of thirty, but in itself; it was strikingly original and brilliant, and was at once recognised as the work of a scholar of the first rank. Nothing of the kind, nor perhaps anything approaching it, had previously been done on the Greek tragedians. While he breathed fresh life into the play itself, the effect of his work went further; for it suggested what might be done for other legacies of the Attic stage, interest in which seemed to be steadily sinking into the mere formal respect one pays to a dull old man whose former dignities do not permit him to be quite ignored. The volume was welcomed with delight and admiration, and I think I recognise the hand of Professor Tyrrell in a long and frankly eulogistic article unearthed from the file of the *Saturday Review*. The textual restorations, of which something will be said below, naturally attracted special attention, and confirmed to their author, if they did not originate, the half-jesting, half-earnest *sobriquet* 'Splendid Emendax.' But this part of the work was by no means the chief or the most valuable. Other merits were found in rare and perhaps unprecedented combination : a peculiarly delicate appreciation of the subtleties of the language, a fine discrimination between expressions superficially identical, a subtle appreciation of the poet's skill in delineation of character, and an acute perception of the necessities and possibilities of a dramatic situation. In the two last Verrall had no rival among his predecessors, and few if any equals then or later among his contemporaries. As one perused the text afresh after digesting the commentary, one found the scenes leap into life, one saw and heard the drama in progress ; or rather—but here we have first to thank Euripides—one felt one was in the presence of a living Medea and a living Jason. The notes were enriched with illustrations drawn from English literature and even (as the writer in the *Saturday Review* notes) a parallel from *Lohengrin*, 'which to a commentator of the older school would have appeared unpardonably frivolous.'

Of these qualities of the book there was but one opinion, but the textual work divided readers into two camps. While the teachable, old or young, were only grateful, there were some who were offended by the originality and alarmed at the

brilliance. They mistrusted the cleverness of emen-
dations which took their breath away, making
familiar passages unrecognisable, and they feared
the effects of a pernicious example. Thus did the
mediaeval world regard Galileo. It is an attitude
towards Verrall's work as a textual critic—whether
here or in later books—which has always filled me
with astonishment, for his methods were essentially
sound. As all his labours in this department show,
his decisions were not based on mere guess-work
(of which he always spoke with some impatience),
but were conclusions arrived at from the evidence
furnished by the MSS. themselves. Where he differed from others was in the possession of unusual inductive powers, which enabled him to *see further*; and
these powers were assisted by a rare sense of literary and dramatic fitness, an apparently complete
acquaintance with the extant vocabulary of classical
Greek, and an exceptional memory. We may, if
we please, sum up all this as 'ingenuity,' but if we
do, we must not use the word in a disparaging sense.
Of course, and he used readily to admit it, the
sharp-edged tool sometimes slipped. Impatient of
the 'fluffy' explanation that does not explain, he
was occasionally tempted to offer something which
still fails to satisfy, and which only he could have
made plausible. Again, as some think, he sometimes finds a point where none was intended. It
may be so, but it is surely well to err on the side of
respect for one's author, and if we do not believe
in pointless lines in Aristophanes, why should we

tolerate them in the texts of the tragedians? And
after all, to accompany Verrall even on an incon-
clusive quest, is to learn things by the way which
are perhaps as valuable as what we may have set
out to seek.

In emendation he kept two ruling principles
always before him: he did not accept or offer a
correction as more than possible, unless the supposed corruption were accounted for, either by the
correction itself or otherwise; and he held that an
*odd* variant, just because of its oddness or grotesque-
ness or absurdity, might possibly conceal the true
reading, as against the passable respectability of the
*textus receptus*. The first, of course, was a well
established canon, though one freely ignored; the
potentialities of the second had been but dimly apprehended. Three examples, taken from the *Medea*,
will show his methods at work.

At *v.* 668,

$$τί δ' ὀμφαλὸν γῆς θεσπιῳδὸν ἐστάλης;$$

is the text of all the MSS.; but the second hand in B
(one of the inferior class s) has superscribed ἱκάνεις.
ἐστάλης is irreproachable, but ἱκάνεις cannot be a
gloss on it, and Verrall deduces ἱζάνεις as the true
reading. If anyone cannot see this, there is no
more to be said; in the name of all that is dull, let
him hug his ἐστάλης and be happy.

At *v.* 531 the 'superior' class of MSS. give

$$ὡς Ἔρως σ' ἠνάγκασε$$
$$πόνων ἀφύκτων τοὐμὸν ἐκσῶσαι δέμας.$$

The 'inferior' class give τόξοις ἀφύκτοις. Paley's note is, 'There is a variant τόξοις ἀφύκτοις, approved by Elmsley,' and he passes on with the crowd. Verrall was not so easily satisfied. Both variants are passable though feeble, but their presence as alternatives is unaccounted for, and he offers τόνοις ἀφύκτοις as the common original. If anyone thinks there was no problem to be solved, again there is no more to be said.

At *v.* 1183 the 'superior' MSS. have

ἡ δ' ἐξ ἀναύδου καὶ μύσαντος ὄμματος
δεινὸν στενάξασ' ἡ τάλαιν' ἠγείρετο.

The 'inferior' class give a variant ἀπώλλυτο. No one had seen that ἀναύδου (ἀναύγου, Verrall) required correction, and since ἀπώλλυτο passed unheeded, ἠγείρετο of course incurred no suspicion. But it is just from this absurd ἀπώλλυτο, as a correction of ΑΝΩΜΜΑΤΟΥ, a misreading of a mis-spelt ΑΝΩΜΑΤΟΥ, that our 'daring' editor restores ΑΝΩΜ-ΜΑΤΟΥ. Unfortunately ἀνομματῶ is not an extant word, and that fact has been to some, in this case and others, a stumbling-block in the way of acceptance. One reviewer solemnly deprecated 'these attempts to enrich the Greek language.' The logic is somewhat Chinese, but minds work variously. In China the scholar himself, on returning from a journey, is in danger of being refused recognition by his family, argue as he may, unless he can produce the tally which is the one sure proof that he is not a masquerading devil. So the English editor

should perhaps not be surprised if, when he says
'Take my word for it,' his word is regarded as some
such masquerading devil, unless he can produce
from the lexicon a reference to its respectability.
There is naturally no trace in Verrall's *Medea* of
the theory of Euripides' art which he afterwards
elaborated, and the one miraculous incident in the
play, the dragon-chariot, is passed over without
special comment. One paragraph in the Introduction is, however, noteworthy in this connexion. It
was a traditional commonplace that the poet's concern in the stories which he dramatized was pre-
dominantly with their human interest, but so far as
I am aware, no one had previously laid stress on the
significant completeness with which the marvellous
and all reference to it are excluded from the *Medea*,
at any rate until the play's proper climax has been
reached. The observation appears to have been
fruitful.

> To Euripides, therefore, the story of Medea is interesting
> wholly as a plot of passion, and all other aspects of it are
> thrown into the background. Indeed, considering the rich
> fabric of romance with which her name had been interwoven,
> it is not a little curious to observe how strictly it is reduced
> by the dramatist to its human and ethical elements. The
> splendid and marvellous story of the Argonauts is of course
> a necessary presumption, but the allusions to it are so curt
> and so colourless that, even with the story before us, it is
> sometimes a matter of difficulty to interpret them (*Med.* 479,
> 487); and it is plain that any other story would have been
> as acceptable, which furnished or admitted the essential points
> of the situation, the proud barbarian wife and mother aban-
> donèd by the Greek husband to whom she has sacrificed all.

Even the chorus in their lyric songs occupy themselves with the ethic and pathetic aspects only, with the social and intellectual position of woman, the virtue of self-control, the blessings and trials of parents, the sanctity of hospitable Athens, with anything, in short, rather than the clashing rocks and the fire-breathing bulls, the ram of Phrixos and the cauldron of Pelias. (p. xviii.)

In 1882 (June 17) he married Margaret de Gaudrion Merrifield, daughter of Frederic Merrifield, Barrister-at-law, of Brighton, now Clerk of the Peace of East and West Sussex. Miss Merrifield, after a study of Latin and Greek extending over practically no more than the period of her University life, had taken honours in the Classical Tripos Examination of 1880, and was at the time a resident Classical Lecturer at Newnham College. For many years after her marriage Mrs Verrall continued to take part in the classical teaching at Newnham, and her valuable work in connexion with the Society for Psychical Research during the last ten years is well known to a large section of the public. Of the married life of these my dearest friends I cannot trust myself to say more than that the union seemed to be as ideal as that of Robert and Elizabeth Browning, and to realise to the utmost the beautiful vision of *The Princess* :

> Two heads in council, two beside the hearth,
> Two in the tangled business of the world,
> Two in the liberal offices of life,
> Two plummets dropt for one to sound the abyss
> Of science, and the secrets of the mind.

There is one daughter of the marriage, Miss Helen de G. Verrall, who has inherited largely both the gifts and qualities of her parents. She obtained a First Class in the Classical Tripos Part I in 1905, and a First Class in Part II in 1906.

Verrall's next book, *Studies in Horace*, published in 1883 and now out of print, is a collection of essays on the *Odes* of Horace. The volume is written with charming freshness, and the poems discussed gain a new life and often a quite unexpected interest from the originality and independence of the criticisms. The most important essay is the one entitled *Murena*. Identifying the famous conspirator of that name with the Murena of III 19 and the Lucius Licinius Varro Murena whose 'sister' Maecenas married (and on this identification the main weight of the contention rests), Verrall endeavours to show that the first three books of the Odes were not published before B.C. 19, as against the generally accepted lowest date B.C. 23.

Although he failed to commend his view on either point to some of those best entitled to form an opinion, nevertheless both questions are still matters of dispute, and an eminent Italian historian, ignorant of the existence of Verrall's book, has recently expressed agreement with him so far as to hold that the *Odes* 'are a single poetic work, animated by a central idea, and not a miscellany of disconnected verse.'

Scattered through the volume are vivid pictures of Roman society in the Augustan age, drawn with a rare dexterity, and the power exhibited in appraising the significance of historical events, the liveliness and sureness of touch with which they are described, and the insight which marks the pourtrayal of character, show that when we gained a scholar and critic, we perhaps lost an unusually gifted historian. A great Latinist wrote at the time : 'The essay on Murena was to me the one of most fascinating interest. If a drama or historical romance on the personages and incidents of the Augustan age were to be written, the writer would find his materials in that essay.' The following brief extract may serve as a specimen of much more that is equally striking.

> For the difficulty lies not in the fact of the allusion to Murena, but in the tone of it. That Horace, writing or publishing after the conspiracy, would pass the history of Murena in silence can in no way be presumed. As a poet, indeed, he could ill afford to do so. A theme more suggestive for poetry of a tragic cast, especially as the ancients conceived of tragedy, it would be difficult to imagine. The whole story from prologue to catastrophe—the hard lessons of experience learnt and forgotten, the humiliation, the sudden rise and ill-sustained prosperity, the insolent tongue which made enemies when it was the time to propitiate envy, the doubtful guilt and certain ruin, the wide-spread sympathy not unmixed with horror—all that our authorities give us unites in a subject such as Aeschylus chose, a veritable τραγῳδία of real life, acted not in the theatre of Dionysus but in the midst of the society of Rome. Nor would the relation between the poet and Maecenas forbid the subject, if only it were touched in a proper spirit. What was the private opinion of Maecenas on Murena's crime and the emperor's justice, it would be vain to conjecture. But on no view could he desire silence. (p. 31.)

From 1886 to the summer of 1889, in addition to his other work, he lectured at Pembroke College. An interesting anecdote falls somewhere in this period. On a certain Saturday he was going to London for the day. On the following Monday the Trinity lecturers would be wanting to distribute to their pupils printed copies of a piece of English for translation into Latin hexameters. It was Verrall's turn to set this piece, and at the Cambridge station he remembered that he had not done so. Moreover, his Latin version of the piece should be in the lecturers' hands on the Tuesday morning. From London he telegraphed to the University Press to print and send out to the lecturers that day '*Merchant of Venice*, Act v. sc. 1, from "The moon shines bright" to "footing of a man,"' and he composed the version, from a perfect recollection of the English, during the day. A few final touches were given next day, and the copy sent off to press. It will be found, with about a score more from his pen, in *Cambridge Compositions* (1899). He wrote Greek and Latin with almost as much facility as English, and in a style that has the true ring, as a man writes a language which he speaks. All his compositions possess distinction and individuality, and some of his verse is such as an ancient poet might have published with advantage to his reputation. One merit of his versions is sufficiently uncommon, even in the best work of this kind, to deserve special mention: he never failed to catch the spirit of the original. I regret that there is not space to quote here the copy referred to above, for it affords an excellent illustration of this, reproducing with an absolute fidelity (so at least it seems to me) the extremely delicate tone of Shakspeare's sole but perfect idyll.

In 1887 he published an edition of the *Septem contra Thebas* of Aeschylus. The play offers no scope for such a comprehensive view of the poet's art as we have in the commentaries on the great trilogy, but this volume inaugurated a new era in the interpretation of the play and in the study of Aeschylus as a whole. The same faculties which had been so fruitful in the case of the *Medea* were brought to bear, and now by a reconstruction of the text, now by a more satisfying interpretation, he gave to passage after passage fresh or fuller significance. At the same time he did much to quicken and enlarge our appreciation of the characteristic qualities of Aeschylean diction and style. There were of course, here and there, instances of the inevitable over-subtlety,—he expected it himself, no less than did his readers ; but we have learned to regard these things as mere spots on the sun, which are, I believe, due to uprushes of excessive energy from the solar subliminal, and doubtless not without their use. No man was less disposed to hold to 'a poor thing' because it was 'his own,' and I can remember points, both in this play and in others, which upon discussion he instantly abandoned when a reasonable objection was presented. Sometimes (and every scholar could illustrate this from his own case) the obvious view had simply not occurred to him. One day, during my last visit, I was reading over in his presence an unpublished MS. which he had written on a passage in Lucan, and in which reference was made to a statuette possessed by Alexander the Great,

quam comitem occasus secum portabat et ortus.

Verrall had translated, 'whether he went east or west,' and I interrupted my reading to ask him why he did not think the meaning was 'night and morning.' His immediate answer was, 'I did not think of it.'

Perhaps the most valuable of Verrall's contributions to our enjoyment of the *Septem* is one which affects the whole play, and concerns a matter on which no one dreamed that there could be anything novel to say. By general consent it was agreed that the play was wanting in true dramatic interest. There was a wealth of gorgeous and majestic poetry, and a succession of stirring scenes, which nevertheless failed to give the genuine tragic thrill. There was none of the suspense and painful interest that is produced as we watch the action steadily working up to a *supreme moment*; none of the 'horror and pity' to which we are moved when at that moment the blow of fate is suddenly struck, without warning, and in a manner that its victim had never suspected. By a master-stroke of dramatic instinct Verrall restored the deficiency, and showed that the meeting of the brothers, usually supposed to be foreseen, was on the contrary an unexpected *peripeteia* developed on the stage. This makes tragedy indeed; but a reviewer, as I remember, 'confessed that he thought the new view made no difference,'—and this, though he was writing under no compulsion.

In 1889 he became one of the four Tutors at Trinity. He accepted the office with a deep sense of its responsibilities. Its duties, he felt, included the cultivation of really human relations with the men, a thing involving considerable expenditure of time and energy, but an expenditure that must be made, he believed, if the work was to be properly performed. For this closer intercourse, which was to him and Mrs Verrall a source of genuine pleasure, opportunities were made in a manner at that time almost unknown among Tutors, by the exercise of frequent hospitality at Selwyn Gardens. All the freshmen, some fifty in number, were invited to dinner in their first term, which involved a dinner-party two or three times a week, and tennis and croquet parties on Tuesdays and Fridays were a regular institution of the May term. It was in this way, besides others, that he sowed the seeds of that affection which most of his men came to feel towards him. 'You know how much more than a merely official relation Dr Verrall made of his tutorship,' writes one; and another, 'he made a man feel he was more than one in a long list.'

Mr E. H. Marsh, C.M.G., a former pupil, who has kindly sent me some reminiscences, writes,

He was an extraordinarily sound, just, and sympathetic judge of character. No one valued cleverness and originality more, but there were plenty of rather commonplace good fellows whom he not only appreciated for their 'English' qualities, but thoroughly liked. I remember his going through the list of freshers on his 'side' one year,—'No,' he said when he came to the end, 'they are not a galaxy'; but before their first year was over I am sure he had made personal friends with a great majority of them. He seemed rather formidable of course at first sight, but no one could mistake the perfect simplicity of character which he combined with that unusual complication of mind; and as he always steered between talking down to people and talking over their heads, everyone was soon at ease with him. He used to have croquet parties in old days, and though I don't remember his playing himself, he used to throw himself into the games and devise complicated tactics for the players— the balls almost became characters in a subtle Euripidean plot.

He was a very successful president at smoking-concerts, etc. I remember how everyone shrieked with laughter when he excused himself for having been prevented from preparing an after-dinner speech by 'a succession of incalculable circumstances over *whom* I had no control.' He was never on a high horse for a moment; he used to tell delightedly how, when the son of an old friend paid his first visit, the talk fell on Shelley, and Verrall said he had never read *The Revolt of Islam*. 'Ah,' said the youth, 'that's sheer indolence of mind.'

With the Tutorship he combined his ordinary work as lecturer. This was not usual, but he made it for himself a condition of undertaking the office, and managed the double work easily for most of the period of ten years over which the Tutorship usually extends.

Verrall's reputation as a lecturer and teacher

grew year by year, and of the value of this part of his work there is but one opinion. To my own lasting regret, I heard him lecture twice only, although he was my most intimate friend for more than thirty years. For the present purpose, however, this matters little, for I am fortunately able to give the reader the life-like impression of him in this aspect contained in a letter kindly contributed by Mr F. M. Cornford, Fellow and Lecturer of Trinity College. The following pages are from Mr Cornford's pen, down to the place where his signature appears (p. xlviii).

## *Letter from Mr F. M. Cornford.*

You have honoured me by asking me, as one who was first a pupil, and later a colleague, of Verrall at Trinity College, to write some account of him as a teacher and lecturer. Several Trinity men have helped me by sending their impressions of him. They all agree, as we should expect, in saying that it was, above all else, his personality that counted ; one or two of them speak as if contact with him had changed the whole current of their intellectual life. To describe that personality is another matter, but it cannot be left out in any account of his teaching and lecturing.

It was in this part of his work that his extraordinary gifts had fullest play; yet, when I call up my memory of him, it is neither as 'lecturer' nor as 'teacher' that I can think of him. In both these words there is an undernote of pedantry ; and, in the rear of the two respectable nouns comes a flock of woolly epithets—'painstaking,' 'conscientious,' and the rest—which in this case are, all of them, thoroughly deserved, but convey nothing of the quality and distinction of Verrall's genius. He did take unlimited pains, not only because he was 'conscientious,' but because to him teaching was the means of expression in which he felt the passion and the joy of an artist. His emotion seemed, at least in his last years, to have fused with his intellect in a way that is rare among northerners : it strengthened the impression that he must have had a strain of Latin blood—an impression given by his dark colouring and the particular clear-cut and dignified beauty of his features, the long fine aquiline nose and oval cheeks. This passionate intellectuality, moving most easily at a height of rarefied atmosphere where few could follow him, combined with something aristocratic in his nature to tinge his pupil's admiration with awe. He was, to many people, always a little terrifying ; but he became much less so to those who found out that he genuinely cared, not only to set their minds working, but to win their sympathy. I was slow to discover this : it was long before it occurred to me that he could mind what I thought about his theories, or want others to share his delight in the things he enjoyed. There must be something in the relation of pupil to master which makes it hard to perceive such a need ; for with Verrall it was

very strong and characteristic, and to a great extent
the secret of his influence. Without it, he might
have been too remote; but, as it was, it moved him
to exert his marvellous powers of exposition to the
utmost, so as to bring the slowest minds under his
spell.

Perhaps only an acute reader would detect this
trait in his books. In writing, his sensitive courtesy
never allowed him to forget that he was addressing
strangers; there is a certain formality of style, which,
together with his scrupulous use of words and the
polish of his dexterous sentences, would leave anyone
who had merely read his books with only a faint
notion of what it was to hear him speak to an
audience whom he knew. In conversation, again,
there was scope for his wit and for that adorable
silliness in which an intellect incapable of foolishness
can bubble over; but in conversation only the
pompous can be eloquent; and of pompousness he
had not a grain. It was only when he lectured that
he could let loose all his rhetorical powers and yet
keep the explosive flash and exuberance of his talk.
On informal occasions in his own class-room, his
delight in some absurdity would vent itself in that
strange noise, which was at once a laugh, a crow,
and a shriek. But, being never afraid of losing his
dignity, he never lost it; and, for all his need of
sympathy, he neither flattered his hearers nor traded
on his charm. He was too completely absorbed in
the point he was making: and this—whatever it
was, from a subtlety of Euripidean psychology to

a detail of syntax—seemed to everyone, because it seemed to him, the only thing in the universe that mattered for the moment.

Mr E. H. Marsh writes :

> Did you hear his lectures on the *Choephori*? Those are the ones I have the clearest recollection of. You know how he used to sit, in a subdued frenzy of impatience, waiting till everyone was there and seated, and how, if the noise of settling down went on a moment after he had hoped it was over, there was an agony, shown only by his martyred face and the drumming of his pencil on the desk. There was never any noise when once he had begun, and the high rich shrillness of his voice came streaming out, under the closed eyelids in his ivory face. We are not likely to see anything more resembling the phenomena of inspiration. I find my mental picture has completed itself with curls of pale blue smoke from a tripod.
>
> He could work us up into excruciating suspense, as when he unfolded Ridgeway's theory of why Electra recognised Orestes' hair and footmark. And how beautifully he told the story of the man who had only time to write '*πάρεστι*' before he was overwhelmed by the mud avalanche! It was all far too exciting to take notes. I used to put a dot under each word that he noticed, and he put everything so perfectly that I scarcely ever found I had forgotten what the dots meant. I was usually convinced by everything, and always felt at least that, if Verrall's own theory was not certain, at any rate all the others were impossible.

This description brings out what is quite true, that a lecture by Verrall was definitely a performance, prepared down to small details with an orator's sense of effect. The performance, however, was not a display of fireworks, but dramatic, requiring (as I

have said) the sympathy, and therefore the understanding, of the whole audience. This is not an
easy end to achieve in lecturing to a class which
covers the whole range of ability and knowledge
lying between the first and last divisions of a Classical
Honours list. To bring in the third class man,
elementary truths must be mentioned which were
known to the first class man years before he left
school. How to instruct the most backward without
boring the advanced, is a problem that few can
solve. Verrall managed it so cunningly that one
could never see how it was done; he neither talked
over their heads, nor yet seemed to talk down to
them. It was partly that, in lecturing as in talking,
he had the art of thinking aloud and taking his
audience through all the processes by which he
reached his conclusion. Often he followed what
one may call a *Ring-and-the-Book* method, repeating
the same thing again and again, but so as to put
a finer edge on it each time. This was, of course,
most delightful in ordinary talk, because then he
started without knowing himself where he would get
to : as he went on, the idea cropped up and sprouted
and branched and flowered under your eyes. His
wit was never expressed in the dry drawl of an
academic epigram; his best jokes broke cover in the
heat of some excited discourse, and, once they were
sighted, he spared them no turn or double of the
chase. In lecturing, the excitement was even more
intense, for he only allowed his pack to scent the
quarry from afar, so as to give them their share in

the passion of pursuit as well as the joy of being in at the death.

The following extract is from a letter written by one of his most recent pupils, Mr J. R. M. Butler :

I think the first thing about Verrall's lecturing which struck one coming from school was the way in which he forced you to take no literary judgment for granted, but to justify your opinions at first hand. He challenged everything that occurred to you as a truism, and his paradoxes could not be answered by stock arguments out of books. And by discussing with you on equal terms—as he did in the notes he scribbled on your papers—he gave you a self-respect in literary things and made you ashamed of being dishonest.

That was one thing—forcing you to criticise. Another was the desire his own strange theories gave you to discover new and hidden things yourself. There might be endless secrets lurking in the best-known places, and Classics became a delightful and adventurous thing.

I don't think we believed very much what he said; he always said he was as likely to be wrong as right. But he made all Classics so gloriously new and living. He made us criticise by standards of common sense, and presume that the tragedians were not fools, and that they did mean something. They were not to be taken as antiques privileged to use conventions that would be nonsense in anyone else....

He was good about keeping in touch with his class. I remember once he sent for me to his house, to ask if I could suggest any reason why he was not getting satisfactory papers done, and if I thought he ought to make any change in his own method.

It is interesting to compare this writer's ' I don't think we believed very much what he said,' with Mr Marsh's ' I was usually convinced by everything.' But both letters equally show how little it mattered whether this or that statement bore the cold light of reconsideration. The point was to witness the reaction of this astonishing intellect upon literature which to him, and to all whom he made see it with his eyes, was the subtlest form of art. He was, I suppose, one of the first lecturers in Cambridge who resolutely insisted on always treating the Classics as works of art and not as masses of so much Greek and Latin, from which samples of dubious grammar could be extracted and held up with the warning : 'Not for imitation!' He was not, by modern standards, a very learned man ; he knew the ancient writings that deserve to be called literature up and down, but he was a little impatient when he was made to attend to archaeological lore. Not, of course, that he either despised or neglected it ; but his private name for it was 'stuffage.' And, as a civilised man, with a preference for civilised products, he disliked the grim remains of prehistoric savagery which, as he felt, are now being pinned to the skirts of Hellenism. What he loved to analyse was the intended qualities of technique and design, and all the unconscious effects of style. He realised that a Greek play, for instance, must be interpreted primarily from itself, not buried under a load of more or less relevant learning, still less used as a text for a general disquisition on grammar. This may seem obvious enough ; but, if we compare his editions, which in this respect are like his lectures, with the commentaries of an older generation, we see that he was one of the first who made it obvious. Many generations of pupils got from him their first revelation of literature as an art. At school, they had necessarily—or so, at any rate, it used to be considered—spent their time in struggling with the difficulties of learning to read and write the ancient languages. At that stage, the Classics are used as textbooks ; and, while it is dimly apparent to the schoolboy that as textbooks they leave much to be desired both in subject and style, it is not always possible for him to see that their authors had any other purpose in view. In Verrall's lecture-room the light broke upon them. Some speech in Euripides which had seemed a dry tissue of commonplaces suddenly began to glow with passion and flash with wit ; and as he lit up the large outlines of the piece and showed how one part gained its meaning from its relation to another, undreamed-of prospects opened out.

Verrall's manner in reciting poetry naturally produced different effects on various temperaments. I quote two extracts from letters which, as it happens, refer to the same occasion. Mr H. A. Hollond writes :

> Too rare, we thought, were the occasions on which he exercised his wonderful gift of reading aloud in order to illustrate his point. No word-music has left with me so vivid a memory as his rendering of Horace's *Solvitur acris hiems*. I feel, as if it were yesterday that I listened, the passionateness, at its beginning, of the sentence : *Pallida mors aequo pulsat pede...* dying away into the whispered sibilant at its close. A long pause, and then the sad but calm philosophy : *O beate Sesti, vitae summa brevis spem nos vetat inchoare*

*longam*; and last of all the courageous change of mood into the forced gaiety about young Lycidas. On that day Verrall must have been giving us much of himself.

Another correspondent says :

> He gave you a new idea of the importance of language and sound in poetry, by chanting Horace, Catullus, etc. It was often fantastic, as when, in *Solvitur acris hiems*, he said 'regumque turres' meant the approach of thunder, or that 'Hadria' in *Donec gratus eram* ought to be laughed—'Ha-ha-ha-dria'; but it made you believe in the power of subtle word-building. In reciting *Vivamus, mea Lesbia*, he showed wonderfully how the change of sound meant change of thought. I think the finest of all was when he declaimed Creusa's monody in the *Ion*, at a University Extension lecture; καὶ...σός γ'...ἀμαθής was extraordinarily dramatic.

In teaching composition to individual pupils, Verrall had nothing in common with the school of teachers whose favourite words are 'grinding' and 'grounding.' Instead of setting himself to fake a goose till it should pass, in the examiner's eyes, for a swan, he was content to help the creature to see what it was to be a swan, and, with gentle derision, when it was deserved, to make it feel what a goose it had been. But, if he pounced upon stupidity, he watched eagerly for every symptom of intelligence, and encouraged it with generous praise.

> He had, writes Mr Marsh, the most scrupulous sense I have ever known of the value of exactness in language. There was nothing academic in this: no one took more pleasure in novelty or audacity of expression, if, on close inspection, it was justified and held water; but he would never tolerate an approximation to the meaning required. I suppose very few of the greatest writers always came up to

his standard! Do you remember how particular he was
about not misleading the reader (except, of course, on
purpose, when he loved it) as to the form a sentence was
going to take? Any such inelegance would cut him like
a knife.

He had beautiful manners as a teacher, and never made
one feel a fool when one wasn't. When he did, it was
delightfully done. I remember dining with him once, as
a mature wise second-year man, to help with three freshmen.
After dinner modern novels were discussed, and one of the
freshmen contributed his view as follows : 'Well, Dr Verrall,
I must avow that in my opinion Edna Lyall is the first of
contemporary novelists.' Verrall was taken aback for a
moment; but then : 'Well, if you think so, you're quite right
to *avow* it, you know...*ur*...' (the long high *ur*, between a
laugh and a crow). His sense of justice made him approve
the young man's candour, but his humour couldn't resist the
handle given him by the unlucky word 'avow.'

## Another pupil says :

I think that Verrall's personal teaching was exactly com-
plementary to the stimulus of his written work. Whereas the
latter, whether convincing or not, teaches one to try to see
what the author really felt and meant, conversely his teaching
of composition showed one how to shape one's mind to the
formal mould on which our ideas must be impressed if they
are to seem to be the utterances of Greeks or Romans. So
many scholars who write admirable Greek or Latin are quite
unable to point out to a learner what are the features which
cause it to be idiomatic. They can tell you intuitively 'That
won't do,' but not why it won't do. Verrall's own Greek and
Latin did not always seem to have quite the quality of that of
some of his colleagues ; he sometimes strained the language ;
but he seized unhesitatingly the merits of another's fair copy
and showed exactly why an effect in the English piece, of
emphasis for example, could only be produced in the translation by a device of a completely different character. For

instance, he was continually pointing out the use which can be made in Latin of alliteration, of the repetition of an important word, of compact phrasing. In correcting a verse composition he would urge us to look at the structure of the piece as a whole and to avoid uniformity and monotony of rhythm, whereas so many teachers content themselves with indicating the faults—grammatical, syntactical or metrical—of each particular sentence.

I have the feeling—do you know whether anyone shares it with me?—that Verrall, however enthusiastic he was about Greek literature, nevertheless understood the Latin mind better, or, at any rate, Latin modes of thought and expression.

The extremely difficult, and often impossible, task of translating English poetry into Greek or Latin taxed all his peculiar powers, and he rejoiced in it. If he had been imprisoned till such time as he should have rendered (say) Stubbs' *Select Constitutional Charters* into Greek Iambics, I believe he would have emerged in a surprisingly short time, refreshed in spirit; and Stubbs' treatise would thenceforth have been better reading than it is. This curious form of art, beloved of English scholars, provided him with just what he most liked—a strictly limited problem, only to be solved by the utmost stretch of dexterity and the finest sense of word-values in both languages. His versions were brilliant. He used to say that he was not sure that composition could be taught in any other way than by the master's letting the learner see how he did it himself.

To his colleagues, Verrall was generous and considerate. Staff meetings are commonly dull enough, but if he was present, there was sure to be fun. One never knew what he would say next, or how his whimsical humour would twist the banalities of business into every shape of absurdity. He had not, at least when I knew him, the temper of a reformer. The traditional system of teaching satisfied him ; within its limitations he found room to do all that he wanted. But, though he seldom initiated changes, he never obstructed, but always listened readily to others who recommended them, giving his support, if he was convinced. He was, all his life, steadfast to Liberalism in politics, and the passion that went with his reason was quickly fired in any cause of justice or liberty; yet he had in his composition something of the conservative. With an instinct for ceremony, he always liked a decency to be observed. This feeling for tradition was connected with his devotion to the College to which he gave his best work. It is hard to tell how far it is possible for one man to affect the life of an institution where the generations come and go in rapid succession ; but it is certain that Verrall's influence will be felt so long as anyone who knew him remains connected with Trinity College, and his lectures and books have permanently affected the tradition of teaching.

Before ending, I should like to be allowed to recall one of his most exquisite and characteristic performances. It was at a College meeting which met in January, 1906, to discuss certain changes in the papers set in the Fellowship Examination at

Trinity. The old 'Philosophy papers' were to be remodelled and their range extended to include questions on the general aspects of science, art and history. Literature, for some reason, had been omitted from this list. I believe Sir Richard Jebb had intended to move for the insertion of it; but before the meeting was held, Sir Richard was dead, and Verrall took up the proposal in his place. He had been deeply moved by Jebb's death. He delivered his speech sitting in his chair (he was too crippled to stand) and, as usual, with closed eyes. Ostensibly, he was outlining the sort of questions about literature that might be set in the examination ; they were questions, it is true, that few but himself could have thought of, much less answered. But as the speech went on, his audience began to realise that they were listening to a funeral oration, though he said nothing about Jebb, and I doubt if he mentioned his name. It was, perhaps, the most audacious thing that Verrall ever did. College meetings are extremely impatient of long speeches, and he ran the risk of being interrupted at any moment by an appeal to the chairman to check his irrelevancy. Who else could have trusted his power of holding such an audience, and who else could have succeeded ? The climax came when he contrived to recite a passage from Massillon's *Oraison Funèbre de Louis le Grand*, in which a quotation from the Vulgate is several times repeated : *Quando interrogaverint vos filii vestri, dicentes : Quid sibi volunt isti lapides ?* His pronunciation of French was singularly pure ;

his musical intonation rendered the melancholy pomp of echoing sounds and slow, massive rhythms ; and he made the recurrent *Quando* (pronounced, of course, with the French nasal *n* and a long-drawn *a*) strike through them like the passing bell with its harsh clang at long intervals : *Quando interrogaverint vos filii vestri, dicentes : Quid sibi volunt isti lapides?*

With my correspondents' help, I have tried to give some idea of Verrall's influence on the men he taught. But, as I look back, what fills me with admiration and gratitude is not so much his teaching as the splendid spectacle of his triumph over physical pain. He will live in my memory as he was in the last years of his life, when his mind seemed to have withdrawn inside the last defences, gallantly defying the encroaching disease that had crippled and emaciated his frame. Beaten back from point to point, as one activity after another was taken from him, he kept the flag flying as gaily as ever. When his body failed him he treated it with contempt. He thrust his infirmity aside as a tiresome accident, about which the less said the better. Latterly, his mind was like a fire that smouldered through hours of bodily exhaustion, and then would suddenly shoot up in flashes of white flame. As soon as this happened, his illness was utterly ignored. It was impossible to remember that every movement was pain ; he made one forget it, as he forgot it himself. There was in this no hint of an heroical pose. Probably no man of equal rhetorical gifts ever so completely kept rhetoric out of his life. Nor was it resignation ; but rather the magnificent pride of the spirit setting its heel upon the flesh.

Much as his friends have learnt from him, it is above all for this last conquest of a courageous and noble mind that they will always hold his memory in reverence and honour.

F. M. CORNFORD.

Numerous other letters received from former pupils confirm one point or another of Mr Cornford's impression. One writes :—

> There was no one of his generation at Cambridge who meant so much as he did to us younger men. It was not only the immense pleasure and stimulus of hearing him either on his own subject or any subject, but besides that his constant kindness and readiness to give sympathy and advice were a very great help and a thing for which I shall always be grateful.

And another, to the same effect :—

> My intellectual debt to him is greater than I can estimate ; but even more than the brilliance of his mind, it was the fearless directness of his character and the inspiring ardour of his enthusiasm which endeared him to those who had the good fortune to come under his influence.

Another writes that, to know Verrall 'meant an awakening all round, and something of "the rapture of the forward view."'

In 1889 Verrall published his *Agamemnon* of Aeschylus, and in the general judgement the book at once established him in a position of supremacy among the poet's interpreters. The position was confirmed later by his *Choephori* and *Eumenides*, but it was assured to him by this work alone. As an instrument of expression, for flexibility and range, for delicacy and subtlety as for force, the Greek language confessedly has no rival. To judge from his work on Aeschylus, Verrall would seem to have come near to grasping its utmost possibilities. By a fearless recognition of the boldness and pregnancy of Aeschylean phraseology, and of the freedom of Aeschylean syntax, he enlarged our conceptions of the whole language. He, so to speak, extended its reach. We may sometimes be tempted to think that he claims for Aeschylus a latitude of expression which the poet would not have claimed for himself, but when that occurs, it may serve to give us pause before condemning, to recall that Tennyson in a certain place wrote

'and felt the boat shock earth.'

If he thought of *strike* (with the poet, however, *la parole suit la pensée*), he rejected it, to give us something peculiarly Tennysonian and better, if we can see it,—but, like much in Aeschylus, at once audacious and 'unexampled'! On the other hand, Verrall's surer judgement rejected not a few extravagances, both of language and grammar, which less discriminating editors would father on the poet; nor could he be beguiled into believing that what was on universal principles false in taste, might nevertheless be Aeschylean. Again, not once nor twice nor thrice, his mere command of the language enabled him to give meaning to what others had found untranslatable or unsatisfactory ; and in many a familiar passage his more than Oedipodean acuteness as a solver of riddles detected a point or allusion which had hitherto been missed. Not a few passages he restored to sense by no more than a change in the punctuation or re-division of the words.

But the unique value of the book consists in something more than all this. If any new thing was less expected than another in connexion with the *Agamemnon* (as with the *Septem*), it was the discovery that our conception of the plot was in essential features wholly wrong. Verrall declared that it was, and propounded a view which fell on the classical world like a bomb-shell.

> No edition known to me ventures to tell without disguise the story of the *Agamemnon*. I do not of course mean merely that the story told is not correct. This would be to assume the very point we are to discuss. I mean that the story, as it is commonly understood, is not told without concealment and practical misrepresentation.

With cruel frankness he makes good these editorial laches. He relates the story as it 'is still, with whatever dissatisfaction, accepted,' and goes on to ask,

> Is it possible that the story above told really represents the intention of Aeschylus? That a man who had spent most of his life in writing plays, when he came to lay down the lines of his supreme masterpiece should encumber himself at

starting with absurdities so glaring, so dangerous, so gratuitous, as this fable exhibits in all its parts?

To sweep away any lingering traces of delusion as to what the story amounts to when seen in its naked simplicity, he adds :—

As I see no reason to think that the popular mind in the time of Aeschylus was in this respect very different from the popular mind now, I will offer a Socratic parallel, not the less just because it is homely.—Scene : A room in London. Time: Early morning. Servants discovered preparing the room. From their conversation it appears that the master of the house has been for some time in Africa, and that the conduct of his wife, in relation to a person too often received, is causing them much anxiety and a strong desire for the master's return. They have learnt with satisfaction that their mistress is expecting soon to hear that he is on his way home. A telegram arrives for the lady, who presently appears and informs them that it is from her husband, and was despatched last night from Lake Nyanza. Being asked by a servant whether there is a telegraph at the Lake, she explains that the wires have just been extended so far by the result of her husband's enterprise. He intends to return forthwith. She wonders what sort of breakfast he is having in Africa, and hopes that he will not meet with any accident on the road back. The table is laid, and the lady is sitting down to it, when there is a ring at the bell. Enter the husband's courier, who announces that his master is detained for a few minutes at the terminus, but is coming immediately. He dilates upon the discomforts of the overland route and the breaking-down of an Italian train. The husband follows accordingly. He describes the success of his explorations. The lady receives him with rapture but without any surprise. In conversation with him she says nothing of the telegram, nor he to her. And so ends the first scene.—Now, at this point of the story we might either know the key to the riddle (if the author were dramatizing a popular novel) or we might wait for the solution in the sequel. But what would be the bewilderment and the dismay of the audience if it should prove that there was no solution, and that the mysterious telegram, introduced with so much circumstance, had no bearing on the story whatever! I submit that this is not the way in which the crowns of the drama may be won, and that the most rigorous proof should be required before we assume that it ever was. (p. xxiv.)

Verrall's solution of the tangle will be found in his Introduction, which, as also all the Euripidean volumes, can be readily understood and enjoyed even by those who have no knowledge of Greek. The power with which the exposition is worked out, and the skill with which the threads of the argument are gathered and combined, alike from innumerable hints scattered through the play and from the necessities of the whole situation, are beyond praise. It is a masterpiece of induction, and we are left staggered, but convinced and satisfied. The play which we had admired for little more than the great scenes which follow the king's entrance—being a little bored (to tell the truth) by the want of dramatic interest in what precedes, despite the magnificence of the poetry— we now see has a close-knit unity which keeps us enthralled from beginning to end.

It is notoriously difficult to lay aside deep-rooted prejudices, and accordingly this account of the plot was greeted by some with murmurs of disapprobation or doubt; but it may be safely prophesied that the Byzantine view of the *Agamemnon* will not again

find a serious champion. There is one little dilemma
to be faced by such a defender at the outset. If
Verrall's story is not what Aeschylus had in his
mind, then some Maxwell 'sorting demon,' with a
literary turn, must have been having the time of his
life, as he popped in note after note of his own *leit-
motiv*, in faultless accord, under the poet's very
nose! The suggestion, made some three years ago,
that an interval of several days may be assumed
between *vv.* 493 and 494, is sufficiently condemned
by an examination of the text at this point,—to say
nothing of other serious objections.

In the editions of the *Choephori* (1893) and
the *Eumenides* (1908) there is the same luminous
exposition of details, fresh evidence of that characteristic faculty of seeing in one view the drama and
its purpose, the same skill in presenting it to the
reader, the same incomparable dramatic instinct.
Who but Verrall could have offered such a solution
as he offers of the problem raised by the sudden
conversion of the Erinyes?

> *Ath.* (*coming closer*). I am not to be wearied of pleading
> with thee what is good [etc.].
> (*She is now in the midst of them, and speaks as for
> them alone.*)
> Ah, if sacred Suasion be holy unto thee, the appeasement
> of my tongue, the soothing... (*Her voice ceases to be heard,
> and for a while she seems to commune with them in silence.
> They become suddenly calm, and show in their behaviour a
> great awe.*)
> ...So thou wilt belike abide ;...

We cannot be sure that this is the manner in

which the wondrous reconciliation was effected, but who would not be profoundly grateful for the conception, and that, if only because it inspired the following noble and eloquent passage?

Now here [in the conversion of the Erinyes] is a solution indeed, a solution not of any particular casuistical or judicial problem (we may notice that after the trial the specific crime of Orestes is ignored completely), but of the universal problem, the discordance of principles, the antithesis of Right against Right. If the Inexorable can indeed be pacified, then there is somewhere One Right, one universal principle, something upon which 'the fallen house of Justice' may be builded again. Let us but know *why* this pacification takes place, upon what grounds and by what persuasions, and we shall be admitted to the very secret of things. We turn to the speech which effects all this, but—no explanation appears. At a certain point it is *assumed* by Athena that the adversaries are content, as they prove to be; it is *assumed* that this content proceeds from something just said or done. And just before stands—an unfinished sentence. *Ah, if sacred Suasion be holy unto thee, the appeasement of my tongue, and the soothing…. Thou, then, wilt belike abide, or if it should be thy will not to abide*—but that is not their will. A hiatus (it would appear), an injury singularly deplorable, has obliterated the words of the Eternal and the wisdom of the Most High. But never (we may hope) were they written. It is a gap which Aeschylus could no more have filled, nor would, than Dante could have told us what was the song which, on the Mount of Purgatory, hailed the forgiveness of sin and the restoration of man: 'I understood it not, nor here is sung the hymn which that folk then sang.' Not Aeschylus, nor any one who had felt, like him, that 'burden of thought' which can be lifted away only in the name of Zeus, would pretend to tell us what thought or thing it was with which Athena won the Erinyes. He that would put it in words, in his own words, would not be worth our hearing

Such a conciliation, if it is to command faith, cannot and must not be explicit. Something there must be which by men is not understood nor even heard, some place for the miraculous, mystic, and incomprehensible. (p. xxxii.)

And this—

> Indeed the strongest reason for believing, provisionally and until the contrary is proved, that the mystic and miraculous conversion of Vengeance to Grace, the sudden revelation that, in some incomprehensible way, Vengeance and Grace are the same, punishment and prosperity parts and aspects of one Providence, was the thought, substantially new and original, of Aeschylus himself, is its profound unlikeness and immense superiority to the common religious products of the Greek mind. It has the stamp of Aeschylus, perhaps the only Greek who shows a strong genius for religious invention, not metaphysical, or moral, or artistic, or imaginative, or ritual, or anything else but religious. The conversion of the Erinyes is a religious idea, awful, dark, and intensely satisfying. (p. xliii.)

In the summer of 1890, at the request of the Syndics of the University Press, and with a view to the performance of the play at Cambridge in the coming term, he prepared and published an edition of the *Ion*. The commentary, though intentionally limited in scope, gives an adequate explanation of the text, and as was to be expected, throws new light on a considerable number of passages. The dialogue is admirably translated into blank verse, with occasional deviations into the rhyming couplet, and the lyric portions of the play are rendered in a variety of metres adapted to the subject-matter of each. The following is the version of the passage beginning Ὦ Πανὸς θακήματα (*v.* 492), and for spirit, music, and rhythm, would seem to be hardly capable of being bettered. The reader will observe the felicity with which the sad note of the thrice-recurring ὤ of the original (Ὦ Πανός...ὤ Πάν... ὤ μελέα) is echoed in the burden of the version.

> O Athens, what thy cliff hath seen!
> The northward scar, Pan's cavern-seat,
> With rocks before and grassy floor,
> Where dancing tread the Aglaurids' feet
> Their triple measure on the green
>           Neath Pallas' fane,
> Whene'er the god in his retreat
> Times on the reed a quavering strain:
>   O Athens, what thy cliff hath seen!
> It saw the ravish'd maiden's pang,
> The babe she bare to Phoebus there
> Cast to the talon and the fang,
> There on the same insulting scene!
>           Of any born
> 'Twixt god and man none ever sang,
> None ever told, but tales forlorn.
>   O Athens, what thy cliff hath seen!

The chief interest of the book, however, lies in the Introduction, where we have the earliest of those studies in the work of Euripides by which Verrall attained what is perhaps his greatest and most lasting distinction. For these studies have achieved a result which, in all its circumstances, is unique in the history of literature. The admiration of the poet's contemporaries for his dramas knew no bounds, and the judgement of the whole ancient world, Greek and Roman, ranked him, howsoever different the quality of his genius, as the equal of Aeschylus and Sophocles. His right to the place was not discussed, it was taken for granted. In the popular favour he stood far above his two great rivals, and the picture drawn by Browning in *Balaustion's Adventure*, though heightened by poetical expression, represents in spirit an enthusiasm which was universally felt. In contrast to the ancient estimate of Euripides, the modern world, since the Revival of Learning, while not blind to his merits as a poet, found him as a playwright, in almost every one of his extant works, frankly beneath contempt. He was a botcher and bungler, a mere patcher of theatrical quilts which lacked all unity of design.

> Story! God bless you, I have none to tell, sir;—

or at least he could not tell it intelligibly, or without making it impossible and ridiculous. When he seemed to be desiring to rouse the hearer to emotion, with incredible perversity or stupidity he would kill the nascent feeling by a dash of the grotesque. Even when he had touched on something like success, he would spoil his own effect, and you would have the preposterous god or goddess contradicting from the clumsy machine all you had been led to expect, and failing to unravel the tangled skein after all. In a word, what stood for the plot did not work; and the dubious thing which he offered as drama, though 'good in parts,' as a whole failed to please, if it did not actually

stink in the critical nostril.  It was left for Verrall
to do for the whole work of Euripides what he had
done for the *Agamemnon* and *Septem*—to solve the
enigma by recovering the old-world point of view,
and to justify the ancient enthusiasm by showing
that we have before us not only sane, peculiarly
sane, art but also a supreme artist.

Thus in the prologue of the *Ion* Hermes tells us
that Apollo intends to guide the day's events in a
particular way : in the sequel these events go their
own way, in defiance of the intention of the prophetic
god.  In the course of the play the Oracle makes
a certain statement about Ion's parentage, but circumstantial evidence, furnished by the Delphian
authorities themselves, convinces the boy later that
the statement is false.  When he realises the contradiction his simple soul is 'horrified'—*for the oracle
must have lied*—and he turns to enter the shrine
and ask Apollo for an explanation.  At this moment
Athena appears above the temple roof.  The
following account is no travesty of the speech which
she proceeds to deliver ; Verrall has only added the
touch of an inimitable raillery to the common impression of its effect.

> Such being the knot to be solved, let us now consider the
> solution.  To say that Athena cuts it, without untying, is to
> pay her an unmerited compliment.  She does not touch the
> *nodus* at all.  Whatever she said, how could she?  This
> goddess, or this part of a goddess (for we seem not to be
> shown the whole of her, though we doubtless see all that
> there is), this divine πρόσωπον, heaved up by the machine, is
> herself a walking or rather a swinging fallacy, a personified

*ignoratio elenchi*! A goddess of Olympus, and a goddess 'rising above' the Delphian temple, is to give bail for the Oracle of Delphi! And where then is the security for herself? As is the speaker, so is her speech. It ignores the question, and Ion bluntly tells her so. More than half of it is spurious legend, complimentary to Athens but nothing to the matter. In the other half she repeats, point for point and almost without change, the explanations which Creusa has already offered in vain, and which now fall the flatter after exposure. Her apology comes to this : ' Yes, the facts are precisely as you can hardly believe. You, Ion, are the son of Creusa and Phoebus, who is indeed the selfish, brutal being that, on that hypothesis, he has been freely called. (In fact it is because he is ashamed to show himself, that I am here.) He did tell, and through his oracle, the lie in question; his motive, if that mattered, was no better, but a trifle worse, than Creusa has said ; and he does propose to save his credit by the quirk which has been treated with such contempt. As to the question asked, whether then the Delphian oracle is worthy of credence or not, I do not choose to answer directly ; but I leave you to suppose, if you please, that it is not. I have only to add, that (since Ion will grow up into an excellent father and hero of the Ionian race) all this is of no importance, and you may all go happily home, convinced that revelation is a fraud, and faith a delusion. And of this there is no shadow of doubt, no possible, probable shadow of doubt,— for I am Pallas Athena !'

No wonder that she produces no effect ! (p. xvii.)

Clearly this sort of thing won't do. By 'this sort of thing' I mean, not the echo of the *Gondoliers* —by which, as one grieves to learn, a certain Professor was inexpressibly shocked—but Athena's speech. It won't do. But what if it was not meant to do ? What if in fact the *Ion* conveys, beneath a veil thin enough for sharp eyes to pierce, a deliberate attack upon Delphi and the Olympian religion? Euripides was notoriously a 'free-thinker': *by putting the gods on the stage he persuades the men that they don't exist*, is the complaint of a woman in Aristophanes. Strip the play of its divine prologue and finale, and what have we left? A perfectly constructed drama in which every point tells, and from which every supernormal element is absent, but at the same time a drama in which the purely human story is, with consummate skill, so handled that Delphi is plainly discredited as a fountain of truth. As the pious Ion perceives to his dismay, it can lie. This discovery, however, which forms the climax of the play proper, has more than a polemical purpose; it contributes to the pathos of the story no less than the sufferings and anguish of Creusa. For the shattering of a cherished religious faith is in itself a sufficiently tragic experience, and this Euripides plainly meant to show. Indeed, it is Ion's case, rather than Creusa's, which would seem to have lain closest to the poet's heart; and I hazard a conjecture that as he drew this touching picture of the boy's distress, he was recalling the shock which had 'confounded' his own youthful soul when its early beliefs were swept away.

Such is the scope and purpose of the *Ion*, as revealed by Verrall's analysis: it is an impeachment of Delphi and all its works. The attack is covert, indeed, but it is so by preference as much as by necessity, for Euripides had in his armoury a better weapon than open invective, and one in the use of

which he is unsurpassed. He knew the deadly effect
of innuendo, and Verrall aptly sums up his method in
a quotation from George Meredith, prefixed to one
of his later essays :—'Yes, dear Van! that is how
you should behave. Imply things.' And though
two gods are introduced to deliver speeches, this is
no more than a concession to convention, and one
that the poet is little loth to make, for the prologue
and finale which he maliciously claps on to his
already finished play are so contrived as to give the
*coup de grace.* As our bloodthirsty old drill-sergeant
used to say at bayonet practice, 'one half-turrn to
the right *makes the wound incurable.'*

What contemporaries of Euripides, who shared
his views, might have thought and said of such
a Day at Delphi as the *Ion* represents, Verrall has
embodied in an epilogue. This epilogue is dramatic
in form, and represents a conversation between the
Delphian authorities and some Athenians who have
been silent spectators of all that has taken place. It
extends to no less than twenty-two pages, and is in
its kind a perfect work of art; one knows not whether
to admire most its originality as a conception, or its
brilliance and truly Athenian wit. To read it is to
receive a positive thrill of intellectual delight. When
the talk is over, the scene is suddenly changed : we
are in Athens, and the curtain has just fallen on
Euripides' play.

> *An Athenian (sadly).* And is there then *no* god, O
> Euripides ?
> *Euripides.* Neither that do I say, or have said, O

Chaerephon. Whence, or from whom, came to that feast
the detecting dove? Who sent that dumb creature to save,
at the cost of her own 'incomprehensible agony,' the life of
the kind-hearted lad who was sorry to kill the birds? Apollo,
Chance, Providence? We know not. Only, for the gods'
sake, do not think that it was the ravisher of Creusa.

Which is more likely? That this frame of the heavens,
this truly divine machine, is governed by beings upon whom
our poor nature cries shame; or that a knot of men, backed
by prejudice and tempted by enormous wealth, should try
by cunning to keep up a once beneficent or harmless delusion
for a little while longer?

For a little while! Χρόνια μὲν τὰ τῶν θεῶν πως, εἰς τέλος
δ' οὐκ ἀσθενῆ. Good night. Let us go to our chambers and
pray, to Pallas, if you must, to Zeus if you will, but let us
pray at least to the Father of men and women and beasts
and birds of the air, and give the verdict according to our
hearts. (p. xlii.)

The recognition of a double purpose in the
Euripidean drama forms the basis of the work by
which Verrall has vindicated Euripides as a dramatic
genius inferior to none, and has rehabilitated indi-
vidually more than half-a-dozen of his plays. He
contends that while, as a poet, Euripides found
sufficient material for his art in the play of human
passion and the tangle of life, he saw his way to
combining with this an attack on a theology and
religious practices which were, in his judgement,
both puerile and harmful,—or rather that the latter
was his life's purpose, which the stage was em-
ployed to subserve. In the conjunction he contrived to strike a tragic note such as had not
been heard before, and the skill with which he has

united the two aims leaves him in this respect absolutely without a rival. If we did not see this before, it is because we did not know the *man* Euripides as Verrall has taught us to know him ; we had failed to recognise the full import of hints, and more than hints, scattered broad-cast over his works. And if any do not now recognise or care for this contexture of tragedy and wit, then Euripides did not write for them ; but the enjoyment of those who do, comes as near as the lapse of ages will permit to that of the poet's contemporaries and the ancient world. All thanks and homage to him who has placed the key to it in our hands.

After the publication of the *Choephori* in 1893 the Euripidean studies were resumed, and bore fruit in *Euripides the Rationalist*, which appeared in 1895. The *Alcestis, Ion* (for a second time) and *Iphigenia in Taurica* are subjected to an exhaustive analysis, and the general result is to establish that view of Euripides as a dramatist which is indicated by the title of the volume, and which had already been shown to be the only view accounting satisfactorily for the phenomena presented by the *Ion*.

Of the novel and startling view taken of the *Alcestis* no extract or summary could give a fair presentation ; the whole essay, which extends to 128 pages, must be read (and more than once) before the cumulative force of the argument can be appreciated. The many who agree with the conclusion arrived at, regard the essay as a marvellous example of inductive reasoning. On the other hand, a reader who for any reason hesitates to yield assent, finds himself again confronted with the 'sorting demon'; for the play is manifestly open to Verrall's interpretation, while from beginning to end it does not present a single refractory feature. Let us make a supposition. Let the story of Alcestis' restoration to life be familiar, but let Euripides' play exist only in one recently discovered copy, still kept secret in the pocket of a happy digger in the Fayum who is a convert to the rationalist view of the poet's work. Let him be challenged to sketch the plot of a covertly rationalistic play on the Alcestis story, after the manner of his Euripides, and let him for answer produce the *Alcestis* that we have. Can it be doubted that by the general vote he would be pronounced to have scored a triumphant success?

In this same year the honorary degree of Litt.D. was conferred upon Verrall by Trinity College, Dublin. As will be seen, the Public Orator did justice both to his theme and to himself.

Maximo meo gaudio ad vos duco Arturum Woollgar Verrall, virum excellenti ingenio, doctrina, industria praeditum, qui nomen meruit nulli secundum eorum quibus Cantabrigia pristinam famam hodie auget. Postquam spatia Academica felici eventu percurrerat, totum se dedit Musis quarum ingenti percussus amore sacra fert. Studiis Aeschyleis, Euripideis, Horatianis operam praecipuam adhibuit. Fabulas Aeschyli tres, Euripidis *Medeam* edidit. Non huius est tritam criticorum orbitam sequi. Pennis non aliis datis

negata temptat iter via
coetusque volgares et udam
spernit humum fugiente penna.

Novas verborum gemmas eruere hunc valde iuvat, novosque flores decerpere unde prius nulli velarunt tempora. Locis obscuris lampada ingenii admovit, sententiamque latentem saepe elicuit quae alios omnes fugerat. Quid? Nonne ab inferis Alcestin revocavit, Stesichori exemplo clamans οὐκ ἔστ᾽ ἔτυμος λόγος οὗτος, negavitque in fabula eam decessisse, ut vulgo perhibetur, argumentisque haud spernendis sententiam suam stabilivit? Ut ingenio dives, ita animo candido ingenuoque est: et ipse pro me testari possum quam libenter auxilium ferat iis quos idem pratum metentes viderit.

Musarum pio sacerdoti interpretique sanctissimo Arturo Woollgar Verrall plaudite.

The year 1897 marks the beginning of the declension in bodily health. There was a definite attack of arthritis, from which, in spite of a visit to Bath, he never made a complete recovery, and the ˙smaller disabilities in the use of the hands and limbs began. In 1899 the Tutorship terminated, and in the summer he went for a 'cure' to Strathpeffer, but without obtaining any appreciable benefit. The next years were uneventful. He pursued further the study of Euripides, and in 1902 wrote, in the Alps, the essay on the *Heracles* which was afterwards published in *Four Plays*. In the October term of 1903 he delivered a lecture on the *Birds*. This was the first of those, given to a general audience, which came to be looked forward to as an invaluable prelude whenever afterwards a Greek play was to be produced in Cambridge. I regret

that I can give no account of it beyond saying
that it was astonishing for brilliance and originality,
and that the enthusiasm of the audience knew no
bounds. It was found necessary to repeat the
lecture for the benefit of many for whom there was
no room at the first delivery. The later lectures on
the *Eumenides* (1906) and the *Wasps* (1909) live
no less, I believe, in the memory of those who were
fortunate enough to hear them. The following
extract from a report of this last in the *Cambridge
Review* will give an idea of the delightful humour
which from moment to moment convulsed with
laughter an audience of nearly a thousand people
in the Examination Schools.

> The Old Man Philocleon is trying to adorn his con-
> versation with the literary anecdote in the true style of the
> day. Unfortunately his fund of stories all date from the
> glorious but old-fashioned times of Peisistratus, and they
> are marred by the fact that in his drunkenness he ends
> off each anecdote or allusion with a piece of scurrility.
> Dr Verrall explained how much of the humour of this
> scene was lost to a modern audience. For instance, we
> can hardly raise a smile at the lines
>> Simonides and Lasus once were rivals:
>> Then Lasus says, 'Pish, I don't care,' says he.
>
> Now, the point lies in the fact that Simonides and Lasus
> are two poets of the Peisistratid period, and reference to
> them sounded grand in the ears of Aristophanes' contem-
> poraries. We might produce something of the same effect
> if we imagined a dispute about the fare between a Festive
> Person and a Cabman. The Festive Person or F. P.
> attempts to silence the Cabman with the following remark:
>> Great Galileo through his optic glass
>> Saw once, as I see now, a silly ass.

A Policeman summoned says F. P. must pay.    Says F. P.,

> Carlyle thought not.  He closed a like dispute
> With Ruskin by the observation 'Scoot!'

The Policeman says there must be an end to this. 'Ah,' says the F. P.,

> Sir Isaac Newton knew that Science springs
> From careful notice of the simplest things,
> And when he rode a coach would never fail
> To keep an eye upon the horse's tail.
> He learn'd a lesson which I recommend
> To your attention : 'All things *have an end.*'

In other matters also is the humour of Aristophanes not obvious to a modern audience.  The Introduction of the Chorus is really a piece of delicate parody.  In Tragedy it had frequently been the custom to introduce a Chorus speculating and questioning as to the absence of the hero.... In the *Wasps* the Old Dicasts come searching for their absent brother, who appears, be it remembered, out of the chimney-pot.  Throughout there is sly imitation of Tragic Drama.  We may partly reproduce the effect in English, by introducing somewhere a parody of English poetry—say of *Locksley Hall*:

> What constrains him,
> What detains him?
> May the cause of his arrest
> Be some injury?  Or how, sirs,
> If he have mislaid a vest,
> Shirt, or coat, or even trousers?
> Or perchance the mischief's root
> Is a tightness of the boot?

Comrades, let us wait a little, while as yet 'tis early morn,
Wait, and if our friend should want us, help him with the
    shoeing-horn.

V. L. E.                                                          *e*

Verrall was an active member of the Greek Play Committee, and in connexion with the performance of the *Eumenides* in 1885 and the *Oedipus Tyrannus* in 1887 executed the *tour de force* of rendering the lyrics of these plays into rhymed verse which could be sung to Stanford's music, composed for the Greek text.

In 1905 the work of the poet who had now perhaps become his favourite—at least among the ancients—was examined afresh in *Four Plays of Euripides*. The plays discussed were *Andromache, Helen, Heracles, Orestes*. With characteristic aptness in the selection of titles, the essays are headed respectively, 'A Greek Borgia,' 'Euripides' Apology,' 'A Soul's Tragedy,' 'A Fire from Hell.' The first essay and the two last—these last especially—were hailed as masterpieces of analysis and criticism ; and the volume, together with *Euripides the Rationalist* and the essay on the *Bacchants* afterwards published, has no doubt settled the main questions of Euripidean interpretation for all time. The view propounded of the origin of the *Helen* is, from its nature, not such as could be more than suggested. The true answer to the riddle may lie elsewhere, but even if we remain unconvinced, and regard Verrall's solution as no more than a clever guess (which would be to do it great injustice), we are far from regretting that the essay was written. There is the expected originality in the way in which the whole problem is handled, the familiar but always astonishing 'ingenuity,' with humour, fancy, playfulness, wit, *tout ce qu'il y a de plus Verrallesque,*—in a word, Verrall in his lighter vein at his very best. The following passage gives one of the many reasons which compel him to regard the play as a jest.

Whether the cardinal miracle of the phantom Helen and its astounding disappearance could by any treatment be made credible to the imagination, we need not speculatively enquire. What is certain is, that Euripides does not so treat it. Never for an instant do the personages of the drama exhibit the sort of emotion which such an event must be expected to excite. They neither speak nor behave as if it were real. A single quotation will settle the point. *Where then is the evil thing which was sent to Troy instead of you?* asks Theoclymenus of Helen when he has been informed that Menelaus has died at sea. *The cloud-image, you mean,* she answers; *it vanished into air. Ah Priam!* sighs the amiable prince, *and ah Troy town, destroyed for nought!*—and then without another word on the subject they settle the details of a funeral ceremony for Menelaus. We do no disrespect to the author of such a dialogue, but conceive on the contrary that we are following his clear direction, when we say that it recalls not even the midsummer night's dream, but another famous dream, which I need not specify, in which the cat asks what became of the baby. 'It turned into a pig.' 'I thought it would,' says the cat, and closes the incident by vanishing. (p. 46.)

The following, from 'A Soul's Tragedy,' is a remarkable piece of writing, independently of its bearing on the play.

But among the conceivable factors of legend, among the many ways in which things might come to be believed though they never happened at all, or at any rate not as they were related, there was one upon which Euripides, whether guided or not by any predecessor, had meditated, as a tragedian, with special and specially justifiable interest. That the topic of madness and mental aberration was attractive to him, is noted by ancient critics, and is indeed obvious....[Illustrations are here given from various plays.]

These, however, were but steps on the road. It is in the _Heracles_ that this conception is applied on the largest scale, with most skill, with most insight, and most profoundly tragic effect. For power, for truth, for poignancy, for depth of penetration into the nature and history of man, this picture of the Hellenic hero may be matched against anything in art.

Although both in fact and in fiction madness is most commonly associated with crime, this conjunction is neither the only one in which mental extravagance is actually found, nor that in which it may with most profit be studied and depicted. Great hearts, as well as great wits, are to madness near allied; and among the consecrated benefactors of mankind there are perhaps few whose intellectual constitution appears to have been particularly sane, while in many the vigour of delusion has been proportional to the general strength of the faculties and character. Euripides needed not to look beyond the market-place of Athens for a personality scarcely more distinguished from the mass by acuteness and benevolence than by eccentricity of spiritual imagination. Nor are these higher types of aberration exempt, any more than the vulgar sort, from fluctuation and intermittence. The madman of genius or virtue may swing, like another, between sanity and insanity, and may be great in both. Now let us suppose (and the supposition is surely entertainable) that in the dark ages of superstition in the very dawn of civilized life and intelligent speculation, there arose a hero physically, mentally, and morally far superior to his contemporaries, but curst from his birth with a taint in his blood, a recurrent and progressive malady of the brain. Let such an one, in ardent and solitary meditation, have so far purged his notions of man and God from the grossness and barbarity around him, as to grasp at least

in vision the hint of philosophies still unbuilt, the principles
of creeds and religions long after to be preached and established. All this has been achieved by many a 'madman,'
whose thoughts, by the favour of circumstances, have passed
into circulation and are famous to this day; and doubtless
(as Euripides justly divined) it has also been achieved by
many and many another, whose voice was not heard nor
even raised, and whose meditation effected nothing but the
uplifting of his own heart and the ennobling of his own life.
Let our hero have done his duty faithfully up to and beyond
the demand and standard of the time, loving his home
and family, devoted in friendship, fighting gallantly and
victoriously for the little struggling community to which he
belonged. Let him have lent his services without stint to
the largest and most beneficial enterprises which the state of
things presented, to penetrate as pioneer the uncleared and
unknown waste, peopled in reality by savage beasts and men,
and supposed to be the haunt of monsters yet more terrible.
By the vulgar herd, nay, even by his nearest and dearest,
the source and nature of his greatness will be ignorantly
misconceived, and most of all by those who admire most.
On all sides he will hear his praises translated into language
which he loathes and contemns. His superiority to others
will be explained by the fiction of a divine parentage, which
to his better thoughts will seem a revolting blasphemy. His
genuine achievements will be enlarged and travestied by a
huge appendix of incongruous falsehood. And worst of all,
because of that taint in his blood, because he is not only
inspired but also, in the plain and gross sense of the word,
mad, because he has his hours of darkness as well as his
hours of illumination, he himself will sometimes lend his
authority to confirm the tales which he abhors, will repeat
the abominable nonsense with which his ears are fed, pro-
claiming himself that which he knows he is not, and painting
the good deeds of which he is proud, with the crude,
disgusting colours of folly and misbelief. In process of
time he will become aware that he does these things.

Long before anyone else, he will know how it is with him. Self-hatred and self-suspicion will aggravate the inner mischief from which they spring. And at last, upon the occasion of some special excitement, in a few moments and without any effective warning, the thin partition of his brain will break, and a burst of cruel fury will exhibit the benefactor of humanity, for some horrible hours, in the secondary but not less genuine character of a fiend. Such is the Heracles of Euripides. (p. 139.)

As a constructive study in the psychology of madness, based not upon observation but on intuition, and for sheer eloquence, the passage stirs in me a greater admiration than I dare express.

In 1910 was published *The Bacchants of Euripides*, a volume which contains seven other essays besides that which gives its name to it. The essay on the *Bacchae* is a worthy companion of those on Euripides previously published, both in power of analysis and in literary grace and vigour. But it was much more than a mere addition to its predecessors; it formed the indispensable completion of the work which Verrall purposed to do in connexion with the poet. Other remaining plays could easily be brought into line by application of the principles of interpretation already laid down, but in the *Bacchae* the miraculous, or seemingly miraculous, appears not in a detachable prologue or finale, but interwoven with the whole action of the play. What countenance, if any, Euripides intended to give to the cult of Dionysus, had long been a matter of debate with scholars; to Verrall the question naturally presented itself in another form. What puzzled him was the presence of the miraculous element at all, and its contradiction of the poet's practice in other plays offered a problem which he had long felt demanded solution before he could himself consider his views to be securely established. After much pondering this last riddle was guessed, and with the discovery that in the *Bacchae* the miraculous was after all intended to be no more than clever wizardry or the familiar exaggeration of hearsay, his last difficulty was removed, and the rationalistic interpretation of the Euripidean drama was rounded off into a harmonious whole.

As a critic Verrall possessed certain qualities of mind which gave his work a peculiar *differentia*. In their combination and in the degree of their development, so far as I am aware, he stands alone. Perhaps the most distinguishing mark of his genius was his power of reconstructing his author. I do not mean his author's works, nor his author as a writer, but as a man. In the case of modern or even ancient writers, if a moderate amount of biographical information is available, such reconstruction is not difficult, and the thing has often been admirably done; but when this information is wanting or negligible in quantity, as in the case of Aeschylus and Euripides, the task is of an altogether different nature. Verrall's rare insight and inductive powers, brought to bear on little more than the text of these authors (on no more in the case of Aeschylus), enabled him to trace the workings of their minds as it were from within, and so to embody with some measure of completeness the living, thinking man behind. He seemed to know them as one knows a personal friend, the natural current of whose thoughts one can in given circumstances divine, and of whom one can affirm with some certainty (as in deciphering, say an illegible passage in a letter) that he would, or would not, have written this or that. To this power of psychological reconstruction we are indebted for a more profound and comprehensive conception of the genius and aims of Aeschylus, and for a presentation of Euripides which we can well believe touches close upon the truth. In the long monologue put into the poet's mouth in *Euripides the Rationalist* (pp. 106 ff.) we feel that we are listening to a living man, in comparison with whom the personages in Landor's *Imaginary Conversations* are hardly more than marionettes. Clever, again, as is the *New Lucian* of H. D. Traill, the author has all the advantage that comes from the selection of modern characters and well-known public men. Verrall did better with much less promising material. It was because Euripides had come to be alive to him, no less than by critical observation directed to the play, that he was led to his wonderful interpretation of the *Heracles* : if this man handled the story at all, this is the Heracles he would have pourtrayed, and being Euripides, he *could not have pourtrayed any other*. Indeed, it was, I think, because Verrall thus realised Aeschylus and Euripides as living men that he bestowed so much loving labour on their works.

Though the aims of the two poets were so widely divergent, he felt a sympathy, at once moral and intellectual, with both; he came to know each as being, according to his lights, a man of noble purpose, worthy. In the art of Sophocles, great as was of course his admiration of it, his interest was of a totally different kind, and comparatively weak. Even if the field had not been already occupied by the great scholar whose genius was so completely in sympathy with that of the poet, he would never, I believe, have been drawn to producing an edition of Sophocles. The mere artist,

εὔκολος μὲν ἐνθάδ᾽, εὔκολος δ᾽ ἐκεῖ,

awakened no enthusiasm; there was no man to be discovered behind the artist, or at any rate no man whom Verrall would greatly care to know.

Another predominant trait, in respect of which I find it difficult to imagine that any man could surpass him, was his extraordinary intellectual alertness. In the ordinary relations of life it was a characteristic which could not escape notice, so that if Athena (not she of the *Ion*) had chanced to meet him on one of the many likely occasions that Cambridge society affords, she could hardly have helped quoting herself in gracious approbation,

οὕνεκ᾽ ἐπητής ἐσσι καὶ ἀγχίνοος καὶ ἐχέφρων.

The company would have agreed that each epithet was deserved, but they would have had little doubt that it was the ἀγχίνοια which brought the line to her mind. Of his published work it is one of the most conspicuous features. He seems, as he read, to have missed nothing. No point, unnoticed by others, but which the author must have intended, would pass unobserved (there is a striking instance in the note on ὑπτίασμα at Aesch. *Ag.* 1263); no text which obscured such a point would remain unchallenged. That he was always right, his most whole-hearted admirers would be the last to contend; but it is his distinction, that in the whole range of classical literature and elsewhere he saw much, very much, that predecessors and contemporaries alike had failed to see. Few men can have raised or discussed more problems in familiar fields, and few can have contributed more to their solution; and if we cannot always discern what he discerned, well— the eye can only see what it has the power of seeing. Thus a reviewer failed to see, even when it was pointed out, the effect produced by the turn which Agamemnon gives to his term of address at *Ag.* 905. The following note left him unconvinced.

> Λήδας γένεθλον : a significant opening. Clytaemnestra was the daughter of one false wife and the sister of another, and her husband, who calls her by no other name or title but this,—neither 'wife,' nor 'queen,' nor even 'Clytaemnestra,' —gives her to know that he has not forgotten the fact.

This would make our Aeschylus too clever!

Problems were indeed a meat that Verrall's soul loved; and if it were the modern fashion to give additional surnames to others than sailors and soldiers, in commemoration of notable achievement, one might venture to affirm that he would be known to posterity as Problematicus. Leaving out of account the minor questions which confront the editor of an ancient author at every turn, more than half of Verrall's published work, which runs to twelve volumes, is addressed to the solution of problems properly so called. No less than five, from Greek, Roman, and Italian literature, are discussed in the present volume. The whole of his work on Euripides, excepting the *Medea*, centres round one great problem, and we must include under this head the *Studies in Horace*, and the Introductions to the *Septem*, *Agamemnon*, and *Eumenides*. In *The Bacchants of Euripides* we have essays on The First Homer, the Mutiny of Idomeneus (a little discovery of his own), the Death of Cyrsilus, and Christ before Herod ; and a problem is the starting point of half the papers now republished in *Collected Classical Studies*. The variety exhibited by the list is significant : whenever and wherever in his reading he came across what in the language of private life he called a 'boggle,' he could not rest until he had made an effort to get to the bottom of it. The origin of the essay on Christ before Herod is typical. He happened, during a holiday in the country, to be reading Loisy's ponderous tomes on the Synoptic Gospels, and discovered that a difficulty of some importance had been raised, but not solved, in connexion with the two Trials. The subject was entirely outside his usual range, but as he said to me with a whimsical air of apology 'there was the boggle.'

Another faculty he possessed, which must have
been observed by all who knew him or have read
his books : he had the genuine dramatic instinct.
He showed it in the way in which he narrated a
story or anecdote in conversation, in his lectures
(it is noted in Mr Cornford's account), and in the
form in which he cast his essays and many an
editorial note. He does not jump to his point,
but skilfully prepares the ground piece by piece,
so that the reader shall grasp the situation as it
is in all its bearings ; and when expectation has
been sufficiently aroused, and the suspense long
enough maintained, then and not till then, he
launches his conclusion, with proportionately telling
effect. In his editorial work the faculty proved of
special service, and not only in the matter of verbal
interpretation. He never forgot—it seems odd to
have to note this—that a Greek play is a thing that
was once actually *performed*—a δρᾶμα, and the
details of the stage-management were always present
to his mind. Yet, as he found it necessary to observe, the ancient dramas have been read and
interpreted as though a dramatist who wished to
produce a play on the stage, had nothing more to
do than write his dialogue and place the MS., without
explanation, in the hands of the actors. Even with
our own dramatists readers would fare ill if the
printed book contained no more than the words
to be spoken ; and how much turns on effective
stage-management, and sometimes solely on that,
needs no saying. In numerous passages of the

plays with which he has dealt, Verrall has saved us from error, or enlarged our understanding of the scene, simply by supplying necessary stage-directions. He has pointed out how much could and must have been expressed on the Attic stage by grouping, by gesture, by a mere change of attitude or position, by intonation and emphasis.

Evidence of yet another fruitful gift is given by five essays in the volume of *Collected Classical Studies*, and by many an occasional observation in other parts of his works. He had a peculiarly delicate ear for rhythm. The essays referred to are that on Eur. *Andr.* 655 f., *The Latin Sapphic*, *The Metrical Division of Compound Words in Virgil*, *A Metrical Jest of Catullus*, and *On a Metrical Practice in Greek Tragedy*. Each was born of that unerring instinct for musical balance in language which is illustrated by many passages in his own prose and verse, and each is a master-piece of constructive criticism. So imperfectly were the rules for the senarius of Greek Tragedy understood, that though the two lines in the *Andromache* had been suspected, no one had thought of rejecting them decisively, as Verrall does, on metrical grounds alone, and the essay forms a valuable guide for numerous other passages. The conclusions arrived at in the two last essays must have awakened some dismay in the hearts of not a few who had found delight in writing Latin hendecasyllabics or Greek iambics, and if any such composers have not read them, they would do well to let their Muse rest until they have! For they will find—what they will find. Besides these essays he wrote the articles on metre in the *Companion to Greek Studies* and the *Companion to Latin Studies*. To the latter he also contributed the article on Latin Literature to the end of the Augustan period. Some original and valuable observations on rhythm were also made in the Clark lectures.

Mr Cornford, who gives expression to the universal verdict, has spoken of Verrall's exceptionally stimulating power as a lecturer. The same quality is found in his books. It is not merely that he writes with conviction, as many others have written : he does this, and it is part of the secret of his force, but he does more. Some authors write as though chiefly anxious to maintain an opinion, for their own satisfaction, as it were. Most write as though their business were done, as perhaps it is, when they have delivered their message,—with an air of indifference as to whether the message be accepted or not. Verrall wrote as one concerned to convince, to convince *you*, the individual reader. There is a personal air about it all. It is as though he began by saying, 'Here is something that interests me immensely, and I want to interest you too.' He wishes to do his reader a friendly service : ' Let me introduce you to Euripides ; you will find him worth knowing.' It is an effect which few writers, and very few editors of the ancient classics, manage to produce. In Verrall's case, while even those who have not known him are sensible of the impression, with those who have, it is reinforced by a peculiar experience. He wrote easily and naturally, and so vividly does the literary style represent the man, that sentence after sentence produces the illusion of hearing the written words spoken by the living voice, with all the familiar intonations. Vitality of this kind stimulates, and not merely with the stimulus of awakened interest and the sense of refreshment. It encourages, and has already encouraged not a few, to fresh study on the same lines. For Verrall never left the impression that he had exhausted his subject, but rather that there was more left to be done, that the familiar ground is still full of buried treasure.

The two following extracts from obituary notices refer to his work on Euripides.

> It is largely due to Dr Verrall that the reputation of Euripides has been rehabilitated; at present owing to his work and to Professor Murray's translations, the last of the three dramatists occupies in the esteem both of the critics and the public a position which, if foreshadowed by Milton's view of him, would have been surprising to many of his readers in the middle of the last century. (*The Times*, June 19, 1912.)

> The scholars had long considered Euripides' plays unsatisfactory; but by riveting their attention upon details they were able to hush the fact up, and continued in a mechanical way to acclaim him the equal of Aeschylus and Sophocles. Verrall's first business was to tear aside the veil, and to show that, if the scholars' view of such a play as *Ion* was correct, honest opinion must pronounce its author hopelessly stupid and incompetent. This, however, led to a dilemma, for such excellent judges as Aristotle had a very different opinion of

Euripides. It is well known how...Verrall proposed a solution for this dilemma. Whether it is the correct one is a highly controversial question; but it may be asserted with some confidence that the correct solution will be found upon Verrall's lines. In any case the dilemma itself remains and can no longer be shirked; and it was this power of forcing a clear-cut intellectual problem upon those who would always prefer not to face one that was the great merit of his mind. (_Spectator_, June 22, 1912.)

I do not quite understand the writer in the _Spectator_ when he says that the correct solution of the Euripidean dilemma will at any rate 'be found upon Verrall's lines.' Setting aside certain professedly conjectural suggestions duly marked as such, and which do not concern the main question, Verrall's 'lines' are not speculative but logical, and it is difficult to see how they could lead to any but his own conclusions. That these conclusions should not yet be generally accepted, need cause no surprise, nor should the fact tempt younger students to mistrust their own unbiassed judgement of Verrall's arguments. Busy men read books with haste, and so may fail to appreciate their force, and towards middle age most men notoriously find it difficult to change their views on any subject. No doubt, also, there will always be those who cannot see that a door must be either open or shut. Moreover, we British cherish an inborn mistrust of all subtlety of mind and of some forms of originality, and a writer who combines these qualities with what we call 'brilliance,' is likely to find his very merits a bar to the ready acceptance of his message. If

Verrall had written in France for French scholars, their only hesitation, I fancy, would have been as to which to do first—kiss him on both cheeks or lay wreaths on their copies of Euripides. There is a question which we ought to ask ourselves, and which some of us have not asked, and it is this. If the ancient and (may I add?) correct estimate of Euripides as a consummate artist was ever to be recovered, was this recovery likely to be made, considering the conditions of the problem, except in a manner at once daring, original, subtle, brilliant, startling or even shocking? Was the riddle for any chance guesser? Was less than a Verrall needed, and *were we not to expect to be astonished by the answer?* Some critics would seem hardly to have realised the magnitude of the issue, and the fundamental change of view which *any* solution of the question must involve. The very strangeness of the solution of such a problem is in its favour, so long as the steps by which it is reached are logically sound,—as Verrall's are. The *Spectator* also speaks of the correctness of Verrall's solution as 'a highly controversial question.' This may be so, but one looks in vain for the controversy. It is now twenty-three years ago that Verrall first blew his trumpet and entered the lists on *Ion*, and three times since he has sounded his challenge and thrown down his glove. And all have praised his high port, and the beauty of his armour, and the skill of his *manège*, and some have muttered that bold though he be and ful of sotyl devys, yet are there many weak joints in the rich harness, and that his is not to be the victor's garland, but *no man has taken up Verrall's gage.* Meanwhile the onlookers are drawing their own conclusions, and for myself I take leave to express without reserve the conviction that before this generation has passed away, Verrall's view of the work of Euripides will be the accepted view, and that mere murmurs of disapproval will cease to command attention.

From 1904 the arthritis remained practically stationary for about five years. He could walk with assistance, and save for this and some other slight physical disabilities, lived the usual life, doing his ordinary work, and going out in his trailer or for drives in a carriage. Journeys by train were accomplished without great inconvenience, and during this period he paid many visits to friends, and travelled to various places to lecture. It may be interesting to note that *Aristophanes on Tennyson* in the present volume originally formed part of a lecture delivered at Newcastle.

In the October term of 1909, besides the 'historic lecture' on the *Wasps* already mentioned, and the Henry Sidgwick Memorial Lecture, the substance of which appears in the present volume in the essay entitled *The Prose of Sir Walter Scott,* Verrall delivered also the first six of the Clark Lectures. Six more were given in the following term. To illustrate his main theme, the Victorian Poets, the following authors were selected: Tennyson, Robert

Browning, Matthew Arnold, D. G. Rossetti, and Swinburne. The lectures were given in a large double lecture-room at Trinity, accommodating about 200 people. The room was always filled to its utmost capacity, and the men among the audience greatly outnumbered the women, 'a fact most rare in the history of Cambridge lectures on English Literature or on Art.' A characteristic feature of the lectures, to which he himself attached great importance, was the reading aloud of a considerable number of selected passages. I quote the following from the *Cambridge Review* :—

> Dr Verrall's method of reading is unique and overwhelming. His voice is under the most wonderful control for shades of pitch, volume, and expression. In Greek we have long known it, we know it in English now. Dr Verrall's reading gives the hearer something, many things, that no criticism in the world, not even Dr Verrall's own, could ever give. The poems are suddenly alive. No one who heard 'Blush it thro' the East,'...will ever forget the experience.

It is to be regretted that these lectures are preserved only in the memories of those who had the good fortune to hear them, but from their very nature they were incapable of being committed to paper. Verrall himself would make no attempt to give them to the press, for he held that in such lectures the living voice must always play an indispensable part. This opinion he expressed in the Inaugural Lecture delivered from the English Chair in May, 1911. In a report of that lecture the *Cambridge*

*f* 2

*Review* writes of him as speaking to the following effect :—

> All languages, and English more than most, depend largely upon effects of stress and intonation, which are incapable of reproduction in writing, but in conveying which the *viva vox* can be of great service: an instance is the much quoted and much misunderstood line, 'We needs must love the highest when we see it.' Especially is this the case with poetry written in an elaborate and difficult metre—for instance, Shelley's *Ode to the Skylark*.

The appointment to the King Edward VII Professorship of English Literature, which is made by the Crown, came in February, 1911. The chair was founded at the end of 1910 by Sir Harold Harmsworth, who expressed a desire that in promoting the study of 'English Literature from the days of Chaucer onwards,' the Professor should follow 'literary and critical rather than philological and linguistic lines.' Verrall was the first holder of the office. Before accepting the appointment he consulted his medical man and a few friends. There had been some increase of the arthritis in the spring of 1910, and he was carried upstairs to the two last Clark lectures, after which time he never again walked. In the summer, however, there had been a satisfactory recovery, and the medical verdict was that there was no apparent reason why the present condition might not be maintained for a considerable time. His friends were unanimous in urging acceptance of the appointment. The universal opinion was indeed expressed by the Master of Trinity at the 'Annual Gathering' soon after Verrall had passed away; he said that no one who had heard the Clark Lectures could doubt that Verrall was the proper person to be the first King Edward VII Professor. Twelve lectures on Dryden, the only course delivered, were given from the English chair in the October term of the same year. They were marked by the expected originality and freshness of treatment, and though the difficulties of delivery were considerable, showed no least falling off in power. The notes for the lectures have fortunately been preserved, and these are so full and in such form as to be suitable for publication. It is hoped that they may soon appear.

All who have known both Verrall and his books, agree upon one point, that the fascination of his literary work, great as it is, was surpassed by his personal charm. The following is a sample of many letters received by Mrs Verrall:

> Your dear husband had for me an irresistible attraction from the first day I got to know him when I was an undergraduate, and the attraction which he exercised on me was only that which he had for everyone who knew him....I have never forgotten, nor can I ever forget, his kindness to me in the early years after I had taken my degree.

It was my own happiness to enjoy the closest intimacy with him in a friendship extending over half a life-time, and perhaps no man knew him better. What such a friendship was to me would add to his praise if it could be told, but I can only record here that during all the time that I knew him, I was conscious of an ever increasing admiration and affection. To know him was to like him, to know him well was to love him,—and for all that he was. One did not have to make allowances, for there were no contradictions in the character, it was rounded, harmonious, beautiful. The extraordinary subtlety of the mind was united to a nature of rare simplicity, utterly devoid of ostentation and pretence, and without the least tinge of vanity. He never even exhibited such a modest pride in his achievements and distinctions as would have needed no excusing, and I am sure he did not feel it. When he was elected to the English Chair, his crowning University distinction, his one thought was of the things he would now have an opportunity of saying. He was also transparently sincere, and few can have known a man so completely unselfish. Easily roused though he was even to excitement when holding forth on some matter which greatly interested him, his usual manner was extremely gentle, the natural outcome of a kindly and affectionate disposition. His sympathy was instinctive and peculiarly real, and his interest in the fortunes of his friends seemed greater than in his own, if indeed they had not become his own. If you went to his house on a visit, he would inquire particularly about each member of the family, asking for details, and this not out of mere politeness, but because he wanted to know. Even in the case of

strangers or those who were no more than acquaint-
ances, news of a misfortune touched a chord of real
feeling, and as his swift imagination vividly pictured
how things must be with the sufferers, he actually
experienced, I believe, something like what he
would have felt had the trouble fallen upon himself.
It was a literal συμπάθεια. I have myself observed
this many times, and instances will occur to others
who knew him. Thus, in a letter written home
from Chamonix, there is a quite long account of the
sorrows of a poor man who had lost a mule; and
another letter written from Normandy depicts the
desolation of a 'personally conducted' party of
tourists who had missed connexion with their con-
ductor, with almost as much concern as if he had
been one of them. A letter from Strathpeffer tells
how sorry he was for a young bride who was being
married, 'Scottish fashion,' in a sort of open shelter
in the hotel garden, in full view of the residents,
and how relieved he was to learn afterwards that
she 'didn't mind a bit!' His love for children was
uncommon in a man. He understood them and
their ways, and found great delight in watching and
talking to them. How generous he was of his time
and of his counsel, many an old pupil has testified,—
how he would 'put himself out' to do a man a kindness. Thus one correspondent recalls an occasion
when 'he carried me off to Brighton with him for a
change, when I was in bad health before my Tripos';
and few of his friends are not his debtors for some
service out of the common.

Not the least of his charms was his exquisite courtesy, which was not, as it is so often, just a veneer, but natural and spontaneous. No doubt it was the mark of sincerity which made the following incident live in the mind of the writer.

> ...I have a very vivid recollection of the first time Dr Verrall spoke to me. It was in my second year, and we had rooms on adjoining staircases and shared the same bedmaker. One day he was wanting to call Mrs Chapman and climbed the stairs to the first storey. I was just behind, on the way to my rooms, and as his illness was then beginning to take a firm hold upon him, I was kept waiting a little on the staircase. As I passed him at the first storey landing, he turned and apologized for delaying me, and such courtesy to an insignificant strange youth touched me deeply....

One can imagine the winning smile with which the apology was made. It was by these and a dozen other delightful traits that Verrall won men's hearts; but there was more still behind, for all were combined in a character of singular rectitude and rare purity of mind and heart.

As Mr Marsh has said, he was a good judge of character. Yet he was never a harsh one; his broad sympathies were always ready with an excuse for human weakness. But he had more than the insight needed to make a judge of character; he had the quality of constructive psychological intuition which goes to the making of men of the type of Robert Browning, and I have often thought that it needed but a touch to transform him into something out of the common as a dramatist or poet. How near he came to this may be seen if, for a moment, we combine in one view his gift of musical verse and his instinct for the dramatic with the masterly pourtrayal of the Euripidean Heracles.

'His presence, his voice' (to quote Professor Gilbert Murray) 'were full of inspiration'; and this was true even of the latter years, when the body was a wreck and the voice had lost something of its *timbre*. There was still the fine head and face—the broad full brow, the harmonious contour of the cheeks and well-proportioned nose, the kindly lines about the mouth, and the large, dark, expressive eyes that spoke with no less eloquence than the compelling voice. During the later lectures he said, ' I could lecture as well as ever, if they would only get my tiresome voice right.' Nor was this far from the truth. So long as the voice, with its clear articulation, and tones according instinctively with his theme, responded not inadequately, one could not fail to feel, through eye and ear, that quickening effect which is justly called inspiration.

Verrall was not a wide reader, as reading goes among scholars to whom we apply the term 'learned'; but he was something better than ' learned,' and he turned his reading, which was really wide, to better account than many a ' learned' scholar has done. For mere information he did not care overmuch, he preferred *multum legere potius quam multa*. What he asked for from serious books was nutriment, and this he got better (if I may pursue the horrid metaphor) by repeated mastication than by the hasty omnivorous feeding which makes assimilation

impossible. Certain books and authors he read over
and over again until they became part of him, bone
of his bone. Among these, besides some of the
English poets, were Shakspeare, Dante, Dryden,
Macaulay, Thackeray, Fielding, Scott, Louis Stevenson, Jane Austen, *The Egoist*, Racine, Bossuet and
other famous French orators, on which last he lectured in early days at Newnham. Jane Austen was
an especial favourite, and it is characteristic that in
her works he found abundant room for emendation
in the countless printers' errors perpetuated from
the first editions to the latest. He published an
article on them in the *Cambridge Observer* (1892),
and two others reprinted in *The Book of the Cambridge Review*. While some of the corrections are
obvious enough, many are emphatically not, but
needed—well, a Verrall. I regret that there is not
room to quote the note on 'his *direct* holidays might
with justice be instantly given to' [his friends at
Mansfield Park] (*M. P.* vol. 1, p. 240, Brimley
Johnson's edition). The correction *derelict* is typical
of his skill in this line, and the arguments by which
it is justified are another illustration of his remarkable power of reconstructing for himself an author's
mind. Shakspeare and Macaulay's History were
never out of his hands for long, and I believe he
had read the history from end to end some half-a-
dozen times, and many parts much oftener. He
had in fact prepared for delivery from the professorial chair lectures on Macaulay's works considered
from a literary point of view. Shakspeare, I suppose,

he knew as some of us know, or once knew, our Latin Grammar jingles. His memory, and especially his verbal memory, was extraordinary. Scores of times I have heard him quote the very words of long sentences from prose authors, and long passages from poets ancient and modern. Verse in particular he seemed simply unable to forget, and he would often repeat stanzas which he had read only once. There seemed to be nothing for which he could not instantly find a quotation that fitted, and only a week or two before we were to hear the loved voice no more, something—a mere word—called up a stanza of Thackeray's verse which he had not seen for years. He 'boggled' over the ending of one line, but the rest he declared was correct.

For dogmatism in every form Verrall had a strong dislike, and in the matter of religious faith the dogmas of orthodoxy and heterodoxy alike failed to appeal to him. He believed that the truth lay deeper. At the same time his reverence for religion was deep, and the life—for 'all that is true, all that is noble, all that is right, all that is pure, all that is loved, all that is fair-speaking, be there virtue, be there praise'—was such as many who hold a more definite faith might look upon with self-reproach. His was the *anima naturaliter Christiana*. In politics, in which his interest was keen, he was a strong Liberal, stronger than many friends whose opinions differed, were aware; for he hated controversy, and while he delighted in a political talk with those who thought with him, he never himself introduced the subject with those who did not, though he would listen with genuine interest to their expositions of the adverse view. His liberalism was of the true sort. G. K. Chesterton writes, in his book on Browning,—

> A Liberal may be defined approximately as a man who, if he could by waving his hand in a dark room stop the mouths of all the deceivers of mankind for ever, would not wave his hand. Browning was a Liberal in this sense.

And such a Liberal was Verrall, as he himself used to say. Miss Jane Harrison tells a confirmatory story :—

> I remember saying to him *apropos* of some scholar from whom I differed, 'It is intolerable that people should be allowed to go on talking and teaching such nonsense !' He screwed up a whimsical eye at me and said, 'All right, let's have back the Inquisition.'

He believed in thrashing out things, everything, by the freest and fullest discussion, for only so, he thought, could the ultimate truth, for which he cared supremely, be attained. No established view or theory, on any subject, had for him any claim to acceptance just because it was established ; all must stand the test of examination, and every side must be heard. He would encourage every investigation which gave promise of tangible fruit. Thus he took the liveliest interest in Mrs Verrall's work in psychical research, and in the work of the Society generally, and himself originated and pursued one most valuable and interesting telepathic experiment, the famous one on μονόπωλον ἐς Ἀῶ. And he was more than content that his daughter should devote her rare intellectual powers, as she has done, to work in the same scientific field.

To his predominant enthusiasm for literature he added a love of art in any shape, for he had the artist's instinct, and the artist's eye readily responsive to beauty of colour or of form. Architecture in particular appealed to him. His knowledge of its principles and developments was considerable, and probably few men were better acquainted with the great European churches, either through having visited them or through books and photographs. Music gave him intense delight. He felt it, like all true lovers, in his very marrow. As he listened, he lived in it, totally absorbed, alert to every refinement of expression and responding to every mood. He was a regular attendant at concerts in Cambridge until the physical difficulties made this impossible, and in the last months the skilful and sympathetic interpretations of a friend who used to come and play the pianoforte to him, were among the welcome solaces of that sad time. He loved nature in every aspect. A cycling or walking tour, in England or abroad, was a source of perpetual enjoyment, for he missed no beauty of the scene, however simple, no transforming effect of light. The Alps, Swiss or Italian, he of course loved best, though alas! he was no mountaineer; the most moderate precipice made him giddy. The resolute spirit did its best to master the flesh, but it was of little use, and the passage of such places, if accomplished, was always attended with anguish. It seems to have been the only thing for which the dear head was no good at all.

It is needless to add that he was, to an unusual degree, a man of many friends,—real friends, who were much to him, as he to them.

Of his conversation Professor Murray writes in the *Oxford Review* :—

> His conversation, even at a time when he had been crippled by years of arthritis and must have suffered great pain, was indescribably brilliant, ranging over politics, literature, classical learning, and often taking refuge in pure nonsense. Seldom indeed can so keen a wit have been so utterly devoid of malice. In a friendship of about twenty years I never heard him tell a story to any one's discredit, nor even defend himself against criticism with any resentment or bitterness. I remember nothing worse than a genial ' W——— is an owl,' and then attention to business. His style in controversy was courtesy itself. He could make an opponent feel ridiculous and even—*experto crede*—laugh at himself; but there was not a word to resent, not a phrase that left a feeling of unfair treatment. It is perhaps owing to these qualities, combined with his unflagging love of justice and the extraordinary courage with which he rose superior to his long and terrible illness, that Verrall has left upon those who knew him well an impression of greatness and of nobility, far outweighing the normal admiration due to a famous scholar.

It remains to say something more of a trait touched upon in this extract and also in the obituary notice in the *Spectator*, from which the following is taken.

> Though his body was crippled by a painful illness, his mind never seemed subdued by it. It was always active and

at times irrepressibly gay, as willing to discuss *The Mystery of the Yellow Room* as a Pindaric ode, ready to break out into a snatch from the Mikado or a *tirade* from *Andromaque.*

The trait I mean is one that is never absent from a mental picture of the man we loved,—his natural gaiety of heart and love of nonsense for its own sake. His wit was always ready, as for instance when, overhearing on a hot and smelly day in Rome, some tourists asking for the *Cloaca Maxima*, he quietly observed, ' I should rather have expected them to ask for the *Cloaca Minima*!' Another story, which I tell in Mr Marsh's words, shows his power of extracting amusement from unpromising materials. At a meeting of 'revisers' to the O. and C. Board the Latin verse papers from Eton were produced. 'Now for *susurrus*!' said Verrall. 'What do you mean?' asked a colleague. 'Why, did you ever see a copy of Eton verses without *susurrus*?' Then he looked at the English, and gave up hope; there seemed to be absolutely no opening for *susurrus*. He went on sadly to read the first copy till he came to a line in which 'And universal silence reigned alone' was rendered by *nullusque susurrus*! 'My point is completely established!' he screamed. 'If there was *any* sound, it was *susurrus*; if there was *no* sound, there was *nullus susurrus*! U-u-ur!'

But the joy of joys was his manner of reciting humorous verse or pure nonsense, and to find (if it was your first experience of him in this vein) that

he took as intimate a delight in it as you did yourself. 'Tragedy!' he once said to me suddenly in
the early days; 'Did you ever hear this?' And
he proceeded to chant slowly, in rolling, melancholy
tones, a once famous song of Toole's (metre strictly
dactylic)—

> A norrible tale I 'ave to tell
>   Of the sad di-sasters that befell
> A noble family as once re-sided
>   In the very same thoroughfare as I did. (etc.)

Or it might be Dan Leno's parody of 'The Honey-
suckle and the Bee,' in which the Wasp vainly
makes love to a hard-boiled egg :—

> And what a silly wasp for 'just a word' to beg,
> For you *can't* get any sense out of a hard-boiled egg!

It is impossible to give any idea of what Mr Marsh
well calls 'the kind of augustness which remained
with him in all his wildest nonsense. He seemed
always to be a priest of fun, pouring it out with the
same power and authority with which he recited
the most magnificent poetry.' He seemed indeed
at such moments to be literally *possessed* by the
spirit of mirth, and it was enough 'to shake the
midriff of despair with laughter.' Scraps from the
*Ingoldsby Legends* would bubble up on the slightest
provocation, and it does me good to recall the tones
with which he would bring out such things as

> She drank prussic acid without any water,
> And died like a Duke and a Duchess's daughter!

Or

But is it *O Sanctissima* she sings in dulcet tone,
Or *Angels ever bright and fair?*—Ah no, it's *Bobbing Joan*!

Sometimes some musical rhythm running in his head would seem to have touched the spring, as when he would say without warning,—

> The CALLIPYGE 's injured behind,
> 𝕭𝖑𝖔𝖚𝖉𝖎𝖊 𝕵𝖆𝖈𝖐𝖊!
> The DE' MEDICI 's injured before;
> And the ANADYOMENE 's injured in so many
> Places, I think there's a score,
> If not more,
> Of her fingers and toes on the floor.

He was also a prolific inventor of extempore comicalities in verse, and this not only in waking moments. He said one morning, only four days before the end, that between sleeping and waking he had been fancying that Charles the First's children were presenting a petition to Cromwell, when he found what he used to call his 'head,' as distinguished from himself (for such experiences were not uncommon) saying—

> And then this strange complaint the list of querimonies
> led off:
> 'We can't get back our poor papa, they've been and cut
> his head off.'
> I wouldn't listen longer to these slangy little princes,
> For when the language mocks the rank, the mental palate
> winces.

As a jest of the παρὰ προσδοκίαν type, or any type, the following dream is, I should suppose, unequalled. It is of much older date than the preceding. He dreamed he was in a train. The train stopped at a station. Someone in the carriage asked what place it was, and someone else said *Miletus*. Verrall put his head out of the window and saw close at hand a factory, on the blank wall of which was painted in large letters

EPIC CYCLE WORKS, LIMITED.

---

What remains to tell may be told briefly, and perhaps best so. Although, as has been said, there was a satisfactory recovery after the illness in April 1910, it would seem that the ground lost was never completely recovered. In the late autumn he felt the strain of a great anxiety, lasting for some weeks, about the health of Henry Butcher, and Butcher's death in December was a crushing blow. Nevertheless he gradually recovered his usual spirits, and during the early summer was very well, all things considered, and occupied himself in preparing the professorial lectures. In August, however, there was a grave illness, and though he was able to deliver the English lectures in the October term, and although, as those lectures show, the mental vigour was in no way impaired, it was only too clear that the bodily strength was steadily ebbing. The next course of lectures, which was to deal with Macaulay, was indeed prepared, but it was found necessary to postpone their delivery. The

May term was looked forward to, and there was reasonable hope that he would then be able to lecture; but the following months brought no accession of strength, and the proposed May term lectures were in consequence abandoned.

When, as was the case after the end of 1911, he ceased to go away from the house and garden, it was a delight to him to be still kept in touch with the outside world by more frequent visits from friends, both from Cambridge and from a distance. The visitors from the neighbourhood were arranged for by a sort of *rota* for each week, and a few of the most intimate, such as Mr Duff and Dr Parry, came of course with special frequency. During these visits he would talk with the old alertness and something like the old vivacity; and when at last talking became difficult he would still take pleasure in listening to the conversation of others. During all this period his days were filled up with reading or hearing books read to him. Nor were the books selected light ones: the one in hand at the last was Clarendon's *History of the Great Rebellion*.

Through all the fifteen years of his illness, he never lost heart or interest. From the time when the physical disabilities first became serious, there was no repining, no complaint, no hint of rebellion. Some momentary uneasiness might call forth just a fretful word, but even this was extremely rare,— and it was all. Each successive infirmity was accepted with calmness and patience, as a disagreeable factor indeed, to be reckoned with and arranged for, but then as far as possible ignored. With a resolution that never wavered, the unconquerable spirit, unshaken and at peace within itself, insisted on continuing to live its own separate life. Some of his best literary work was done at times when the least involuntary movement was attended with pain and the general discomfort was continual ; and he lectured when the hands could no longer turn the leaves of a book or lift a glass of water. Years of suffering failed to crush him, and what might remain to be endured he faced without dismay. A condition which would have dulled the intellect and withered the heart of most men, would have soured them and made them peevish or morose, left that rare nature serene, interested, lovable, to the last. It was wonderful and beautiful, but oh, the pity of it !

The end came with some suddenness on June 18, 1912. In the morning, after being carried down into the study, he asked the day of the week, and when told, said, 'Ah, Parry's coming.' He then asked the day of the month, and on learning that it was the 18th, said 'Wellington College Day.' At half-past two the pure, noble, steadfast soul passed peacefully to the larger life.

M. A. B.

*Inscription on Memorial Tablet in Antechapel
of Trinity College.*

ARTVRVS WOOLLGAR
VERRALL
SOCIVS TVTOR PROFESSOR
LITTERIS ET ANTIQVIS ET NOVIS
TOTO ANIMO DEDITVS
IN COLLEGIO PER XXXV ANNOS LECTOR
MIRO ACVMINE MIRA ELOQVENTIA
AVDITORES TAMQVAM SIREN
DEVINXIT
IDEM SCRIPTIS SVIS
AESCHYLI ARTEM INLVSTRAVIT
EURIPIDIS FAMAM VINDICAVIT
DENIQVE IN ACADEMIA
LITTERARVM ANGLICARVM PROFESSOR
PRIMVS INSTITVTVS
MVNVS FELICITER VIX INCEPTVM
MORBI MORTISQVE NECESSITATE
DEPOSVIT.
IN HOC VIRO
SINGVLARES INGENII DOTES
COMMENDABAT MORVM SIMPLICITAS
COMMENDABAT EA FORTITVDO
QVA LONGOS CORPORIS DOLORES
SVI SEMPER IMMEMOR
AMICORVM MEMOR
INVICTO ANIMO PERPESSVS EST.
NATVS NON. FEBR. MDCCCLI
OBIIT A.D. XIV KAL. IVL. MCMXII.

# COMMEMORATIVE ADDRESS

*delivered before the Academic Committee of the Royal Society of Literature by John William Mackail, M.A., LL.D.*

ARTHUR VERRALL was not, technically and professionally, a man of letters; he was a classical scholar and student. In that field, he was an able exponent of the fine and contentious art of textual criticism; he was a subtle and also a daring interpreter. On the one hand he was an instance of the old-fashioned scholarship at its best, equal, perhaps, to any scholar of his time in the peculiarly English art of Latin and Greek composition : on the other, he was a potent force in the movement which has transformed scholarship by altering the whole attitude of our minds towards the ancient classics. But to the larger circle of those who practise the art of English letters, or who are its critics and historians, he was little known. In his own University, and among scholars, he was known certainly as a brilliant writer, but as a writer of works of scholarship. The master of a graceful, flexible, and lucid pen, he, in fact, wrote comparatively little. His Clark Lectures, and those few which he was able to give from the Chair of English Literature, were not committed to paper. He was not the author of any single great work. The collection of his literary essays, which is now being made, will not place him among the writers who have in this age made English letters illustrious. Yet he was a strength and an ornament to the Academic Council which is now recording his loss : and when he was chosen by the Crown to be the first Professor of English Literature at Cambridge, the choice was recognised by those most competent to judge as not only justifiable, but singularly happy.

It should not indeed be necessary, if the relations between scholarship and literature were such as they ought to be, to draw a line between men of letters and classical scholars. For the classical writers received and retain that name, because their works represent the highest and best of what has been created in the art of letters. Just as our whole civilisation is based on, grows out of, that created and established by the Greek and the Latin genius, so the whole of modern letters have the ancient masterpieces before them as patterns of excellence, beneath them as a soil from which they draw nutriment. But in fact, as we all know—as the opponents of classical education triumphantly point out, and as its defenders must candidly, if not ruefully, acknowledge—it is not the case that all scholars have a genius for letters, any more than that all writers of genius are scholars. Education based on those ancient masterpieces, life spent in their study, too often are an illiberal education, and a wasted life. The creative artist has often never possessed scholarship, or has flung away what he possessed of it. What has been his loss, what may have been his incidental gain, by being thus cut away from the traditions of the past, or by cutting them away through his own act, is a large question. But this much at least can be said : that a writer to whom scholarship is meaningless can have no trained sense of the organic continuity of the art of letters : he has forgone, from circumstances which may or may not have been inevitable, for reasons which may or may not be judged adequate, the power of placing himself in the stream of history. It will not, to be sure, profit him to have gained touch with the past if he has lost touch with the present, and submerged his own genius. But neither is it to be expected that his own genius can thrive on a sustenance which is of the day only. All live art is a new birth ; but the present is the integration of the past, and the art of the present is but one manifestation of a single continuous art. On the other hand, it will not be denied that the scholar has often contracted into a pedant, for whom literature is not a living art, out of touch with the creative and imaginative movement of his own time. For scholars of this kind the noblest of all arts has little vital reality, the actual movement of the human mind has but a faint interest. They are linguists, archaeologists, critics ; but they move like laborious ghosts, out of the daylight, immersed in a dead world.

This Verrall was not: we are not following a grammarian's funeral. For him letters, both ancient and modern, were a world crowdedly and intensely alive. He brought to the study of the classics—of those masterpieces which have been so thumbed and worn by long currency—the fresh mind at whose contact they sprang into fresh vitality. He brought the same fresh interest and enjoyment to English letters and the literary art of his own day. To hear him discourse on modern authors was to realise that they were not separated in his mind from the ancient authors among whom he worked professionally. To both alike he applied the same rapid intelligence, in both alike he felt the same living interest. And that was the interest neither of classicism nor of modernism; it was the interest of literature as a fine art.

It is as an exponent or representative of English letters that we have to regard him here. But English letters are part of a larger community. A sane literary nationalism not only keeps touch with, but reinforces, the solidarity of the Republic of Letters: just as the living art of the day is rooted in vital appreciation of the no less living art of the past, and in conscious kinship with it. For in literature, as in all the arts of life, art is one thing, and artists, of all schools and periods, are one household.

In that art he concentrated his study, not on periods, but on qualities; not on particular writers or particular works for the sake either of their prestige or of their novelty, but for the sake of the artistic quality which he found in them; not on a single province of letters—poetry, history, oratory and the like—as such, but on all these as literature. That his work, so far as it is recorded and accessible, does deal mainly with certain periods and writers, only means that, having to deal with these in the course of his duties, or finding in them the literary quality, as he conceived it, specially prominent, or requiring special prominence to be given to it, he took them as instances, and turned upon them the critical spirit in which he read not only them, but all that he read. If we can fancy a mind so rapid and alert as his pausing to describe its own operation as a system, we may think of him as saying, whenever he took up a book : This purports to be a work of art; what sort of art is it? what is the effect of its art upon my mind? and what has to be noted in order to elucidate its art, to enable me or others to appreciate the quality of that art, the process by which the work of art came to be what it is, the meaning that was in the artist's mind? In advice given by him to students entering on a course of modern English literature, this note is struck with emphatic precision. 'Do you honestly enjoy this book, and if so, what in it pleases you? Does your enjoyment increase as you study it, and if so, through what process of thought? Such are the questions which readers should ask themselves.' Such were the questions which he asked himself, and in finding answers to which his study of literature in essence consisted. The word 'enjoyment' should be noted.

For art is, according to the old and sound definition, production with enjoyment and for the sake of enjoyment; and the appreciation of art is the entering into the artist's enjoyment through imaginative sympathy, and in some sense thus renewing his act of creation and the joy of that act.

Art is one thing; it is the organic synthesis of all the arts. And the art of letters is likewise one thing; it is the *élan vital* incarnating itself in verbal structure. Where one artist in letters will differ from another is in his special pursuit of one or another element in his art; and where one man's appreciation will differ from another's is in his native or trained affinity for one or another of these elements; in the measure to which he disengages this from other qualities, traces its workings, and makes it in some sort the test or critical moment in all his appreciations.

The element in literature to which Verrall's mind had perhaps the greatest affinity was wit, as he himself somewhere defines that ambiguous word. 'Wit,' he wrote, 'or subtlety on the part of the artist in the manipulation of meanings'; and with this he went on to connect, on the part of the recipient or critic, 'the enjoyment of such subtlety for its own sake, and as the source of a distinct intellectual pleasure.'

Subtlety in the manipulation of meanings—this was at once Verrall's distinctive strength in dealing with literature, and in some measure also his besetting temptation. His enjoyment in it was almost a passion. By its exercise he did much towards the modern revivification of scholarship. His effective work lies not so much in any published writings as in the impulse which as a stimulating teacher, and even more perhaps as a brilliant talker, he communicated to pupils and friends. He never brought to any book, were it ancient or modern, the dulled mind. He took no orthodoxy for granted. In his reading he was always poised ready for a pounce on some shade of meaning, some implication or suggestion ; and he followed out their traces acutely, adroitly, alluringly. Sagacity in its literal sense, the keen scent after things hidden, was the habit of his mind. If, as was once said by a remarkable thinker, imagination is nothing else than the faculty of tracing out consequences fully, Verrall had imagination to a singular degree.

To this power of scenting and tracing, of quick and continued apprehensiveness, must be added another if work is to be sound. That other power is comprehensiveness ; the power of seeing things in their proportion to one another, and not exaggerating what is secondary, or losing grasp of the whole plan in curious consideration of some detail or byway. It is, in fact, good sense. Without it, the sagacity of which I have spoken leads straight to paradox. Self-hypnotised by absorption in a certain train of reasoning, the mind insensibly sways aside, and the judgment loses its centre. This is a danger which always attaches to fresh interpretations. The essence of paradox is that, however startling, it

is true ; its vice is that, however true, it is truth
placed in disproportion, and thus distorted.

It may be said of Verrall that he did not wholly
avoid this danger. His quick insight into subtleties
of meaning, and his delight in tracing them out, led
him, more than once, into paradox pursued beyond
measure, novelty of view passing into a more or less
conscious whimsicality. It made him fond, perhaps
too fond, of a fascinating but dangerous occupation,
that of rehabilitating names in the commonwealth of
letters which had either found or sunk below their
due level, and reinterpreting in a new sense works
(like the *Odes* of Horace), upon which the world
had formed a settled, and, it might seem, an un-
alterable judgment. In this his example has affected
a whole school of his pupils, some at least of whom
may be thought to have given way to the temptation
of reinterpreting everything, to the pursuit of clues
spun by themselves, and the finding of hidden meanings where he who hides finds. A sentence from
one of his essays is very characteristic of his own
attitude towards the authors on whom he turned his
dancing searchlight : 'What Dante alleges about
Statius, he could not have found unless he had
sought it with singular determination ; but find it
he did.' But any reservation to be made here as
regards Verrall's own work would only be just if
accompanied by generous recognition of two things ;
first, of his delightful love of nonsense, what I may
venture to call his attractive and humane impishness ;
secondly, of the great service he did to literature by

approaching it always with fresh eyes, by realising, for himself and for others, the truth that all works of genius are alive and possess the mobility of life ; that they lend themselves perpetually to fresh interpretation, and have stored in them an unexhausted potential energy.

To all his favourite authors Verrall brought this vitalising force of a subtle and dexterous intellect. He was an accomplished sophist, in the best sense of that needlessly discredited word. He was a master in the art of exposition and the art of persuasion. The power of the live voice, a thing nowadays too little enforced and too little cultivated, was an element in his genius. It made him a fascinating lecturer, but this kind of accomplishment leaves no written record. The printed page only shows imperfectly with what adroit and ingratiating skill he handled the work of poets and historians, of orators or dramatists or novelists, and showed the live intelligence taking shape in it. His own range of reading was wide, over the whole field of French as well as English letters. His affinity was for the writers, in either language, in whom wit and subtlety are predominant. But he did not pursue these qualities simply for their own sake, or allow them a monopoly in his interest. His two favourite French authors were Racine in poetry and Bossuet in prose, writers of the classical period who renewed, and not as copyists, the authentic classical note. So in English likewise, he found his choicest and closest friends among the writers of the central movement—

Dryden, Fielding, Scott, Macaulay—the masters of spacious construction and large sanity. An essay on Dryden, the last work on which he was engaged, would have been a real help towards the appreciation of that fertile and perplexing genius, and of the whole age in English letters to which he has given its name.

This is not the occasion for personal record, and my task is not that of the biographer. But a friendship of more than five-and-twenty years may be allowed a concluding word of more intimate tribute. For what Verrall's friends remember is not so much his fine intellect and brilliant accomplishments as his courtesy and geniality, his kindly nature and winning manners, a natural gaiety and clarity never clouded by circumstance, the total absence in him of jealousy and self-assertion, and, above all, the unconquerable spirit which bore him up through the last years in which, crippled by long wasting illness, he never allowed himself to repine, to be beaten down, or to lose heart. Of the courage, not less than heroic, with which he bore that load of bodily weakness and great pain, the less said the better; it is a thing to admire, not to praise. If I venture to touch upon it now, it is because in such an example we may see how the art of letters can sustain and reinforce the art of living; how commerce with great writers may and does kindle in their students some corresponding greatness of soul; and how literature is not a region abstract and apart, but a real thing, the image and interpretation of human life.

# A ROMAN OF GREATER ROME

THE proverb would lead us to suppose that for a bad name some dogs have actually been hanged. It is certain that this kind of justice has been exercised not seldom by "the judgment of posterity" and at the "bar of history." Such compendious condemnation has been passed not only on individuals, but on whole states, whole periods, and whole civilizations. And no culprit was ever more unlucky than the Roman Empire in that period which precedes the definite appearance of Christianity in the West. The first century (the second fares rather better) is scarcely known but in denunciation. It has armed with instances all the satirists and all the preachers who have come since, and is commonly described as one vast field of tyranny, servility, and corruption, full of the seeds of a just and scarcely regrettable decay. The mark of Tacitus and of Juvenal is upon it all. It would be useless to ask for a reversal of this verdict, partly because there is truth in it. But we ought perhaps, once in a way, to remind ourselves that there was another side, and spare a word of thanks to benefactors not less real because for the most part anonymous.

In spite of many warnings, it is difficult well to remember the enormous part of accident in giving the colour to historical evidence. Nineteen-twentieths (or some other imposing fraction) of that evidence is literature, so much of literature as is preserved. Speaking generally, it is preserved according to its merit; and its merit—this is familiar enough, but is often ignored all the same—has scarcely anything to do with its true and proportional value as material for history. There are at any given time a few men, most probably a very few, whose words will stand for the chief monument of the age. Each of these must be capable of giving literary permanence only to a very small part of the life about him. All of them are under the strongest temptation—we may almost say necessity—to copy each other and fall into each other's ways. What does not get into their pages will, not indeed in effect but in the memory of men, soon exist no more than if it had never been at all. We need not go far back or far away for instances. Are not they now complaining in France that their recent literature misrepresents them; that their writers have been working a certain vein, because they have lighted on it and come by suitable tools, not because it is really wider and deeper than others that lie about? It is certain that these complaints have truth; yet it is odds that, as between the literature and the protest, if either has any long life, the literature will have the best of it. We need not even go to France. At this very moment most of what is truly important in the internal history of eighteenth-century England, a history made up of obscure multifarious effort in the direction of social improvement, is fast slipping into the irrecoverable gulf, because it has no attraction for art. The enterprise of treating it truly and effectively becomes daily more difficult; and though it is not for those who have done nothing to speak ungratefully of what has been done, no book exists yet which is likely to make Walpole's England (another *hanging* name) appreciable by the good it had, and not by the good it wanted. And if we are already in some difficulty with the eighteenth century, how is it likely to be with the first?

The fact is that, of the true work, the greatest work, of that time we know scarcely anything, and never shall know anything adequate. I do not now speak of the grave personal limitations and disabilities which affect our chief witnesses; these have been often pointed out and as often practically dismissed from notice. Most of them are professed scandal-mongers, most of them reactionaries, out of temper with themselves and their times. But what is much more damaging is this: almost all their interest is fixed in Rome. It was not in Rome that the work was being done; it was not even mainly in the East, where the seedling of Christianity was preparing for future transplantation. The bed meanwhile was preparing for the flower, and for the moment this part of the labour had the lead. If we could have bargained with the writers of the age, we might well have foregone a great part of their laments over what was dead for a glimpse of what was growing, for some picture of Africa, of Gaul, and of Spain. The Romanising of the Western provinces in particular was probably the most brilliant service, as it was certainly one of the most vital, ever rendered to civilization. Our side of Europe was twice saved from moral destruction, and very narrowly saved, by the vigorous Romanism of Gaul. There is something ludicrous, pathetic, and yet consoling at the same time, in the thought that Roman Gaul was being made, and with marvellous rapidity, all the while that morbid and sensational declaimers in Rome were painting the world as a crowd of profligate slaves. At the fall of the Republic, about 50 years before Christ, Toulouse was a mere military outpost in the "backwoods." A century later it was a celebrated seat of learning. Cordova, formerly a not remarkable place of trade, rose in even less time to send from a single house three leaders of the first rank to rule the literature of the capital : though Lucan and the two Senecas unluckily learnt in that intellectual society to repeat too much of its futile dreams and spurious cant.

Little more than half a century from the death of Horace, a Spaniard could at least talk, in a moment of exuberance, of matching him with a Horace from Spain :

> The Tagus dares, in Lucius' praise,
> Challenge Venusia for the bays.
> Be Argos praised as Argos will
> By Argos, Thebes by Thebans still;

> Be Rhodes renowned by other tongue
> Than ours, be Lacedaemon sung;
> We, Celtic or Iberian born,
> Of Celtic towns will take no scorn.
> If Spanish names be rude, they chime,
> Think we, not ill in Spanish rime.

And it must be remembered, as this boast reminds us, that Corduba, Tolosa, and a hundred creations like them, were produced in great part not by the destruction, but by the instruction and self-instruction, of the native peoples. All this work, to which we are all deeply indebted this day, was achieved by the early emperors, or rather by the men, mostly unknown, who supported and carried out the imperial policy. It was begun when the sword of Julius opened the senate-house to the foreigner. How it was done so fast and so well is what we really want to know about the first ages of the Empire. It never can be known with any completeness. Most of our informants, belonging to a select circle which greatly mistook its own importance, are occupied with dramas of high life and of personal politics, which seldom touch the vital matter. The greater their art, the more they take our attention from the right place. We have however one writer, who indirectly lets us see something of the spirit which made the work possible—a Roman Spaniard who never forgot that he was a *Spanish* Roman, who never learnt the false "patriotism" and theatrical "indignation" of the metropolitan cliques, who was a loyal and enthusiastic citizen of the Greater Rome.

History has scarcely used enough the representative evidence of Martial. Tacitus is a grave personage. Juvenal takes himself somewhat more than seriously. Both profess to instruct us, and both for reasons good and bad are very angry with their contemporaries. It is not surprising that historians, who like the rest of us take men at their own valuation and, for accidental reasons, have too often read their "first century" to get up an indictment, let Tacitus and Juvenal give the tone. All the literary men of the same age must be in many ways much alike. They learn their art from each other. Martial and Juvenal illustrate each other at every turn, and have been quoted side by side till they are half confounded, Juvenal being mostly taken for the witness of real importance. But between Martial and all the rest there is a spiritual gulf. Taken as a whole, the literature of the first century leaves for its chief impression—weariness. The spectacle of life seems to give the writers no direct pleasure. They take a sullen satisfaction in enduring, and a fierce satisfaction in denouncing. These are the springs of feeling; and writers who cannot live upon these (such as is for the most part Statius) are much in want of something to live upon. With Martial it is utterly different. It would be hard to find another poet, equal in bulk, whose tone is so uniformly cheerful. Never was so bright and so interesting a world! He is ready to touch off any subject, and every subject suggests a not unagreeable contemplation. Trifles do not weary him, nor graver thoughts depress. He enjoys beauty without discontent and ugliness without malice. His satire is such as one can hardly call by that terrible name. It is thoroughly good-humoured, and carefully guarded from personal application. He enjoys the splendour of the imperial city; he enjoys, but without spite, the thousand little embarrassments of a city population. He enjoys the country, not in the philosophic manner of Horace, nor in the artificial manner of Virgil, but rustically and simply, in the way we commonly call modern. In the beneficent destiny of the Roman Empire—and here is the grand distinction, the key to all the rest—he believes heartily and without reserve. He is the only writer of this time who uses comfortably and unaffectedly the language of the genuine imperial religion, the worship of the monarch.

> King of heaven, whose power is proven
>   While it guards our prince below!
> Though mankind besiege thee, seeking
>   What, O gods, ye can bestow;
> If for me I ask thee nothing,
>   'Tis not, Jove, in scorn of thee.
> I should pray to thee for Caesar
> And to Caesar pray for me.

Here indeed Martial, whose religion has naturally something of himself, is playing with the subject, as (to say nothing of the rest) he sufficiently shows by the humorous little reservation "quae dei potestis." The sermons which have been read to him hereupon for his "disgusting adulation" are a sad waste of

preaching.   But he is sometimes serious enough.
It is thus that he praises the emperor for repealing
a sentence of banishment :

> Kinder than bolts from heaven thy thunder's course
> Turns in mid air and stays the fatal force.
> Were Jove thus merciful!   Then both alike
> Should often stint your strength and seldom strike.

Strong language, but not to be judged as if Martial
did or could regard "Jove" as the moral ideal.   He
only expresses in his way what Dryden, applauded
by vast numbers of Christian Englishmen, expressed
in *his* way, when he said of Charles II :

> If mildness ill with stubborn Israel suit,
> His crime is God's beloved attribute.

Such language belongs to epochs (that of Louis XIV
in France is another case) when the dearest interests
of millions have depended, or seemed to depend, on
a strong government, and strong government has
demanded, or seemed to demand, the reinforcement
of personal power.   It would be ridiculous to represent Martial as calling a man "a god," if indeed that
could give the man much pleasure, in order to be paid
for it, which he was not, and, as far as we know, had
no reason to think that he would be.

This "worship of the emperor" is a matter exceedingly hard for us now to approach with sympathetic
understanding.   We are apt to fancy it mere slavish-
ness and profanity.   It was most assuredly neither
one nor the other, but the best and truest form which
religion took in that "inter-religious" period—if we

may coin a term. As to the profanity, that is answered
by observing that the Roman, had he used capital
letters, would still have written "deus" with a little
"d." It was not the fault of the provincials that
Latin was beggarly in terms of spiritual distinction.
When they called the emperor "deus," they took the
simplest way of saying that the empire deserved from
them, as human beings, gratitude and veneration.
And so it did. The disestablishment of the Roman
oligarchy at once rescued and vastly extended the
benefits of culture. If the rapture of those for whom
civil peace was only saved, found natural vent, as
with Virgil and Horace, in the language of religious
imagination, what was the strength of that feeling
among men highly capable of civilization, and swept
in the way of it then for the first time? The altar
of Augustus at Lyons, with its solemn annual cele-
bration maintained by all Roman Gaul, represented,
if ever an altar did, a moral and reasonable zeal. In
the capital, mainly for reasons intelligible but not
creditable, the enthusiasm soon died away. Juvenal
bestows on the altar of Lyons, and on the excitement
of those who served it, a brutal sneer. We cannot
decently applaud him. It is lucky for us that Lyons
did not find the ceremony ridiculous.

Martial, we have said, is first and last a provincial,
a Roman of the Greater Rome. He was born at
Bilbilis in Northern Spain, a place celebrated for its
ironworks, and one of the thousand places which took
life or new life from the consolidation of the provinces
with Rome. His silence and his hints alike assure

us that, despite his Roman name (which proves
nothing), he was a Roman only by name and political adoption, a genuine Spaniard by blood. Almost
all his working life was spent in Rome and Italy.
He came to the capital a young man, in the last
years of Nero (about 65 A.D.), to make his living by
literature, and returned at the close of the century to
his native town, being then near sixty years old, to
spend his old age and to die. He must have taken
with him to Rome an admirable literary education,
an education astonishing when we reflect that
Northern Spain had only been in a settled condition about sixty years when Martial was born. It
is quite possible that his provincial breeding accounts
partly for the form of his work. He composes entirely in short highly finished pieces, each expressing
a single thought, a complete anecdote, an entire
picture. (The name of "epigram," given to such
compositions in ancient literature, has so changed
its sense as to be now misleading.) An author
writing in a learnt language (and we know, from
Martial himself that the exact academic idiom of
literary Rome was not often heard in Bilbilis) is
safer in a short flight. His danger is much greater
if he lets himself go. At any rate Martial never
does let himself go. Sometimes it is a little story
of the bazaar—how A.B. went from stall to stall,
now asking the price of an expensive bronze, now
selecting a set of elaborate crystals, calling for this
tapestry to be taken down and that piece of furniture
set out, and finally took two mugs for a penny, which

he carried away himself. Often we have the figure of the poor man who strolls the colonnades, the gardens, and the baths for the chance of an invitation to dinner. He looks, we are told in one place, so depressed and so seedy, that when he returns as a last chance to the colonnade of Europa, where the heroine was represented upon her bull, the association of ideas inevitably recalls the scarecrows which were tossed about by the bulls of the amphitheatre, and the looker-on breathes a charitable prayer that, failing all other resources, the wanderer may perchance be "entertained by the bull." In one piece the poet laments gracefully over the lovely landscape covered by the lava of Vesuvius:

> Is this Vesuvius, late so freshly trimmed
> With vines, and rich with vats at vintage overbrimmed?
> Are these the hills that Bacchus chose to grace
> More than his Nysa? This the Satyrs' revelling place?
> Is this the land renowned of Hercules?
> The haunts to Venus dear more than Cythera these?
> Burned, blasted, overwhelmed! It is a sight
> To make the almighty rue the license of their might.

At another time he laments with deeper feeling over the tomb of a little slave. This child, Erôtion, seems to have been born in the poet's household, and was brought up by him as an orphan. He loved her dearly, and was deeply affected by her early death. It would be rash to attempt here either the beautiful verses (v 34) in which he commends the poor little ghost to the protection of her dead parents among the terrors of the unseen world, or those, still more tender (x 61), written years afterwards and in the prospect of his return to Spain, in which he begs whosoever might succeed him as the proprietor of his Italian plot, not to neglect the little grave. But there is another tribute to her memory (v 37), of which some general idea may be given. It is a curious piece. The poet's habitual mood asserts itself oddly in the hour of grief. He plays with his sorrow fancifully, and ends with a grimace, as pathetic perhaps in its fashion as tears.

> I had a maid, a little maid,
>     More soft than swans or lambkins be,
> More fine, more delicately made
>     Than finest cates, than jewelry.
>
> Snow, lilies, ivory new, would seem
>     Beside her fairness scarcely fair :
> No fleece or fur of golden gleam
>     Could match the golden of her hair.
>
> Her breath was as the air that smells
>     Of roses in the Paestan land,
> Or honey fresh from Attic cells,
>     Or amber from a lady's hand.
>
> Matched with her poses and her play
>     The graceful peacock wanted grace ;
> The squirrel seemed but clumsy ; nay,
>     The phœnix had been commonplace.
>
> Erôtion ! Six—not six years old,
>     And dead, my plaything and my pet !
> This hour they burned her, and the mould,
>     She mixed with, feels some warmness yet.
>
> And Paetus chides : "Be brave," says he,
>     "*I* have just carried to the grave
> A noble dame of high degree—
>     And wealth (he sighs), no little slave !

"It does not break my heart, although
 She was my wife. I see you start."
What courage! What an awful blow!
*A fortune* does not break his heart!

The way in which the illustrations are here piled up is characteristic. But it is more commonly used merely to make entertainment out of some simple idea. A good specimen is the poem in which a person presented with a garden-farm[1] expresses his disappointment that it is not bigger. "It is a mere window-box. A grasshopper's wing would cover it. A cucumber could not lie straight in it. There is not room for the whole of a snake. The one gnat is dead of starvation. A mushroom in spreading, a fig in swelling, a pansy in opening, would go over the edge. A building swallow takes the whole hay-crop. The corn could be carried in a spoon, and the wine made in a nutshell." This sort of miscellany, set off by phrasing and versification generally fault-less, and everywhere sustained by a frank, unaffected, and impartial human interest, will at any rate just tempt an indolent reader from page to page: and this is Martial's proclaimed ambition.

The mere delight in a complex and yet orderly existence, in material civilization, has perhaps never been expressed with such force as by Martial. It seldom was achieved so suddenly and so happily as by the men of his country and time. I propose to

---

[1] It has been supposed that Martial is the donee, and that the circumstances are real. This certainly cannot be proved, and I take them to be fictitious.

present here, as best I can, a few of those poems
which seem to me representative of this feeling.
I need hardly say that I do not pretend to give a
full equivalent or an exact rendering. This paper
is not for those who can read their Martial, and do
it. Others will perhaps be indulgent, and then, as
Martial himself might say, they may get to the end
if they do not stop sooner.

We will take first a piece (IX 61) expressing
perhaps in the form least liable to modern objection
the enthusiasm of the new Romans for the work of
the Caesars. All suspicion of flattery is here at least
impossible. The Caesar celebrated, the "deified"
Julius, was dead more than 100 years ago when it
was written. The rivalry of Caesarian and Pompeian
was as much a matter of history as it is now. It is
impossible to attribute the zeal of the poet to any
motive but honest reverence for the creator of imperial Spain. That his memory should have been
worshipped at Cordova is the more noticeable because, when every allowance is made for exaggeration,
Cordova must have paid dearly at the moment for
the bloody inauguration of the new world. The
subject here is a house, which had lodged the divine
hero and still showed "Caesar's tree."

> Where golden soil with native richness dyes
>   On living flocks the fleece of Western lands;
> Where Cordova by generous Baetis lies
>   Well-pleased, a mansion monumental stands:
>     There Caesar stayed. A plane-tree spreading wide
>     Enfolds the court in shade from side to side:

This Caesar planted.  From his conquering hands
　The wand auspiciously commenced to rise;
And still, as conscious of his high commands,
　Aspires with lusty boughs to climb the skies.
There oft the reeling Fauns at hour unmeet
　With merry pipe scare Silence from her bed;
There oft to baffle Pan's pursuing feet
　Through lone dark fields the woodland fay hath fled.
　　With perfume Bacchus' rout the rooms hath filled;
　　Lush grew the leafage from the wine they spilled;
At morn the grass with pile of roses shed,
　Which no man knew for his, was flushed and sweet.
Then, tree of gods, hold high thy deathless head,
　Fear no profaning steel, no furnace heat.
　　Pompeian slips may perish with the name,
　　Thy planter planted for eternal fame.

We are not going now to pursue this Caesarian
topic any further, though Martial offers plenty of
illustrations.  We have looked at it only to see what
faith the writer had in him.  Long imaginative
labours (and Martial must have worked exceedingly
hard) can scarcely be sustained without a belief in
something.  Martial believed cordially in the empire
and its business of civilization.  "If you would move
my tears, yourself must feel the grief."  If you would
be interesting, you must be interested.  The mark
of Martial, as already said, is just this: that the
machinery and goings-on of civilized life are so
universally interesting to him, and in him become
so interesting.  Nothing excites him more, nothing
lifts him to so high a level, as that special product
of material civilization, household comfort.  He is
perhaps the only writer in whom plate and tapestry,

earthenware and hardware, beds and sofas, become truly poetic, as all deserving readers would allow that they do. This is not to be attributed merely to the man's individual character. It is the result of his time and situation. Convenience of life has a nobler aspect in him than elsewhere, because it was for his time, and relatively to those whom he represented, a nobler and more elevating thing than it commonly is. He delights in pleasant houses. He loves the urban palace; he is not insensible to suburban snugness; but, above all, he loves that highest achievement of comfort, the rich man's fancy-farm. To the honour of this he sacrifices the palace, with its weary ceremony, and the suburban garden, which leaves you after all dependent on the market. Bassus has such a garden. He has been seen on the road near Rome with a whole carriage-full of pleasant things—vegetables, game, and poultry; even the running footmen had eggs to carry:

> So plenteous was the freight in every sort
> Of rural breed and boon. Our friend, in short,
> Was on his way between his "farm" and town.
> "Yes, coming up." Oh no, sir;—*going down!*

Here, as often in Martial, the jest at the close merely serves to frame the picture, the poem being written for the picture itself. This is still more the case in the noble sequel (III 58), where Bassus appears again, and a genuine country-place is described to him by way of contrast. The poet has few things better:

> That is no "country" where the myrtle grows,
> Bassus, in rigid rows,

And shaven box, and planes without a vine
  In many a useless line.
For "country," see Faustinus' acres, tilled
  To the last corner, filled
With fruitful corn; see many a storing-room
  With autumn's rich perfume
Replenished yearly, till, November past,
  The raisin's gathered last.
Wild in the glen the bull-calves fight and fret
  Their foreheads smooth as yet,
The grown bulls bellow free.   The feathered train
  Spreads in a roomy plain:
There the shrill goose and starry peacock run,
  Flamingoes, like the sun
Setting, and many a wing of speck and spot
  And curious-painted blot,
Numidian, Phasian, Rhodian.   Housed above,
  The pigeon-kind make love,
And coo to coo replies.   Here, rough and rude,
  The pushing swine for food
Follow the farm-wife's apron; there the lamb
  Looks, helpless, for its dam.
The hearth within, where cheery logs abound,
  Shows chubby faces round;
No pale and sedentary tapster there!
  (Your draught is the free air)
No foul gymnasium!   Hunt, and fish, and toil,
  And you may spare your oil.
The footman in his glory will not shirk
  A little garden-work,
And lads who ran from tasks, no more afraid,
  Run willing to the spade.
The country "callers" from the neighbouring lands
  Come not with empty hands;
With gift of honey in the comb they come,
  With shapely cheeses some,
With dormice half asleep, with this and that,
  Kidlings or capons fat.

Eggs in a basket, or such housewife thing,
  The stately lasses bring
"With mother's duty."—Hours with labour blest
  Bring supper and a guest.
The country table, certain not to fail,
  Saves nothing to be stale;
The menials, with their bellyful at least,
  Contented serve the feast.—
See, Bassus, see all this; then boast me not
  Your mean suburban plot,
Some laurels and a scarecrow (this for show,
  To make believe things grow).
The porridge of your artificial clown
  Comes from a shop in town.
The sum of your "farm-labour" is to cart
  Down from the city mart
Eggs, cheese, greens, poultry, fruit.   Why drive so far?
  You were in town—*and are.*

Strange, in all this modernness, are the occasional touches that tell us the time; the gymnasium and the "oil" as the type of town-exercise, and the page-lads, slaves in training for various duties in the great household, for whom in town there would be lessons to do, while in the country they are set, to their great relief, at the garden.   The "dormice" surprise us in the list; but doubtless there would be enough for a dish, a favourite dish.   But no detail is so remarkable as the diffused delight in the apparatus of life, which quickens the whole : if, indeed, I can hope that anything of this survives in the translation. I cannot forbear to quote for their sound just two verses; this on the pigeon-house:

    Sonantque turres plausibus columbarum,

and this exquisite description of the rustic girls:

    Grandes proborum virgines colonorum.

The age when this last could be written was assuredly not without its better aspects.

The poet himself had a country cottage and garden in his wealthier days. He makes a point of sending roses from it to a dear friend, but laments that weightier presents have to come "from the shop." Not but that on occasion he can be enthusiastic also over the "rus in urbe." He has one particularly famous picture in this style (IV 64), representing what must really have been a charming house and from its situation a show-place in Rome. One Julius Martialis (no relation to the poet, whose family name was Valerius), a man of some distinction in politics and—at least as a patron and admirer—in literature, had a sort of miniature park on the Janiculan Hill, above the ancient Mulvian Bridge. Lying on the west of Rome, and separated from the mass of it by the winding Tiber, it commanded the most interesting view in the world: the city for foreground, and behind it, right away to the hills, a beautiful country, crowded with legends and memories; all the towns which had fought with Rome when Rome was an ambitious village, now linked to each other by those magnificent roads which were the chief instrument and symbol of the "Roman peace."

> "A little place"—Yet not the blest
> In the Happy Gardens of the West
> Could here pronounce their dwelling best.
>
> Better does Martialis dwell.
> Janiculus with gentle swell
> From low dull air uplifts him well

To skies more pure. His favoured zone
Enjoys a climate of its own,
A heaven brought near for him alone.

All the Seven Hills of queenly Rome
The eye may take from this fair home,
To Alba, Tusculum, may roam,

Fidenae, Rubrae, names of yore,
Perenna's orchard (heretofore
Mishallowed with a maiden's gore)[1].

Two noble ways you hence may trace
And follow there the chariot's pace,
By sight not sound; to this high place

The wheel is dumb. The boatman's cheer,
The bargeman's most vociferous jeer,
Are silent to the sleeping ear.

Yet that's the Mulvian, past a doubt,
That's Tiber, with the craft about.
"Am I in town?" you say, "or out?"

And you would find a welcome there
So frank and free, so debonnair,
As you yourself the master were.

Alcinous-like he shares his state,
Or like Molorchus, grown to great
For keeping of an open gate.

(Odysseus' entertainer, the King of the Phaeacians,
is moderately famous still; but as to Molorchus, some

---

[1] "Et quae virgineo cruore gaudet, Annae pomiferum nemus Perennae." The legend, apparently of the *Iphigenia* type, is not otherwise known in connexion with the old Italian deity, Anna Perenna. For this reason (a poor one, as it seems to me) it has been supposed that there is some error here. The present tense is perhaps "historical"; but it is quite possible that some symbol of the sacrifice was actually kept up.

may not disdain to be informed that he made his
fortune by entertaining Hercules unawares.)

> Ye that all merit see in size,
> Whom all a township scarce supplies
> With one such farm as satisfies :
>
> Seek where you will your ample space,
> If only you will give me grace
> Still to prefer this "little place."

Martial, we see, like other professional persons,
could plead either side of a cause for a proper consideration, and was indeed a man genuinely pleased
with many different things. But he had his bent all
the while. He is never so sparkling and elastic as
when something suggests the prospect of Spain and
of rest among the iron-forges of Bilbilis. We will
put here together, first his good-speed to a fellow-
countryman, who, having made a fortune at law, was
going back to the West (1 50); and secondly the
farewell which he himself, having at length got
enough and meaning soon to return, takes of another
distinguished Spaniard whom he was leaving in Italy
(x 37). (The strangest thing in them, to our eyes,
is the "sport." It must be confessed that the Roman
gentlemen took their sport in a lazy way. I should
not dare, for fear of ruining Martial right out, to produce here certain expostulations which he addresses
to a friend, who had a habit of hard riding after the
hare.) The first of these pieces is among the earliest
work, the second among the very latest, of Martial's
career at Rome. The places are mostly mere names
now, but they have a quaint and interesting sound.

GOOD-SPEED!

O theme for Celtiberian lays,
O worthy name for Spaniards' praise!
And are you, are you bound for Spain,
To see high Bilbilis once again
(For stream and stithy a town of pride)?
Old Gaius' snows, and the mountain side
Whence breaks Vadavero, sacred flood!
Boterdus' screen of fragrant wood,
The garden-goddess' loved retreat!
Shall it be yours, 'twixt cold and heat,
To bathe where Congedus invites
Soft Naiads to his soft delights?
That softness then to brace and cool
In steely Salo's tempering pool?
Then in Voberca's teeming chace
To make your bag from the lunching-place!
Or break the summer's sultry powers
In the deep dark of Tagus' bowers,
With fresh Dercenna and Nutha's drench
Better than ice your thirst to quench!
When enters with December hoar
The bellowing North-wind, fierce and frore,
You'll seek the Tarraconian coast
And "lang-syne" Laletanian host.
There for your nets are fallow deer,
Boars "on the premises" for your spear,
And dodging hares to breathe your horse
(The stags your rustic best may course).
Almost the forest lays its logs
(So near it grows) upon the dogs.
The household gathers in the hall
Easy and happy; just a call
Will bring the huntsman.—Lay aside
The gown, the badge of irksome pride;

Its purple stinks[1]. You need not here
Go shivering to some levée drear.
You wake not here to meet forlorn
Pale business ghastly as the morn,
The pauper's drone, the lady's scorn—
Sleep on. Let others tear the laws
For the sweet poison of applause.
You, in the triumphs of your boy,
Find a more pure, more wholesome joy.
When most of life is paid for fame,
*Life* claims the rest—a modest claim.

As we follow the traveller from region to region of this Roman province, so interesting but for the most part so dim to us, we must wish once more that he had somewhere given us more full and more precise descriptions. Writing almost wholly in Italy, and for a gay pleasure-loving public, it is commonly, as here, for its material ease and abundance that he contrasts his unexhausted country with the "struggle for existence" in the region of the capital. But he could have told us many curious things, if he would. Once (IV 55) he runs over a list of Spanish places, just to laugh (for the benefit of Italians) at their strange sounds, but maintaining at the same time with proper pride that they are very good names, and that Italy had worse. Some of the touches with which he adorns his catalogue must be painfully exciting to a Celtic archaeologist. What was the sanction, religious or secular, which "protected the dances of Rixamae"? In whose name and with

---

[1] This literal fact (for the Tyrian dye was apt to be very unsavoury) is here used with pungent effect.

what ceremony did the folk assemble for "the holiday banquet of Carduae"?   What mysteries did
Burado cover in its "grove of oaks," and for what
mysterious reason must every traveller, however
little disposed to walk, dismount or diverge so as
to pass through it?   What, above all, was there at
Rigae, for which Martial takes the nearest Roman
term to be "our fathers' antique theatre"?    A
"theatre" in the common sense, such as the Romans
copied from the Greeks, his fathers had certainly not
built there.   Was it perhaps a "ring" of banks, or
of great stones, after the Celtic fashion known elsewhere?   But we must leave these disquisitions for
others, and return to our business of seeing Martial
himself to his Spanish home, and of presenting in
English his happy

### FAREWELL.

> King of the Courts, whose lips maintain
> By honest truth their legal reign,
> What orders, friend and fellow-townsman,
>    What orders, hey! for the Spanish main?
>
> Why care you here to pull the line
> For dog-fish (if your chance be fine),
> While there they fling the mullet, wanting
>    His full three pounds, to his native brine?
>
> Why choose to swell a meagre bill
> With sapless whelk or tasteless squill,
> While Spain has oysters, such profusion,
>    The very lackeys may eat their fill?
>
> Why this halloo a fox to scare,
> Stinking and snapping, to the snare?
> My nets in Spain, ere yet from ocean
>    The hemp be dry, will be round a hare.

Here comes your fisher—nothing ta'en;
Your huntsman—of a weasel vain.
The town must keep your seaside table.
What orders, hey! for the Spanish main?

Naturally the poet, when he had got his will, did not find all that he hoped. Who ever did? Nothing proves that he ever regretted his return. But he felt more keenly what he had left behind. Doubtless the disadvantages of Bilbilis told more in reality than in fancy. His Roman taste had become more fastidious; and—he was getting old. Some of his last verses come as near melancholy as any of his bright and equal writing. It could not be otherwise. It is pleasant, however, to know that he got a garden, and was able to call himself, as he had called his friends in the capital, "as happy as Alcinous and the Hesperides." He even married a garden, the dower of a certain Marcella of Bilbilis[1], and thanks her gracefully for the gift. He was able to thank her also for nobler consolation. We cannot end better than with the little poem (XII 21) in which he praises her, not without pathos, for her Roman culture. It ought to be remembered, when vials

[1] Whether he had ever been married before is uncertain. Some of his poems mention a "wife," but she is never named, and it is impossible to say in his writings how much is literary fiction. Marcella certainly did not become his wife till after his return. It should, perhaps, be noticed, that she has been supposed to have been the poet's patron, and not his wife. The evidence is chiefly contained in the above poem, which, I confess, leaves little doubt in my mind. She was in any case his best and most intimate friend, and the question scarcely concerns us here.

of wrath are poured upon the Rome of Nero and
Domitian, that a man, certainly not without keen
sensibilities of mind and heart, when he wanted to
show how highly he valued the companion whom
he had chosen to be with him till death, could
think of no words higher than these—"You, and you
only, *bring me Rome !* "

Who could believe that such as thou couldst grow
   In this our burgh, by this our iron stream?
Thy thoughts make other music than we know,
   And, heard in Caesar's court, would native seem.

No child of the mid City is thy peer;
   To thee the Capitol's best daughter yields;
To win a Roman heart, for many a year
   No worthier flower shall bloom in foreign fields.

Thou, only thou, dost soothe my fond regret
For that fair Queen.  I have something Roman yet.

# AN OLD LOVE STORY

ABOUT twenty years before Christ, while the first Augustus of the newly established empire, sick in body and sorrowing for the recent death of his only heir, was gone with his legions to set in order the still unquiet East, and to vindicate the national honour by recovering from his Parthian neighbour the standards lost, a generation earlier, at Carrhae, there appeared at Rome, in complete and final shape, a book of verse, destined to exercise through remarkable vicissitudes of fortune a long, and yet unexhausted, effect upon literature. It was divided into Three Parts, and comprised some eighty poems, varying in length from near a hundred lines to six. It was written in the couplets traditionally appropriated to the tender passion, and presented, in the form of a personal confession by the poet, the beginning, consequences, and end of a censurable and unhappy attachment.

Both the author and his *Cynthia* were already well known to the public. The First Part, complete in itself, had come out under the same title before, and the fame of it had spread, we are told, to the steppes of the Dnieper, to the obscure limits of the civilized world. The author, Sextus Propertius, belonged, with Virgil and Horace, to the high court of letters, the circle of the minister Maecenas. And over his pensioned compeers, the son of the farmer and the son of the freedman, he had considerable temporary advantages. By birth he was probably at least the equal of the minister himself, whose pedigree was of the kind suspiciously antique; and in fortune he was independent. He belonged to "what we should call a good county family[1]" of the neighbourhood of Perugia. While he was a child his father died, and he was deprived in some way of a large estate; but he can still speak of himself as "not very rich," and his story requires us to suppose that, in one way or another, his circumstances were easy. If, as it seems, he was not on good terms with Horace, we can easily account for friction between two literary rivals moving in good society, one of whom had the usual passports for entering there, while the other was often reminded unpleasantly that he had not. Of Virgil he speaks with profound deference; but Virgil had written the *Georgics*, and thus placed himself practically beyond competition, before Propertius entered the field.

---

[1] I take this opportunity of acknowledging my debt, as a reader of Propertius, to my friend Dr Postgate. There are naturally points in this article on which he or others might not agree with me, but these pages are not a suitable place for discussion. My references are to the text edited by Prof. A. Palmer, a delightful little book.

It would seem strange, and perhaps absurd, to say of a man whose reputation is not of the first order, and whose chief work was contemporaneous with the *Odes* and the *Aeneid*, that he was in any sense the best poet of his time. And yet, without defiance of common opinion, this might be said of Propertius. We have only to choose appropriately, among the various qualities which go to "poetry," the quality which we will regard as essential. It is a not uncommon view, that the vivid and apparently spontaneous expression of feeling is of the essence of poetry, and that no subtlety of linguistic art can compensate for the want of it. For such a taste Roman literature supplies small satisfaction, and Augustan literature very small indeed, a fact put bluntly by the accomplished critic who said that, after Catullus and Lucretius, the Romans had no poetry at all. The only writer of the Augustan age for whom on these principles much could be said, is Propertius. If he and his rivals could be in some way represented by equivalents of our own time, it is quite possible that by the majority the modern Virgil and the modern Horace would be much more admired than loved ; it is certain that the modern Propertius would become rapidly popular wherever English is read. But the world, now supplied with many good literatures, naturally goes to each for what it offers best ; and has long sought the Roman not for passion at all, but for "lo bello stile che l'ha fatto onore." The *Aeneid* was turned into a school-book the moment it was written, and a school-book of the human race it has been, and will be. For such purposes there could not well be anything less suitable than *Cynthia*. Signs, however, indicate that the long tutelage of mankind by Latin may soon end or be interrupted. Should this take place, one result may be that those who do go to Latin will go to it more for pleasure and less for literary training; and in that case, though Virgil and Horace will not descend, the reputation of Propertius will relatively rise, as in fact it has lately risen. Meanwhile we may at all events spend a few minutes over a book which has made great poetry again and again, and could "spur an imitative zeal" in no less a mind than that of Goethe.

We will look first at the original *Cynthia*, now represented by Part I. It is supposed to have been published near the year 25, when the real Propertius was about twenty-five years old. How much in it was fact and how much fiction we do not and need not know. At the conclusion the poet, after a common Roman fashion, makes a few brief statements about his origin, just sufficient for personal identification. In the rest of the book, as in the two later Parts, there is, for a work of the kind, a remarkable want of detail in place, time, and circumstance. It was plainly never intended for a *roman à clef*. The hero is a youth without occupation, whose first serious love, when the work opens, has lasted a year: he may be supposed, according to Italian ideas, perhaps twenty years old, not more. His story might be that of any such youth. Equally

typical is the description of the heroine. It was believed in the second century A.D., that she answered
to an original in real life, whose name was Hostia ;
but the statement, if true, is of no importance. The
Cynthia of the poems is a woman without position,
family, or connexions (except a mother) of any
kind, sustaining by her beauty and accomplishments
an extravagant life. Her accomplishments include
a fine taste in literature, or at least such is the
persuasion of the enamoured poet. About her
character her lover is never deceived, except wilfully
by himself. His very first words are a lament that
in the pursuit of her he has become utterly im-
provident, and has lost the taste for honest society.
Around the principal figures are grouped three or
four other youths—a Tullus, Gallus, Bassus, Ponticus
—such friends as a gentleman and a poet would be
likely to have, young, passionate, and literary, but
not characterized with much distinctness. Ponticus
is at work on an epic, and looks with much contempt
on lesser ambitions. His elegiac friend thinks the
epic equal to Homer, but warns him that he will
find hexameters of little use when he falls in love,
which presently comes to pass. Bassus is a lyrist
in the " Adeline " and " Madeline " stage, but cannot,
with his gallery of beauties, distract the devotee of
Cynthia. Gallus seems to be a relation, as ardent
as the poet himself, and exchanges with him
rapturous confidences ; while Tullus, a calmer and
not active personage, is his monitor, and his auditor
when he bewails his folly or talks about his family.

The machinery is of the simplest kind, and might have been perfectly uninteresting.

But, such as it is, it is enough for Propertius. Those who, for a study in grammar, have been conducted for some time up and down the undulations of Ovid, would be astonished to find what the compass of the couplet is, when touched by a poet of earnest and delicate feeling. Propertius has all sorts of faults. He is often obscure, he is sometimes dull. He strains his language, brusques his transitions, and twists his thoughts. But there is one word that never applies to him, a word that haunts disagreeably the reader of much Latin literature. He is never vulgar. Every thought, we are sure, has really been thought by this particular man. Even the commonplace, of which he has plenty, is Propertian, and not the commonplace which is common. His grain is grain, and there is no "vacant chaff." Such a man can but very imperfectly speak for himself in translation. But we must do our best when there seems to be a chance.

The remorseful introduction already mentioned is followed by a gentle expostulation with Cynthia upon her needless finery :

> Thou canst not mend thy face: Love, going bare,
> Loves not that beauty should be made with art.

In the third poem the full splendour of the poet breaks out. Deep in the night Cynthia is found asleep, and the youth, from experience, is afraid to awaken her. The picture, in the realism of its grace, was probably then an entirely novel thing.

Neither has it, in its kind, been superseded by the innumerable imitations.

I gazed, with Argus' fixed and wondering look
At Io guised with horns. Anon I took
And softly set on Cynthia's marble brow
The wreath that was upon mine own, and now
Raised the loose hair, and shaped the scattered strands,
Or slipped sly gifts into the open hands,
A fruit, a flower. *Dull slumber took them all,*
*Nor thanked me, and too oft the lap let fall.*
*And if she stirred or sighed, at every turn*
*My folly still a meaning would discern,*
*And thought perchance, my Cynthia, thou didst seem*
*To fly some lover shown thee in a dream.*

The moon from window on to window crept,
And teased at length the eyes that lingering slept,
With gentle ray the seal of slumber brake.
Upon her pillowed arm she rose, and spake:
"At last thou art dismissed, at last I see,
Turned from some other door, thou com'st to me!
Where hast thou been this weary while, that I
Have watched the stars go slowly, slowly by?
To know thy cruelty, thyself must spend
Such long dark hours, and sicken for the end.
How oft, how long, my needle did I tire,
How often wake, for change, the unwilling lyre!
Sometimes, in pity of my lonely state,
I did lament of others' happier fate,
A little, and but gently. Ere I slept
This was the latest thought on which I wept."

I have marked here the passage which I think most characteristic. Nothing surely can be more exquisitely subtle than this half-conscious "folly," which interprets trifles first instinctively, according to what it knows to be true, and then wilfully, by what it chooses to believe. And how superb are the secure falsehoods of the confident beauty!

Perhaps no other poem in the First Part comes up to this. The next four poems, as well as the ninth and tenth, are addressed to the friends, and something has been said of them already. The feeling of them all (and it is their chief merit) is delightfully young and fresh. In the sixth, Tullus, the monitor, has made the reasonable suggestion that the narrator should go with him for a voyage in the East, and has tried the effect of impeaching his courage. He replies that, as far as that goes, he would accompany Tullus to the world's end; but that not for all the sights in the world would he see Cynthia so miserable as she threatens to be :

> What should I gain to see fair Athens' arts,
>   If Cynthia cursed me while the ship was launched?
> When tears of blood ran down her visage blanched,
> What should I care for Asia's ancient marts?

language which long afterwards he was bitterly to remember. In the eighth poem, with a certain irony of contrast, it is found that Cynthia is on the point of leaving with a wealthy suitor for Greece, but she is dissuaded by the poet, who attributes his success wholly to the power of his verse, and flatters himself that after this proof of his strength he is sure for ever. He is soon taught, however, that his Muse can by no means dispense with the material aids of the purse (XI—XV). Cynthia is gone to the great watering-place of Baiae, the Brighton or

Scarborough of the day, whither the poet has not followed her. This seems at first strange, as there is no hint of a quarrel, and he is extremely doleful at the separation; but it is explained when we discover, certainly without surprise, that his affairs are in disorder. This disclosure is made with much humour. In xiv the poet, with some heat, assures Tullus, who would appear to have been improving the occasion, that really he does not care for wealth, being possessed of love :

> Unenvied you, the rich, by Tiber's side,
> Quaffing your priceless cup, may lie at large,
> And wonder that the skiffs so swiftly glide,
> Or wonder that so slowly stems the barge.

These opening lines may be noted in passing for their delicate description of utter indolence. But, alas! the "peril of my fortune" is announced at Baiae, and Cynthia, instead of hurrying back, does not seem to understand that the danger is "ours," and continues to study her daily toilet, unmoved by the poetic assurance that none of the faithful heroines of Greek legend, neither Calypso, Hypsipyle, Evadne, nor Alphesiboea, would have behaved so, and that she is forfeiting the prospect of an equal renown. After this the lover is forced to open his eyes (xvi). He seeks solitude both on sea and on land (xvii, xviii), and is discontented with himself for seeking it. He repeats the beloved and unworthy name to the woods, carves it on the trees, and generally conducts himself in the expected manner. Finally (xix) he falls into an expectation

of death, and builds some hope of reconciliation on
this pathetic subject. There the book ends, so far
as Cynthia is concerned. The last two poems form
the personal epilogue, and, taken together, suggest
the relationship of the author to Gallus. Before
these two is put a piece unconnected either with
Cynthia or with Propertius, a charming and often
imitated version of the story of Hylas carried away
by the water-nymphs. It seems intended as a
specimen of the author's power in narrative proper,
and by an address to Gallus is loosely tacked into
its place.

Such in very brief outline is the First Part of
*Cynthia*. As will have been seen, though the pieces,
where connected by allusion, are naturally placed in
the order of time, the whole can scarcely be called a
story. There is but slight development, and after
the year supposed to have elapsed at the beginning
there is no hint of date. The time allotted to the
proceedings may be whatever the reader thinks
suitable. We may note also of this part that it
really is, what it calls itself, a book in *praise* of
Cynthia. The lover's expostulations are extremely
moderate, and his tenderness is rather increased
than diminished. A more curious point is this.
The introductory poem is full of self-reproach; the
speaker knows himself to be in the way to ruin and
degradation, and would thankfully be rescued, were
it possible. Nothing of the sort occurs in this Part
again; and it may well be suspected that when
*Cynthia* was expanded to its present form, the

introduction was modified to suit, as it does, not the First Part, but the entire work.

For, whatever Propertius may have intended, circumstances did not leave him perfectly free. His reputation opened to him the official circle, and he entered it. The Second Part begins with an address to Maecenas, and we soon discover that we are in an altered atmosphere. He was told, though he did not need to be told, that his new patron had taken him not for performance but for promise. He has defined his position neatly by reference to the rise of Virgil. The minister and the emperor are pressing for a historical Roman epic, for something parallel to the growing *Aeneid*, and Propertius can only answer that he has not risen even to the *Georgics* yet, but is still in the amatory region of the *Idylls*[1]. But indeed he was something worse off than this. His *Cynthia*, so far as it went, went the wrong way. Augustus wanted a reform of manners, and wanted above all to repeople desolate Italy with soldiers and citizens. He was already struggling to legislate in favour of marriage, and against precisely the sort of connexion which *Cynthia* celebrated. How peremptorily he could deal with literature, both Horace and Ovid in different ways were to prove. Evidently, either Propertius must forgo the obvious path of ambition, or *Cynthia* must stop, or *Cynthia* continued must take a new turn. We can easily understand

[1] II 1, and II 10, particularly II 10, 25, 26. See *Georg.* II 176.

why the rising author decided on the third way, and
added to his first picture of enchantment a second of
disillusion, and a third of deliverance. The Second
Part expressly promises the Third, and the two,
though perhaps published separately, were projected
together.

It is of course impossible here to examine the
whole, and we must be content with a glance at the
principal groups. The Second Part, as it is the
longest, is also in my judgment the most interesting.
The mental and physical charms of Cynthia still
exert their full force, and the lover, without real
effort, remains her servant. But he can deceive
himself no longer. A few pieces of eloquent description are followed (v, vi) by a fearful outburst
of rage and denunciation, recurring in various forms
at frequent intervals. The reproach of himself,
which after the introductory warning disappears
from the First Part, is now frequently upon his lips.
But against pressure from without he is fiercely
defiant. A social enactment enforcing marriage has
lately been put forward by the Emperor. The
lover declares that he would sooner die than wed
(for a marriage with Cynthia, it should be observed,
would not have satisfied the law). They rejoice
together when the law is withdrawn, a scene of
telling irony, for in fact the moment is one of the
few glimpses of happiness in this division of the
story, and it is clear that Cynthia, who for the most
part keeps no measures with her victim any longer,
has really been frightened by the proposal into

a passing gentleness. Two other reconciliations occur. The poet, with the same complacency so amusingly presented in the earlier part, attributes each to an artistic success. We will try to show something of both the poems so distinguished, for the opinion of Propertius on his own work is not to be despised. The first time (XIII, XIV, XV) he tries again the familiar pathos of foreseeing his death, a way, as he says with delicate satire, so obvious that he ought not to have missed it. He now goes the length of arranging his funeral:

> No masked procession show my pedigree,
> Nor let the trumpet wail (what use?) for me.
> Lay not the corpse upon an ivory bed,
> No broidered coverlet beneath me spread.
> Give me no train of mourners, give me just
> The meanest following of a pauper's dust.
> A train of *Three* shall satisfy my pride—
> My *Books*, a royal gift for Pluto's bride.
> But thou shalt follow there, and beat thy breast,
> And call my name, and call, and never rest;
> Kiss the cold lips, aye, kiss them, till the pyre
> Is crowned with spices and awaits the fire.
> Then let me, all to dust and ashes turned,
> In vessel small and earthen be inurned.
> And where they burned me, as memorial due,
> Set me a bay for shade, and verses two:
> "The slave, whose relics this is set above,
> Had but one only Lord, whose name was Love."

Posterity has confirmed the poet's judgment, and has given this poem a wide and perpetual fame. It has also generally agreed with him in admiring still more the other professedly successful piece in the

book, a desperate effort which follows the dead
failure of an allusion to the old topics of death and
poetic immortality (xxiv, xxv, xxvi).   He tries a
different pathos.

> I dreamed.  Ah, dearest!  near a sinking ship
>   I saw thee faintly beat the drowning sea.
> Drenched was thy heavy hair, and ah!  thy lip
>   Confessed the falsehoods it hath told to me.
>
> Thus Helle, when the golden beast she rode,
>   Tossed on the waves, thought I in deadly fear.
> Like Helle, Cynthia too, my thought forbode,
>   May name a sea, and ask the traveller's tear.
>
> I cried to heaven, to Neptune, Leda's Twain,
>   Leucothea too, a woman once as thou.
> Thy hands are lifted feebly from the main,
>   Thou criest on me, and thou art dying now!
>
> Had but the merman king beheld thine eyes,
>   Thou must have been his queen.   The whitest face,
> The bluest locks in ocean, with surprise
>   And jealous murmur, must have given thee place.
>
> But see, a dolphin darting to thy side!
>   (The same Arion, harping, rode upon?)
> I would have flung me in the waves; I tried,
>   I struggled, agonized—the dream was gone.

The reader may find here, as high as it can be
traced, the beginning of many a fertile stream of
poetry.   There is a detail which, though not important in the piece itself, affords afterwards a
curious illustration of the variety of Propertius in
working up his topics.   One would scarcely suspect
anything personal to Cynthia in the "blueness" of
the sea-nymphs' tresses; for Cynthia's hair was

brown. But a new light is thrown back on it afterwards, when in another mood the lover twits the
lady with her small success in a whimsical attempt
at *black*:

> If one I know will turn her tresses *blue*,
> Say, does that prove it a becoming hue?

But beautiful as are these golden threads in the
Second Part, they are far more effective in the web.
The last in particular comes as a delicious relief
after a frantic episode (xxii—xxv), in which the
narrator plunges low indeed in search of dissipa-
tion, with the only result of deepening his disgust
and self-contempt. It is well worth notice that this
incident and all the like element in the book is, so
far as we know, entirely original, a new thing in
literature. Certainly it was not taken from the
Greek. The moment was critical. The *Dipsychus*
was becoming conscious of his two souls, and the
breach was before long to be widened into an agony
which re-created the world. The mental dialogue
which begins thus,

> I, that should have disdained the common road,
> Now drink, delighted, of its very pools!

is worth volumes of declamatory satire.

From the triumph which rewards the "dream"
we pass, by a singularly skilful transition, into a
wholly fresh episode. The dream leads naturally
to the thought, that a death at sea, with Cynthia,
would not be unacceptable, and this to a little piece
of false rhetoric on the theme, that among the
uncertainties of life he alone knows the destined

manner of his death, who will live or die by the
kindness or cruelty of his mistress ; when suddenly
truth avenges itself upon affectation by illustrating
the uncertainty of life in another way.   Cynthia falls
dangerously ill.   In a poem of prayer and pity the
familiar legendary names, the poet's Greek stock-in-
trade, Io, Leucothea, Andromeda, Callisto, Semele,
defile past with a strange and helpless effect.   But
the danger grows ; the last efforts of witchcraft are
exhausted ; the lover throws away his learning and
breaks into the simplicity of despair :

> The wheel runs slack, the spell said o'er ;
>   The ashes in the lembic die ;
> The moon will be bewitched no more,
>   I hear the night-bird's boding cry.
>
> If death for her, then death for me
>   Must set his sail of funeral hue.
> I'll be with her, or cease to be.
>   Is one life nought ?   Yet pity two.
>
> Ah, God !   If you would save my sweet,
>   The hymn that I would make for you !
> And she should sit before your feet
>   And tell you all her peril through[1].

Cynthia recovers, and things return to the accustomed track.   The hero, if such he can now be
called, cannot sink much lower ; but lower he does
sink at the end of this Part (xxxii, xxxiii), where
he actually endeavours to propitiate his tyrant by
artfully defending her offences.

---

[1] The magic *rhombus* was not a "wheel," as Mr Andrew Lang
has discovered for us ; but we cannot well call it a "bull-roarer."

Scattered in this division, of which the above is the merest sketch, runs a topic which takes a larger development in the next. With the revolt of the lover's new feelings mixes very naturally and artistically the stirring of a new literary aspiration. In the address which opens Part II, when first discussing the proposals of Maecenas, he declined, as we saw, the task of national poetry as beyond his strength. But it continues to suggest itself as a true ideal, and begins to take the shape of a duty. It touches with a shade of remorse even the commands for his funeral. He has reasons for renouncing so emphatically the last honours of a Roman citizen.

> Nor let the trumpet wail (what use?) for me.

He recalls himself to the subject sharply a little later (x), registers a promise to undertake it some day, and actually addresses to the emperor a few couplets in praise of his triumphs, excusing himself from attempting more at present with a graceful apology :

> The garland, if the head men cannot touch
> Of some tall statue, at the feet they lay ;
> So we poor poets, when the theme too much
> Exceeds us, bring such incense as we may.

In the heat of the moment he even gets so far as to dismiss, or pretend to dismiss, the topic of Cynthia's praises (xi). His temporary farewell to it is a finished miniature :

> Praise thee who list, if any care, and sow
> His laboured verses in a barren ground.

> All shall be buried with thee, all shall go
> With thee into the low forgotten mound,
> Which men shall pass, nor say, beholding it,
> "This earth was once a woman and a wit."

But the tone of the protest belies its words. He persists in the old manner, and even declares (xxv) that he shall persist in it to the end. However, in the closing poem of Part II, which upon a slight pretext is devoted entirely to his literary hopes, other views are again distinctly seen. Returning to the thoughts of the opening poem, he praises enthusiastically the rising *Aeneid*, and while he takes Virgil himself to witness that it is something to have attained a glory in the parallel of the *Idylls*, asserts with emphasis the superior greatness of the national theme and of the "glories of Actium." It is among such thoughts that Propertius first cites as his model the significant name of Callimachus. Callimachus of Alexandria, himself an elegiac poet, was famous particularly for a work in which he had turned the form of elegy to the service of Greek legendary history. The Roman project which this connexion suggests is henceforth always in view till we lose sight of Propertius, and with an appeal to the precedent of Callimachus the Third Part opens.

Before we dismiss the Second we must notice that *Cynthia*, enlarged into three successive pictures, became something very near a story, and as such now required marks of time. We hear now first of the lapse of months, then of the lapse of years.

Two dates are furnished, each denoted by a great imperial event. Near the end of the Second Part is placed the dedication of the new Palatine temple of Apollo (B.C. 28), towards the end of the Third the death of the emperor's nephew and heir Marcellus (B.C. 23). The former poem is tacked to the main subject of Cynthia, and is in no sense a poem for the occasion ; indeed, it was probably written long after. It is brief, and (except to an archaeologist) of little interest, and is evidently inserted chiefly for the sake of marking the date. The latter is a quasi-official elegy and, we need hardly say, does not mention Cynthia, who indeed by that time is relegated to a colder distance. It was probably composed at the time, and followed before long by the publication of the whole work.

With the Third Part we must be brief. In it are wound up both the threads of the previous part, the amorous and the literary, the two still entangled as before.

In the degraded condition disclosed at the end of the Second Part, in the condition of "slavery," a word of terrible sound to a Roman ear, the narrator spent, as he tells us in the last poem of all, five years. The limits, as already seen, are roughly marked by the two dates, 28 and 23. Of the relations between him and Cynthia we hear directly very little more, some five poems only out of twenty-five being given to it. But this little is significant. Knowing that he is utterly weary, that he is now bound to her, however securely, only by inveterate

habit, the woman had begun to make him scenes.
One such occurs in the Second Part (xx), when
he represses her laments with a peevish tenderness.
But in viii of Part III, a powerful poem, we have
the further stage, when love itself is turned into a
sort of malice, and the lover ruminates with bitter
gusto the enjoyment of yesterday's spectacle—
Cynthia· in the paroxysms of a jealous fury. In
xv the storm is actually raging. But if these
poems present with force the last phase of his
miserable pleasure, the others (vi and xvi) show
with humour, not less artful, the abject facility with
which he went back to it. In vi a message of
reconciliation from Cynthia (for Cynthia in this part
for the first time has to summon) is brought by her
slave, Lygdamus, a name to be linked hereafter with
a tragic mystery. The lover assumes a sceptic air,
and solemnly adjures Lygdamus, "as he hopes for
freedom," to tell him *the truth*. But instead of
waiting for an answer, he shows his resolution not
to be deceived by a series of leading questions,
which put into the messenger's mouth a touching
picture of Cynthia sitting sadly at her modest work,
with not so much as a mirror to be seen, and tear-
fully complaining to Lygdamus of the cruel deserter.
*If* this is true, let Lygdamus bear from him at once
the tenderest reply, and "as he hopes for freedom"
procure an instant cessation of hostilities! In xvi
he makes himself utterly ridiculous, not indeed for
the first time, but with a consciousness of his
absurdity which is ominous. In the middle of the

night a message calls him from Rome to Tibur, a
distance of near twenty miles. He goes, but full
of tremors, which he vainly endeavours to make
pathetic. What if he should be murdered! Will
Cynthia bring garlands to his grave? He is obliged
to confess that this much-abused "grave" is likely
to receive anything but respect from people in
general, and hopes (oh contemptible "grave"!) that
at any rate Cynthia will put it somewhere out of the
way! From this time he sets steadily to the work
of his deliverance.

One only glimpse of anything resembling the
old happiness this Part contains (x)[1]. The connexion, now a thing of years and habit, has become
also a thing of anniversaries. The birthday of
Cynthia will afford, hopes the lover, at least a day's
respite from the fatigue of her tempers. Long
before, when this fatigue was a new feeling, he had
flatteringly compared her eternal complaints to the
mourning of the nightingale and the tears of Niobe[2].
Now, by a dexterous allusion to this, he discreetly
cloaks his request for a brief intermission. The
piece is exceedingly celebrated for poetic grace, and
dramatically also it represents, I think, the author's
highest level. One might spend some time (if the

[1] I do not here forget III 20, but I think it plain, for many
reasons, that this poem is not addressed to Cynthia, but to a
person utterly different, and celebrates the marriage, or at least
the "honourable addresses," of the narrator. It is in fact a step
in the course of his deliverance.

[2] II 20, 5—8.

task were not better left to the reader) in studying
its sharp and delicate delineation.

> Surprised I saw, while yet the sun was red
> This morn, the Muses standing by my bed.
> Three times their joyful hands they clapped, to greet,
> As then I knew, the birthday of my sweet.
> Oh cloudless let it pass, the winds give o'er,
> The waves break gently on the threatened shore!
> *Far from my sight this day let sorrow keep,*
> *Not marble Niobe be seen to weep,*
> *The halcyons hush their plaint, and she, whose lay*
> *Mourns for lost Itys, mourn him not to-day!*
> And thou whose prospered life this day was given,
> Arise, and pay thy grateful dues to heaven;
> Wash thee from sleep with water pure, and fair
> With moulding fingers set thine ordered hair.
> The robe thou hadst, when first thou didst subdue
> Propertius' eyes, put on, a garland too:
> Then pray that still those potent charms may last,
> And still in thy subjection hold me fast:
> The altar wreathe, the atoning incense light,
> Till the glad flame make all the chamber bright.
> Then speed the time till eve: prepare the board,
> The wine, the sense-entrancing perfume poured:
> Tax the hoarse pipe, till night be tired with dance;
> Free be thy jest, and loosely let it glance;
> Banish dull sleep with riot; let the rout
> Fill with its echoes all the street without.
> While we will ask the dice, *as others do,*
> What hearts Love's leaden wings are beating through.
> Last, when the cups have measured many an hour,
> The Priestess shall disclose the mystic bower.
> With annual rite the feast shall duly close,
> And this thy birthday finish in repose.

Meanwhile the great literary project grows in
firmness and fixes in outline. (Fragments of it

were written and are extant, and perhaps it was already commenced before the *Cynthia* came out.) We are told distinctly that the *Cynthia* detains the author only for a while (II), and more precisely that with encouragement from Maecenas, whose admired modesty the author feels constrained to imitate, he will certainly enter on *the poetic history of Rome*, from the earliest legends of Romulus to the overthrow of Antonius at Actium by Augustus himself (IX). The next and decisive step is masterly. Turning from the birthday picture placed here, the poet tries to palliate his servility in the eyes of some censor by excuses from mythologic precedent. And indeed he can plead much nearer precedent. If an Antonius could be slave to Cleopatra—"may not I," he was going to say, "be pardoned?" But the name of Antonius, so lately mentioned with such different hopes, lights like a spark the long prepared train of literary and personal motives. His apology is forgotten, and the *Roman* poet breaks indignantly into that very "theme of Actium" which he had formerly resigned to Virgil. This piece again, familiar as an extract, surpasses itself when read with the context :

> She asked, for price of her profanèd hand,
>   Rome and Rome's Senate subject and enslaved!
> Oh guileful Alexandria, guilty land!
>   Oh Memphian fields, with blood of Romans laved!
> Too deep upon our souls, when Pharos' strand
>   Despoiled thrice-victor Pompey, was it graved,
> That better in the field had Pompey died
> Or 'neath the heel of Caesar laid his pride.

> And dared she then, Canopus' harlot-queen,
>   That sperm of Macedon, our branded shame,
> With dog Anubis front the Thunderer's mien,
>   With threats of Nile the Tiber think to tame?
> With rattles chase our trumpets, and our keen
>   Swift barques with galleons of Egyptian frame?
> On Rome's high rock set up her tented seat,
> And bid the Roman eagles to her feet?

We feel that the Roman Callimachus has actually commenced work, and that, the *Cynthia* finished, a Roman "Scenes of Story" may be with some confidence expected.

The rest of the poems we must pass. lightly. Various in subject, they are variously and sometimes very adroitly shaped to the purpose, as where an elegy on a death at sea, after blaming much the rashness of men's enterprise, concludes with this unexpected turn:

> I shall not brave you, winds. I cannot choose
> But lie at Cynthia's steps, sans fame or use.

All is now ready for the end; and after experimenting on one or two other methods, the rebel recurs after all to the very expedient recommended and rejected years ago—a voyage to Athens and to the cities of the East. To point the parallel and round the whole work, Tullus, the original author of the suggestion (with this exception, the friends of Part I disappear in the continuation), is found resident in Asia Minor, and the poet has the satisfaction of lecturing him on the folly of preferring Asia to Italy, which he lauds in language thoroughly proper to the official school of poetry, and in fact adapted freely from a memorable passage of the *Georgics*,—Italy, whose honourable history is so much more respectable than wild Greek romance, " Italy, Tullus, your natural home, to which you ought at once to return and get married!" Thus Propertius, and we feel that he is changed indeed.

A Roman story could scarcely conclude without a symbolic portent, and here the love-poet loses his professional tablets. As for Cynthia, nothing remains but to dismiss her, with costs, if possible :

> Trust woman, trust the charms no more
> Which cheated once my humble eyes.
> Love lent, I see, the poor disguise:
> I blush to read my verses o'er.
>
> Love, Cynthia, gave each heavenly grace,
> And showed me things that never were,
> And could to rosy morn compare
> The brilliance of a painted face.
>
> My fond disease no medicine moved ;
> Kind seniors sermoned me in vain.
> I would to sea.  Alas ! how fain
> I own the perils I have proved.
>
> Love's cruel dungeon have I tried,
> The stake, the cauldron, and the chain.
> Yet have I 'scaped that Afric main,
> And see in port my vessel ride.
>
> My wounds begin to close, my wits
> Return ; and I myself consign,
> By Jove neglected, to the shrine,
> If such there be, where Reason sits.

This may be all very well, but we could now wish that the ransomed captive had stopped here, and not thought it necessary to hold up to Cynthia the probable miseries of her future. However, such a close is truly Roman and perhaps, if it comes to that, not untrue. If there were any obstinate lovers of "Greek romance" who were inclined to murmur, they were destined to receive an ample satisfaction.

Besides the *Cynthia*, Propertius left a small number of poems and fragments, now subjoined as "Book IV." This numbering, though convenient for reference, is misleading and not a little absurd; for the collection is not a "Book" at all, still less a part of *Cynthia*. Indeed, the "arrangement" of it, if the word applies, is so careless that it can scarcely be attributed to the author[1]. One piece is evidently the opening of that poetic history the projection of which has been traced above, and for the same work most of the others seem to have been intended. Three or four refer to the facts (or fictions) of *Cynthia*. Like the rest of the posthumous collection they are disconnected and without order. They are all distinguished from *Cynthia* by a very different style, and an examination of them shows that (with perhaps one exception)[2] none could have found a proper place in it. But there is one most remarkable poem (not that just excepted), which is in a

---

[1] Dr Postgate rightly insists upon this.

[2] IV 8, which might possibly have stood in Part III, though it is very different in style. Like the other posthumous poems, it shows a great multiplication of *dramatis personae* and scenic details. The absence of these is the characteristic of the *Cynthia*, the defect indeed, as the author would seem to have thought.

certain sense a sequel to *Cynthia*, and cannot be omitted from the briefest notice of it. It is plain that, whatever additions *Cynthia* might have received *within*, if the story were to *proceed* at all, one only further stage had a chance of interest. The deserted woman might die; and Propertius determined to kill her. Her ghost revisits the lover. The scene has a sort of realistic romance quite startling in Latin, and shows, I think, that had Propertius lived or worked longer, he might have changed considerably the course of literature. It is night. It is a very short time after Cynthia's death. The poet has heard of it, and has been somewhat, not very deeply, affected. From the conclusion of *Cynthia* it would be inferred that after the dismissal the lover interested himself in his former mistress no more. The present poem starts from the same assumption. He has heard of her funeral, but was not there, and indeed he does not know (for he has to be told) where she is buried. Of her recent life we must suppose him absolutely ignorant. His mind is wandering in a selfish regret for his departed youth, when—but I will try to give in his own form the manner of the waking:

> There *is* a life beyond the grave. A shade,
>    A pallid wraith escapes the conquering flame.
> *I have seen Cynthia.* She was lately laid
>    Beneath the whispering wayside: yet she came.

(It may be well to remind the reader that Roman graves were made by the roads as a regular practice, and that the words here mean no more than "she is buried,' though they have doubtless a very different poetic effect.)

> To me, who drowsed upon a funeral thought
>     Of love dethroned, came Cynthia from the grave;
> Her hair, her eyes as from the bier she brought,
>     But on her flesh the charrèd vesture clave.

> The gem (I knew it) of her ring betrayed
>     The fire; her blank lips had a Lethe look.
> She sighed and spoke, as though with breath, but made
>     A bony rattle as her hand she shook:

> "False that thou art and false must ever be
>     To woman, canst thou sleep? So quick forgot
> The things that once were done 'twixt thee and me,
>     And all the tender past as though 'twas not!"

She adds a few vivid touches of reminder, and then she tells him that she died without a friend, without anyone who cared to use the strange (but then accredited and common) means to detain a little the parting soul. The call of a beloved voice was supposed to have some power; *his* would have given her one more day. She died, and he knew it; yet he paid not the slightest tribute to her memory:

> "Who at my burial saw thy sunken head,
>     Thy warm tears falling on thy garb of woe?
> Thou couldst not (if no further to be led)
>     Bid to the gate my bier more slowly go!"

He sent no precious spices, no inexpensive flowers. And hereupon, as if to put beyond question that she died not only quite friendless, but also (for a reason which she leaves him to guess) quite weary of life, she suddenly discloses these horrid facts. *She was poisoned by two of her slaves, male and female; she let herself be poisoned; and the murderers, married together, are, without question, enjoying her property, holding in subjection the rest of her household, and stifling her memory by horrible cruelties.*

> Let Lygdamus be tried with fire and brand
>   (I knew the wine's fell colour when I took),
> Let guilty Nomas wash her guarded hand
>   And, if her soul be clear, the ordeal brook.
>
> She, she, the refuse of the public walk,
>   Now trails in dust a golden train of state,
> And if a handmaid of my beauty talk,
>   With double task-work silences her prate.
>
> For garlanding my grave old Petale,
>   Fond, faithful wretch, was loaded with the stocks;
> For begging in my name was Lalage
>   Scourged, while she hanged upon her twisted locks.

The murderess, in her brutal rapacity, actually stole the gilt statuette from the dead, and has melted it down, as an addition to her "marriage portion." Yet Cynthia is not come to reproach Propertius (she acknowledges her debt to his genius), but only to assure him that she is faithful to his memory. She offers a proof, which the poet by his own practice might certainly be estopped from disputing : she has gone to the company of the good women of legend, and in the consoling converse of Elysium gives a report (alas! partial) of Propertius to such admired wives as Andromeda and Hypermnestra. She requests him lastly to take under his protection

two specially dear to her, and to render a small
service to her grave :

> If thou art touched, if Chloris, she whose spell
>   Can hold thee now, permit a thought of me—
> My nurse is palsied; and she used thee well;
>   Let her not starve, my old Parthenie!
>
> And ah ! my darling "Maid" (the name was fit;
>   She held a mirror to me), let her be
> Maid to no other ! And thy verses writ
>   On Cynthia, burn them; keep no "praise" of me!

This, however little we may care for Andromeda
and Hypermnestra, we shall hardly deny to be real
pathos.    It is but too easy to comprehend the wish
that Cynthia's child (for there can be only one
meaning in the explanation added to the name)
should, if possible, never read *Cynthia*.

> So tight with ivy cords my grave is bound,
>   My bones are aching : let me lie at ease.
> In the white clime of Tibur is the mound,
>   Where brooding Anio feeds the orchard trees.
>
> Set me a pillar there, with praises just
>   And brief, that posting travellers may see,
> "Here lieth golden Cynthia, one whose dust
>   Adds something, Anio, to the praise of thee."

Of the "ivy" I have seen no explanation, and should
gladly find one.   That it is not supposed to have
grown on the grave is evident.   The circumstances
make this manifestly inconceivable.   I imagine that
the cords are used, as hazel and other wood is
sometimes used now, to hold together the new
heap ; and I strongly suspect that the tightness of

the binding is connected with the murder, and was a superstitious device for holding down the ghost.

"Soon," she tells him, at the last moment, "soon I, and no woman else, shall have thee, keep thee, press thee, mix with thee bone in bone[1]." The prophecy would seem to have been before very long so far advanced towards fulfilment that Propertius died. At least this is the simplest way of explaining the state of the later collection, and the fact that of his *magnum opus* there is nothing but a few cut stones. These fragments indeed are, many of them, of rare beauty. Perhaps I may return to them another time, and even say something more (I should like to say much more) of *Cynthia*. It is not at all the book to be easily exhausted by selections. Enough if I may have revived some reader's former pleasure, or possibly even directed one to a source of pleasure untried.

---

[1] [The poem is IV 7].

# THE FEAST OF SATURN

SHOULD we like to see sixty thousand people immensely happy? Could we resolve to do it without scolding or grudging? Could we rise to this, even if the president of the feast were to be a traditional villain of the children's story-books—one of those upon whom satire and tragedy, dabbing away in alternate streaks of black and white, happen to have put such a tarry smear as history will never get off? Even if the scene of the feast were a building raised with more blessings and ruined with more curses than any pile of stone in Europe? If so, let us have the pleasure of the spectacle. Let us go back just eighteen centuries. Let us suppose ourselves the subjects of that generous and popular prince (no irony) the Emperor Domitian. We are resident in the capital. It is the middle of December. Let us go to the Coliseum, some fifteen years old, shining white in the sun; let us forget (for to make this Roman holiday no one shall be butchered), let us forget for once to be inviting the Goths to glut their ire (at the cost of what little means of happiness the civilized races have painfully scraped together), and let us, under the guidance of the poets Statius and Martial, attend a revival of the Great Saturnalia.

We must first use our minds a little to the surrounding atmosphere, political, popular, and literary. We must dissociate all the objects round us from the thoughts which long habit has attached to them. We must teach ourselves the socialistic principles of the Roman populace, the true principles, as they held, of the Roman state, vindicated against the rapacious oligarchy by the revolution which founded the Empire, vindicated again against a line of Caesars, false to the democracy through which they rose, by the revolution which threw down the tyrant Nero. Through the work of Vespasian and his sons, particularly under the brilliant reign of the young Domitian, "the Roman people" seemed to themselves to be entering again into their own. The magnificent buildings, most of them destined to popular use, with which the Flavian princes covered the city, were regarded by the citizens of the capital, through whose eyes we are proposing to look, not as bribes for their support, but simply as repayment to them of that "property of the Roman people" which was theirs, but had been treacherously seized and misspent by the degenerate heirs of the deified Julius.

Most strongly, as was natural, did this feeling attach to the buildings and the festivals erected and celebrated within that great area of the city which Nero had occupied with his monstrous palace and park, within the site of the infamous

"Golden House." In the midst of this area, as a crowning monument of popular pleasure substituted for selfish luxury, lay the great Flavian amphitheatre, known later, and by us, as the Coliseum.

It is scarcely possible for a modern to appreciate the sentiment with which this building was regarded at the time. That it should be praised as an all-surpassing "wonder of the world" is intelligible. We can tolerate Martial when he writes :

Boast no more your builded mountains, Memphis ! Babylon, be dumb !
Delos, hide your horn-built altar ; Ephesus, your conqueror's come.
Mention not your Mausoleum, Caria, hanging in the sky.
What is great? The rest be silent. Says the Coliseum, " I."

But this is nothing. Martial distinctly speaks of the amphitheatre (the arena of the lions!) as a "sacred" edifice. And he accompanies the word with explanations which, for the moment, we must try to make our own. It was the strong impression left on the Roman mind by the gigantic greed of Nero which made so keen the sense of renovation for the world when his grasp was unclosed and his prey recovered. Rome seemed at one and the same moment both to be given back to herself and also, by the closer union with the distant provinces, which was the effect of the improved Flavian administration, to become more universal, more worthy of her great enjoyments and splendid popular pomp. There is another piece of Martial

which compresses into a few lines the whole spirit
of the Flavian age, and centres it upon its true
centre, the amphitheatre. He supposes himself to
stand on the site of the "Golden" palace near the
colossus of the Sun, and to be surveying the chief
buildings of Domitian and his family.

> Where midway in the street the scaffold climbs,
>     Raising nigh heaven yon giant crowned with rays,
> One tyrant house devoured in other times
>     The city round, and spread a baleful blaze.
>
> One lake, one private water, yielded room
>     For all that sacred Circle. Where you mark
> Yon swiftly-building Baths, there Nero's doom
>     Made thousands homeless for a single park.
>
> Last to the place of yon fair Colonnade
>     He grasped, still craving.—Caesar, thanks to thee,
> Rome is once more for Romans. Thou hast made
>     The enslaver's pleasance free unto the free.

It was impossible that in any time which possessed a poet at all, or the capacity for poetic
feeling, this union of the world should fail to
kindle the imagination. If in the enumeration of
Gibbon the long defile of races obedient to the
Caesars makes a stately and impressive show, what
must have been the effect of actually seeing the
vast unity, typified in the varied crowd of the
streets, of the colonnades, and, above all, of the
amphitheatre? Possibly this may be read by some
who were present at the opening of the Great
Exhibition in 1851. I was not there myself (for
good reasons), but I have heard it said by men
who were, and who are well entitled to speak on

such a matter, that it was the most "poetic" experience they had ever known or could easily conceive. I am not ashamed to say that I find our various "Inventories" and "Colinderies" in London more poetical than most poetry, and have always wondered a little that scarcely anything of the picturesque and imperial suggestiveness to be found there, and in modern London all over and at all times, has found its way into the later Victorian literature. It has not happened to suit the genius of those among us who have the faculty of expression. We have not for this purpose found our man. Rome did. Among the crowd in the Coliseum sat Martial, noting and translating, in a thousand sharp touches, the thoughts presented by the successive figures. It is true that the unity was much more real and the variety of surface much more striking than in the English "empire" as represented in our capital. Through the same passage of the theatre would pass, in a few minutes, wild horsemen from the Steppes, whose looks at least seemed to authenticate the grossest barbarisms recorded in Herodotus; a group of majestic Arabians, excited for once into something like haste; Germans who had but once seen the Rhine; Africans who had possibly drunk the springs of the Nile—all more or less subjects of Rome, all entering at Caesar's door, and sprinkled as they entered with his cloud of saffron perfume. Among them sometimes would be a mountaineer of Thrace, pale and pensive, who, seeing the press, takes from his wallet a little roll of parchment and holds it tight in his hand as he goes. Martial might well look at him and wonder. He is an ascetic, a brother of the Orphean mystery. He and his like have for centuries preached and practised strange precepts of self-suppression and renunciation. Their little river is at the very point to join and swell a mighty world-stream. What will it not sweep away! Him and all did Martial note. Here is one scrap from his note-book.

> Is there a race so rude,
> So bare of art and nude,
> That comes not, Caesar, to thy glorious show?
> See yon Sarmatian! Think!
> He hath bled his horse for drink!
> Yon Haemian reads his Orpheus 'mid the snow.
> This one, it may be, dips
> In Nilus' fount his lips,
> That hears the breakers of the encircling Main.
> Arabia comes, not last,
> Sabaea hastens fast,
> Cilicia finds her saffron here again.
> See the Sygambrian there,
> Known by his knot of hair;
> The Aethiop, knotted too, but diversely.
> A thousandfold their speech;
> Yet this attuneth each,
> They hail a common father, Sire, in thee!

In a city and age presenting such rich material for the imagination in the walks of daily life, it is not strange that some should have regarded this material as exclusively proper for literature, and should have contrasted with it contemptuously what could be got by treating over and over again the well-worn topics borrowed from Greece. This was the choice : for to the faculty of invention scarcely any school of Roman poetry would pretend, certainly none of those which divided the city under Domitian. The difference of tendency rose to the height of a formal controversy, and is represented to us chiefly by the names of Martial and Statius. But into this controversy we must not now enter very far, nor shall we attempt to estimate the merits of Statius' work on the traditional Greek lines, his epic upon the orthodox epic subject of Thebes. It has had some effect at various times, and may have again. At the present moment, though slightly alive in the schools, in the world it is practically dead, and it has been in this condition for a great part of its existence. A work whose whole motive is borrowed from times in which the writer had only a fictitious interest, has generally something unhealthy in its constitution. There are plenty of English parallels ready to hand. Martial had no doubtful opinion on the subject. He held that, under the Flavian dynasty at all events, the proper subject for Romans was Rome. Despite of civilities, there was evidently friction between Martial and Statius; and the matter is of interest to us here because we are presently to have before us, from the gallery of Statius, perhaps the largest picture remaining of a Flavian festivity. Now this picture is evidently a challenge-piece. It is the chief of Statius' essays in the manner of the rival

school, and probably owes some energy to the
writer's eagerness in proving that he too, when
he chose, could touch off the humours of the town.
A glance, therefore, at these rivalries is a proper
prelude to the subject. Martial offers satire in
abundance ; of which here is a specimen. It should
be remembered, as a help to fixing the point, that the
legends of Thebes and Argos, typified by the names
of Oedipus and Thyestes respectively, make the
whole of Statius' *Thebais*, and that Statius was,
beyond comparison, the chief writer of his school.

Thyestes and Oedipus, folly all that is !
    Your Scyllas, Medeas, what good do they do ?
What's Hylas, or Parthenopaeus, or Attis ?
    Endymion sleeping, what says he to you ?

The pinions of Icarus melted, the slighting
    Of amorous rivers by swains they pursue,—
What help can you get from such pure waste of writing ?
    Here's verse to which Life may write under " 'Tis true !"

No Centaurs, no Gorgons, will here be presented,
    No Harpies ! 'Tis man, sir, man only that speaks.
If you don't like your portrait, and feel discontented
    At seeing yourself, sir—why, go to the Greeks !

A sharp cast of the literary javelin this, at a
time when the favourite poet of culture had "fixed,
O Muse, the barrier of his song at *Oedipus*." It is
clear that to turn aside these and other like missiles
was one object of Statius when, imitating ostentatiously the manner of Martial, he wrote his very
interesting piece on "The Saturnalian Feast of
Domitian."

Of all the feasts by which, as it was held, the "sovereign people" enjoyed their own, the most widely popular, the most typical, was the feast of the *Saturnalia*, held in mid-December, and lasting, in the time of Domitian, five days, of which one was principal. The connexion of the feast with *Saturn*—the Italian god of the field, honoured when the seed was sown, that in due time he might give the increase symbolized by his sickle—had of course long before Flavian times become merely nominal. To suit the facts of the time the Sowing festival of Rome must have then been adapted to the agriculture of Egypt, Pontus, and where not? But the old winter-feast of the farmers fell, for Rome and Italy, at a time of year very well suited to public merry-making. It is otherwise with us. Our Christmas, closely connected in history with the Saturnalia, is made miserable, three years in four, by the weather, and for united public festivals on a large scale it is quite impossible. Our real Saturnalia have long ago migrated to Easter, and from Easter tend constantly to fix themselves practically in our brief summer and delightful autumn. But at Rome, as everyone knows, there is a really enjoyable Christmas for the general public, and there was a really enjoyable Saturnalia. As at our Christmas so at the Saturnalia, public manners required of everyone to make those in his power as easy and comfortable as might be during the five days. Particularly, as with ourselves, this remission was claimed on behalf of the poor and the oppressed. The State contributed to the general rejoicing a relaxation, which is to us odd enough and affords a lesson to the historic imagination. Of gambling the business-like and economical Roman felt a great horror; and at ordinary times both law and public sentiment repressed all games of chance with an extravagant and doubtless self-defeating severity. But both gave way to the imperative desire that everyone in his own fashion should be happy at the Saturnalia, and for five days the Roman might get drunk (which for the most part he did not want to do) and might shake the dice-box (which he wanted very badly indeed), without fear of interference from the aediles. The sentiment, indeed, of the graver sort held out when law had given way. It is laughable, a fine instance of the local humours of Puritanism, to read that Augustus, half a century earlier than our Flavian period, and when the Roman Empire, the "corrupt," the "dissolute," etc., etc., was already established, incurred grave reproach because he, being the guardian of public morals, and bound to set a good example, went so far in Saturnalian licence as to join in a round game for points with his family! *Pro pudor inversique mores!*

To the Roman mind, therefore, a general permission to play in public for stakes seemed to be the seal and assurance of general liberty, and the Feast of Saturn is seldom mentioned without some allusion to this characteristic mark. And it is mentioned often. To Martial in particular, as a caterer for amusement, the season was especially dear. There is some evidence that for a time he published regularly at the Saturnalia—by way of Christmas numbers as it were—special volumes of light verse suited to the holiday reader. He is always pleading the general absolution of the feast as an excuse both for offences against the moral taste, which, to say the truth, are frequent, and for supposed laxities of literary workmanship, which are pretended merely, as a show of humility; for a more exact artist never put stylus to wax. Very delicate and graceful are his excuses for rudeness, and very various; this, for example, where he ingeniously deduces from Saturn's sickle, once used for other purposes, a suggestion of fleeting life and an injunction to make the most of our time:

> When the greybeard with the scythe
> Bids the dice to keep us blythe
>     Days five-fold:
> Merry Mob-cap, Madam Rome,
> Poets for a careless tome
>     Scarce you'll scold.
>
> Will you? No! your smile replies.
> We may write without disguise.
>     Care's man's curse!
> Freedom! Let the casual thought,
> As it ought not, as it ought,
>     Just run verse.

I have myself taken here a certain Saturnalian liberty (as perhaps elsewhere) in the rendering of *pileata Roma*; for to call the *pileus*, properly the

*cap of liberty*, a *mob-cap*, might well be stigmatized
by the severe as nothing more than a bad pun.
But I appeal to the poet. Martial, if any one, must
listen to the excuse that "Christmas comes but
once a year." We will quote yet two more of his
preludes to the Saturnalia. Nowhere is better seen
the spirit of the Hellenized imperial festival—common, nay gross, humanity, frank and unashamed,
exposing itself in forms of singular severity, the
heritage of Greece, and leniently rebuked by public
conscience, the great gift of Rome. Here is a
strange little piece. The tune (if I could catch it)
is the tune of Milton. The thought is—well, not
exactly Miltonic. (It will be seen that the date is
after Domitian, but that does not matter.)

> Hence, sullen Frown, stern rustic heritress
>  Of Cato and Fabricius, come not nigh!
> Go, mask of Pride and mannered Moralness,
>  All things that fall from us in darkness, fly[1]!
> "Hail, Feast of Saturn!" 'Tis a happy cry
> And honest (Nerva giving leave and cause).
> *Grave airs*, I give you warning. It is I.
> Leave me; and read your *Digest of the Laws.*

And here is the other mood, the Roman thought.
Who "Varro" was, whether he really existed, is no
matter. He serves here for a mere type of the mind
to which the holiday is an offensive interruption,
and its harmless game of forfeits an unpardonable
expense of working hours. Impertinent in the

---

[1] *Quidquid et in tenebris non sumus, ite foras*, an epigram, in
its kind, not to be surpassed in Latin or otherwise.

former piece, here Martial chooses to be respectful.
The two moods please.

> *Varro*, whom Sophocles had not disowned
>   For tragedy, nor Horace for the lyre,
> Lay work aside awhile; be Farce postponed,
>   Trim Elegy her hair forget to tire.
> The verse I send, to a December taste,
>   May pass, when smoke and folly seem the rule:
> Regarded, *Varro*, simply as a waste
>   Of time, you cannot find them *worse than pool.*

Freedom then for those who would enjoy, compulsion almost, if need be, for those who would not,
was the key-note of this formidable merry-making.
But the general good-will signified itself in one
way, which, as a *corruptio optimi*, is perhaps the
very worst nuisance which ancient or modern man
has wilfully invented—a mutual giving of presents.
It is true that in Rome, as among ourselves, a certain convention was found, whereby the extreme of
tiresomeness was mitigated. Tablets and napkins
(both doubtless decorated with various "designs")
supplied in Flavian Rome the place of Christmas
cards; and the methods of lighting in use permitted as a third simple usage the handing about
of presentation-tapers. It was thought scarcely fair
to send tablet, napkin, or taper at any other time.
But, as may be supposed, the ingenuity of human
beings in self-annoyance was not to be so easily
balked; and all sorts of other objects, as well as
these three, continued to circulate from house to
house, to flow in with absurd abundance upon those
who were worth courting, and to flow out (for the

Romans managed the matter after their fashion, plain and business-like), to flow out again to the class from which they came, as a cheap kind of liberality, everyone knowing the whole process, and all secretly willing to get as much or give as little as they could. Endless are the varieties of humour which this pernicious and long-lived custom (for it goes on merrily) furnished to the painter of Flavian society. I quote one or two, not for themselves, but because, in order to appreciate the great scene we are presently to see, we must figure to ourselves first the Saturnalia as specially the season of "presents all round." Here is one of many variations on the same fertile theme of the disappointed giver. Very comic when written down in black-and-white are the natural reflections of the hunter for "presents" who has missed his game, and receives, instead of repayment with interest, only satirical assurances that the patron would have been delighted to pass on any little thing he had received, only that, his supply of "gifts" having failed, his generosity is without means. It is the best of the joke, that the man does not in the least feel the absurdity of his anger:

> I sent you a trifle; and, alack!
> Ne'er a trifle has it brought me back.
> Now the Feast is over. Times are bad,
> Say you. Ne'er a present have you had.
> Ne'er a client brought a pot of pickle,
> Coif, or kerchief, pennyweight of nickel?
> Ne'er a grumbler, to assist his suit,
> Backed it with sardines or candied fruit,

> Case of shrivelled figs or olives rotten?
> You're so sorry I should seem forgotten!
> Keep this cheap benevolence for those you
> Still can cheat—and not for ONE WHO KNOWS YOU.

Here is another tragedy of the same type, but
less deeply moving. A gentleman, to whose finances
this commerce of society is important, has failed in
his speculation upon the accustomed bounty of a
certain lady, and ungallantly promises himself to
make things straight next first of March, the Ladies'
Day of the Roman Year:

> Now ushers call the unwilling lad
>     From nuts and marbles back to school.
> The gambler, if his luck be bad,
> Chased from the public, drunk and sad,
>     Tempts the police again, poor fool!
> The Five Days gone! Yet, Galla, you
> Have sent me nothing. Less I had
> Foreseen. But *nothing*, Galla! Phew!
> Ah, well! December's for the men,
> And March for women. Wait till then.
> How shall you like it, Galla, when
> You get your *nothing* back again?

But though the presents might be tiresome
enough, and though Martial, as his business is,
may gaily turn out this and that seam on the
inner side of the popular motley, the Saturnalia
represented feelings real, deep, and sacred. Then,
as at Christmas now with us, was the assembly of
the family for the prearranged evening of festivity,
doubtless difficult sometimes to make "go," but not
to be sneered out of the grateful memory of any

people who know the meaning of "family" and of
"home." What store the Romans set by it is well
seen in a device of their great historian, or rather
tragedian, Tacitus, apt for our present purpose as
if it was made for us. The popular brilliance of
the Flavian house is constantly shown to us against
a background of Neronian horror. It was seen
so by contemporaries. And the blackest of the
Neronian horrors is the horror of murder—that
chain of *parricides* which began when the Emperor's
rival, cousin, and heir, the orphan son of Claudius,
was taken off with poison. And how does Tacitus
think best to make us feel the unkind murder of
the boy Britannicus? By dating the inception of it
from the family feast of the Saturnalia.

At the supper of the imperial family, Nero,
Britannicus, and other young friends were met.
The dice, the dice of the Saturnalia, having raised
Nero to a temporary throne as "king of the forfeits," he laid upon each guest his playful duty to
perform, observing nevertheless the respect due to
each. But when he came to Britannicus he commanded the lad to sing, thinking that he could not
but come off ill, having little experience in gaiety,
and in drinking still less. However, the boy put
him out of countenance, for he came forward,
nothing daunted, and sang a sad enough song,
showing how he who sang was put out of his
own, and oppressed, and had no help. Whereat
the company were much moved (and ashamed, we
will hope), as was easily seen, for the wine made

them free of their looks and words. But the poor
wretch paid dearly for showing his spirit; for the
tyrant, alarmed and angry, resolved to be rid of
him without delay. And so it was. Such had
been the family feast of the Emperor Nero, and
such a story was Tacitus telling about the time of
the particular festival to which we now proceed.

We have now in our minds the chief facts and
thoughts which Statius supposes us to bring to
the reading of his "Great Saturnalia." We are
ready, putting ourselves in the place of the average
Roman at the time, to see in the Emperor not a
bloody tyrant and persecutor but the liberator of
the people; in the Coliseum not a torture-chamber
for martyrs but the revered monument of the great
liberator; in the Saturnalia not a soft name for an
orgy of beasts, but a specially humane ordinance of
public religion, commanding general gladness, wide
benevolence, and summing up, like its successor in
modern times, the charities of the family life. We
can for the moment persuade ourselves to see how
appropriate it was that on the great day of the Five
the "common father" of nations should gather the
people to a common table in the great amphitheatre
and scatter to them his indiscriminate gifts. We
can feel why on such an occasion the poet of artificial Hellenism should have quitted his Parnassus.
It is worth while to make the effort of imagination,
for whatever may be the merits of the verse, very
seldom upon earth has been witnessed a scene more
splendid than Statius has to describe, seldom one

more interesting to a sympathetic mind, not often one more pleasant to an understanding heart.

> Apollo, Pallas, let me play;
> Ye strict and stern, not yours the day.
> Grave Muses, with the opening year
> Return, but leave us. Now and here
> Assist me, Saturn, fetter-free,
>   And gay December, deep in wine.
> Help, wanton Wit and grinning Glee,
>   To picture how our prince benign
> Kept, morn to evening, long and late
> His public Saturnalian state.

The hospitality offered by this giant monarch to his colossal court was nothing less than to feed and amuse, from dawn until far beyond the end of the winter's day, "the people of Rome," that is to say a representative gathering selected from all ranks, which must have numbered some fifty or sixty thousand at the very least. The scene of the entertainment was the amphitheatre, to which the company were doubtless admitted as usual by distributed tickets. How the building was arranged for the particular occasion cannot be ascertained in detail. It is a problem of the antiquary how at ordinary times the awnings were fixed and moved over its vast internal oval of (roughly) 500 feet by 400 feet. But we shall see that for this particular festival the lighting of the building after dark in the manner described would require temporary internal structures on an extensive scale, useful also for other purposes; nor can the expense of such structures, great as it must have been, have told for much in

such a "Christmas bill" as must have been presented to Domitian when the feast was over. The
assembling and placing of the multitude began in
early morning, and must itself have occupied some
hours. Meanwhile they were kept in good humour
by the scattering of confectionery, itself in its variety
a symbol of the power which commanded the whole
resources of the world from far east of the Bosporus
to far west of Gibraltar.

> The day broke showery—such a pour
> Of sweetmeats ne'er was seen before.
> Nuts! All the nuts that Pontus knows,
> All kinds that Idumaea grows;
> Fruits of Damascus, grafts of price,
>     Force-ripened sweetness of the cane
> From Ebusus, the choice, the nice
>     Of East and West, a liberal rain;
> And all that's baked beneath the sun
> Of comfit, biscuit, cake, or bun.
>
> Dates fell as thick, as if unseen
> Some palm-tree overhead had been.
> Not Pleiads shed so loose a shower,
> Nor Hyads in their wildest hour,
> As then from skies unclouded broke
>     Upon the vast theatric throng.
> The storms of Jove, for Roman folk,
>     May waste the earth, yet do no wrong,
> While such peculiar bounties flow
> Provided by our Jove below.

Amid these agreeable preliminaries, with much
crunching and munching, doubtless also much pushing, squeezing, and "Where are you a-shoving to?"
the circle was filled, the arena remaining empty for

a future use. The dinner which followed, Statius expressly tells us, was the same for all; we are, no doubt, to understand that the various ranks were distinguished as usual by their places, and the Emperor's own immediate circle seated on his private platform. The uniformity of the repast is a guarantee that it was good, amazingly good for the quantity. Many illustrious senators must have been cross enough at having to come there at all (for they hated his Majesty), but I would not waste on them one grain of sympathy. The Emperor could not have served them with anything but decent wine, and what he served to them he served to all—not a bad example of taste in a society which is constantly represented as the type of vulgarity.

> The seats are full, in every rank,
> From floor to crown, no single blank;
> When, lo! the attendants mount the tiers,
> And twice as great the crowd appears.
> Like Ganymedes for gest and grace,
>   The cates, the napkins white and fine,
> The viands choice for all they place,
>   And freely pour the mellowed wine.
> Like the round world, this princely treat
> Like that is vast, like that complete.

The "Ganymedes" we are to figure dressed in respectable white, the Roman equivalent for the swallow-tail and shirt front; the company in all the garments worn within the four corners of the earth, even the aristocracy togaless, for the toga was a bore and gladly cast aside, so that the discarding

of it is frequently mentioned as an assurance of
Saturnalian freedom.  Where was Martial?  There,
for certain; perhaps in the Emperor's party, enjoying himself greatly, and making endless mental
notes of figures, costumes, remarks—sighing, perhaps, a little for native Spain and some quiet rustic
pig-sticking, and an evening by the fire telling Celtic
stories under the mistletoe.  Well, he would have
it all soon.  Where was Statius?  In the imperial
party, for certain, from his complacent manner of
assuring the public at large that they were equally
well off; not enjoying himself, I suspect, as much
as Martial, though he does seem on this day to
have been shaken into an unusual state of genuine
excitement.  That simile of the world is very
good; at least, it stirs me strongly.  And his next
is better.

> Gigantic Trade of modern time,
> Feigned plenty of the golden prime,
> All, all are in conception less
> Than this concentred bounteousness.
> Rome at one feast! Sex, ages, ranks
>    Unclassed; none more, none less than free;
> And last, to beggar prayers and thanks,
>    The giver's sacred majesty;
> That so the least of us may say,
> "I with the Prince have dined to-day."
>
> Not sated yet with new delight,
> Taste passes sudden into sight—

We have finished our victuals and wine, we in
the outer rows; a good deal better (as the poet
elegantly but not altogether gracefully reminds us)

than most of us get every day. We have gone back to our dates, figs, ratafias, "cakes of Ameria squashy in the middle," etc., of which in the hours of waiting we collected a little heap, being good at catching. We ruminate peacefully upon these joys; till suddenly even "cakes of Ameria" no longer keep our attention—

> For, lo! the arena fills. A horde,
> By nature soft, and for the sword
> Not formed or fashioned, here forget
> To fear like women, and display
> Their Amazon battalions, set
> In order for a manly fray.
> Hippolyta could scarce have sent
> Such lasses to a tournament.

Now, we are Romans; and it is not one century yet from the birth of Christ. We should not be horrified if these trained girls fell on and did real execution with their swords and javelins. But they are not going to do anything very bloody. From the account of the poet it is clear that this army of women, and the army of dwarfs (amazing proof of organization, when we come to think of it) which enters presently, are sham armies, and that the whole contest is no more than a contest *pour rire*—a laughable Saturnalian parody of those only too real encounters which this gorgeous circle has seen. It is an elaborate mockery of gladiators' performance. They act all the incidents of battle, and the joke of the thing lies in the incongruity of these soft limbs and stunted forms with the horrors and feats which they recall to the imagination. Not a refined pleasure, but for this time not brutal; and such were the spectacles of Rome more often than is sometimes supposed.

> These challenge next a tiny sort,
> Whom nature, knotting them too short,
> Finished as dwarfs.  Heroic rage
> Urges the minions to engage.
> Great is the show of little strokes,
>   Small deaths, and miniature despairs.
> Mars laughs; his grisly partner jokes;
>   While wondering at such pygmy airs
> The cranes above them (see the sequel)
> Allow the pygmy for their equal.

Of these "wondering cranes," who seem to have prompted Statius with a learned comparison between the dwarfs and the crane-fighting Pygmies of Homer, the poet in the sequel gives an explanation not too clear for our modern understandings, and assuredly not made much clearer by the modern expositors.  We shall come to it in a moment, and must hasten on : for the dinner, the dwarfs, and the Amazons have occupied some time, and already the winter light is fading.

> Now, for the day was closing in,
> 'Twas time the scramble should begin.
> "The scramble!" At the exciting call
> Enter the famous beauties, all
> Whose charms of person or of art
>   Possess the stage; the rounded forms
> Of Lydia here, and there apart
>   Lithe limbs of Spain with timbrels; swarms
> Of Syrians, coming still and coming,
> Exclaiming, clapping, dancing, drumming.

The "scramble" was exactly what the name implies to our ears—a scattering of gifts among a crowd, partly for the benefit of the receiver, partly for the amusement of the lookers-on. But what a scene! What a moment, when the hollow ellipse of brilliant and varied colours was filled by a centre of greater brilliance, variety, and beauty! The beauty of the world, literally chosen, gathered, and collected! For mere splendour, for popular splendour (the most admirable sort and the most useful), the world has seen nothing like it before or since.

> Complete at length the motley rout,
> Supers and match-girls not left out.
> All on a sudden from the sky
> Birds, flocks of birds unnumbered, fly!
> The fowls of every climate known,
>     From sacred Nile to freezing Phasis,
> Blown southward from the frigid zone,
>     Blown northward from the warm oasis,
> All kinds but one—no birds of prey,
> Lest they should take the rest away.

These birds, whatever they may have been to the ladies, are a very considerable surprise to us, and a puzzle too. The commentators are nowhere, so to speak. They tell us that these birds were only tickets, scattered among the crowd, each representing a specimen of game or poultry, and entitling the possessor, on application at some place indicated, to the actual bird. Such a method was certainly practised in these amphitheatrical scrambles—the bird, as Martial puts it, preferring the hazard of

the ticket to the certainty of being torn in pieces.
But it is simply impossible that what Statius here
describes was a mere scattering of tickets, con-
vertible into chickens! To say nothing of the
absurd irrelevance of his imagery, the question is
clinched and settled, so far, by the foregoing reference to the *cranes*. The cranes, says the poet in
plain terms, plainer even than my version shows,
were some of the *birds* which descended in the
scramble, and these "cranes" were astonished to
see the exploits of the pygmy paladins in the arena
below. And yet these cranes were only *tickets*?
Not a bit of it. The reader, knowing his or her
Statius, has no doubt a solution of the puzzle. But
"birds" of some sort these birds must have been,
and of course not real, or many a lady would have
been slain on the spot. Privately I guess them to
have been some sort of toy-birds made of rag, tow,
and what not, suspended above, lowered at the
proper time near to the arena, and then allowed
to flutter down. Nothing would make a better
scramble or a more amusing. To each would be
attached the Emperor's gift, that is either the
"ticket" for it or, much more likely, the gift itself.
Objects highly attractive to the assembled fair, and
quite costly enough for a distribution by hundreds and
thousands, could be easily attached to a toy-bird.

> Now all content compare their gains;
> No pocket empty, none complains.
> Then all at once the myriad throats
> Join in one shout their countless notes.

"Hail to the Prince," their sound proclaims,
  "And Feast of Saturn, princely-free!
Hail to his name, to all his names,
  Our Prince—our Master!" "Nay," said he,
And put the flattering phrase away,
"What else ye will; but *master*—nay!"

It is hard that, in spite of this, Domitian—who
has fared worse for less reason than almost any
character in history, and who is frequently abused
from pulpits and otherwise by people who hardly
care to know whether he was or was not the same
as Diocletian—that Domitian should be scolded for
the servility of address which he permitted. He
was a hard master to the Roman nobility, who
perhaps wanted one; but he was a real king and
not a fool. After this last interchange of compliments between him and his company, he had
doubtless had quite enough of the proceedings and
withdrew, we may presume, by his private passage
to a well-earned evening without any round game,
the grandees generally following suit. Nor is it
likely that the fastidious Statius, though the fun
was but just beginning, saw very much more of
it. The arena was lighted up (how, it is hard to
learn from the raptures of the bard), and a sort of
Bartholomew Fair, with shows, stages, and drinking-
bars free, seems to have gone on there *ad libitum*.
Hours afterwards Statius declares himself too sleepy
with the Emperor's wine to tell any more. He had
more probably worked himself out over a first draft
of his poem; which if the reader does not allow to

have some real fire and flavour in it, let the fault
be mine and not the Roman's; for in the original
I find a great glow of pleasure and glory. And
thankful to remember, in this air of mud and smoke,
that ever a multitude was so bright, so happy, so
splendid as were these sixty thousand Romans in
the year Ninety-blank *Anno Domini*, I would conduct the poet, in Roman fashion, most respectfully
to his bed :—

> Scarce night begins to mount the sphere,
> When—see a sun of flames appear!
> Brighter than Ariadne's crown,
> Through gathering shades it settles down
> In mid arena.   Heaven is thick
>     With fires, and darkness banished quite.
> Dull sleep and sloth fled, strangely quick,
>     To other cities at the sight,
> Perceiving that this sun portended
> A feast not easy to be ended.
>
> But how describe the enormous jest
> Of shows and farces and the rest?
> The suppers heaped, the streams of drink—
> I cannot sing, I cannot think.
> Spare, generous Prince, and let me sleep;
>     The memory of this wondrous day—
> Not while thy Rome and river keep
>     Their places, shall it pass away;
> Not till, new given to man by thee,
> Yon Capitol shall cease to be!

# A TRAGI-COMEDY AND A PAGE
# OF HISTORY

A SATIRIST in search of an example by which to show the invincible repugnance of individual tastes in matters of art, and the consequent futility of critical discussion, could scarcely desire a better case for the paradox than the estimate of the poet Euripides. From his own time to the present day it has been the fate of his works to raise a strange and complicated discord of opinions. He was scarcely cold in his grave when Aristophanes hastened to set up the jousts for a tournament of letters, and devoted the most brilliant of his national dramas to a question such as never perhaps before, and seldom since, has been so pompously debated —whether the dead poet had or had not a right to his accredited place as a master supreme in his kind.

And where the question is left by Aristophanes in the *Frogs*, there in effect, and in spite of all changes, it now remains. That vast popularity and influence which the comedy presumes to exist, have never been withdrawn, nor ever ceased to provoke from time to time the same sort of scornful rage which they provoked in the comedian. By the side of Aeschylus and Sophocles he was compelled to place Euripides, and Euripides only; and yet he would gladly have converted the throne to a pillory. So now, in a list of the world's greatest poets, the ducal rank of the literary baronage, no one could omit the name of Euripides without being conscious of the gap. And yet in a general history of Attic drama, it is possible for a scholar to bestow on Euripides a chapter of venomous depreciation, and to back it with respected names[1]. Among the living poets of England one has eloquently defended the unity of the great tragic triad, while another has declared, with something more than his habitual emphasis, the impossibility that anyone worth attention should ever put Euripides in the same class with the other two.

Such a disagreement of doctors might well stop our mouths, if in these few remarks we were aiming at any decision. But the very disagreement is a temptation to ask the cause of it, and why, when most writers who have made a venture for the first rank have been speedily fixed to their places, within or without, by something like a general consent, Euripides alone (for I believe he has no parallel) should be crowned indeed, but with such an uneasy and disputed crown. The fact I take to be that Euripides wrote at a moment in the history of literature not merely, like all moments in history,

---

[1] See the criticism of Schlegel, as reproduced and endorsed by Donaldson in his *Theatre of the Greeks*.

unique, but egregiously and inimitably unique. He swam in the swirl of two strong currents, which, taking their rise in the mind of the same inventor, flowing, clashing, and mixing diversely ever since, threw up around Euripides the spray of their most bewildering conflict.

When Aeschylus, in the phrase of Aristophanes, "first reared the pomp of tragic style," a date which may be put about level with Euripides' birth, his work had two effects, one of which he planned and consciously accomplished, while the other he certainly did not design, nor in its full consequences even comprehend. He perfected the sublime and he made realism inevitable. As for sublimity, it is the essence of him. For the type of his art, antiquity rightly chose the stately and unfamiliar costume by which he strove to raise his personages literally above and out of the common level. He had the faculty of greatness, in theme, style, words, everything. It belonged in part to his age; his contemporary Pindar has it more perhaps than any other except himself. But Aeschylus has it most, and for the exquisite pleasure of elevation there is none like him. To sustain this height he made (we have express, though perhaps needless, testimony that he was the first maker) an extraordinary diction; he borrowed and adapted a peculiar lyrical music; he chose and developed all that was morally grandest in the grotesque abundance of myth and legend ready to his hand. Now in all this there is nothing exclusively proper to the stage; and though Aeschylus was assuredly one of the very greatest of theatrical artists, though his actual work is essentially theatrical, it is nevertheless not in its theatrical quality that his genius as a poet consists. Of which the best proof is that in later literature the most Aeschylean poetry is to be found not in dramas at all. Milton is much more Aeschylean than Shakespeare, and not in scenes quasi-dramatic merely, but in his ordinary narrative.

Nor is this so merely because Milton knew Aeschylus profoundly, and Shakespeare, we may say, not at all; for Dante, who knew not a line of him, is often Aeschylean nevertheless. It is easily conceivable that, under other circumstances, Aeschylus might have applied his unequalled power of elevation to poetry not dramatic in form, and had he done so, he would have been Aeschylus still. But without his sublimity of manner there would have been no Aeschylus, not if he had kept ever so strictly to the form of dialogue and always written for the purpose of recitation from a stage. Indeed the mere spectacular form of tragedy, so far as it was ever invented at all, was invented rather by Athens than by Aeschylus, and was certain to arise, as it did, whenever there should first exist a large free population desiring and able to command the luxuries of the mind.

Nevertheless it was a vital matter, that the strong new spirit of Aeschylus went to raise and to popularise the new form of serious drama. For this form was an instrument not likely, once made, to lie idle for want of hands. Through action and speech, as combined in conversation, we learn the greater part of what we know about each other. It was therefore a prodigious step in the art of showing man to men, when poets took up seriously the composing of dialogues to be recited with action. But Aeschylus, though he took the initial and decisive step, went but a little way himself; and could he have foreseen where the way led and where others soon would go, he would have been but little disposed to congratulate himself upon his lead. In the latest and most developed of his works there is scarcely a sign that the poet feels in his grasp a new tool for carving the likeness of common humanity. His dialogue is but little applied to exhibit the play of thought and emotion as only dialogue can show it. The spectacular possibilities of the drama he grasped completely, but its possible subtlety he did not comprehend or care for. It was indeed alien from his mind. To preserve that noble air of grandeur requires a treatment broad not subtle. You cannot be, at least no one ever has been yet, gigantic in outline and minutely human in detail. However ingeniously the two qualities may be combined, something of the one must be sacrificed to the other.

But the step was taken and was not to be taken back. The realistic analysis of character is a pleasure too keen to be tasted and not to provoke appetite. In the drama of Sophocles it assumes such new proportions as to be really a new thing.

The working of a virtuous mind under temptation, as it is shown in the *Philoctetes*, and could not have been shown without the aid of the dramatic form, offers a kind of intellectual pleasure fertile ever since in literature, but no more to be found in Aeschylus than it is in Homer. Our present space and purpose will not allow us to dwell upon Sophocles, or to consider the skill with which he contrived to hold in combination for a time the discordant elements that were combating for the stage of tragedy. But this we have to remember, that for the conciliation which he effected there was a price to pay. The process of permeating tragedy with the spirit of realistic analysis, without destroying that elevation given to it by Aeschylus, was a process of limited possibility. This is recognised explicitly in the contrasted criticism of Sophocles and Euripides, which is attributed to Sophocles himself; that Sophocles represented humanity according to the requirements of art, while his successor painted it as it is. But what if men should care for the reality more than for the requirements of the Aeschylean art? Or, to put the question more fairly, what if they insisted on having all kinds of intellectual pleasure, a realistic drama as well as the elevated and remote? Even Sophocles is held to have succeeded least in those of his plays (such as the *Philoctetes* and the *Women of Trachis*) where the new element has most part. Who should forbid it then to declare itself altogether independent?

Such was the state of things when Euripides came. Everything was ripe for a tragedy, or comedy, or tragi-comedy of manners; and if there might be a question what it should be called, Athens was not likely to wait, any more than we need delay ourselves now, for a mere scholastic question of classification. Such a tragi-comedy Euripides did in truth create, and if he could have started it frankly in what would now seem the obvious way, half the pother which has vexed his renown might have been avoided. The drama of Euripides, if we look at the essential parts of it and neglect the accidental, is concerned wholly with the life which he actually saw around him. And it ought in the nature of things to have dealt nominally, as well as actually, with common personages and ordinary incidents. Half the criticism of Aristophanes and of many since would cease to apply, if the plays were furnished with a new set of *dramatis personae*, fictitious names without any traditional association. And it is amazing with what facility this could be done, how slight is often the connexion between a play of Euripides and the old-world legend which serves for the scaffolding. With the change of a few verses here and there, the *Medea* might be cut loose from the tale of the Argonauts, with which it has in truth nothing whatever to do. The life of it comes not from romance, but from the homes of Athens. Hippolytus is slain by a miraculous monster; but if he had been killed by the commonest carriage-accident, the play might still be much what it is, and might have made as deep a mark in literature as it has.   The names of Theseus and Phaedra, nay even the very human deities of Aphrodite and Artemis, might all be exchanged for other names and persons, and the drama in its essence would still be there.   There is not a single play of Sophocles which could be subjected to such a process without utter dissolution, and as to Aeschylus, the very thought seems a profanity.   The legends of mythology are the very warp and substance of their compositions ; they are for the most part the mere frame to those of Euripides, and a frame too often imperfectly suited to the texture.

Why the tragi-comedy of Euripides and his contemporaries did not (with exceptions too few to signify) take what now seems the plain road, and strike into independent fiction, is probably to be explained by the quasi-religious character of theatrical performances at Athens.   Probably neither the authorities who licensed and financed the exhibition, nor the audience themselves, would have tolerated all at once so bold an innovation.   The fourth century might have witnessed it ; but the fourth century produced only a Menander and no Euripides.   Serious thought had turned elsewhere, and the great age of Greek poetry was over.   Nor has the true lover of Euripides any reason to regret what actually was done.   The elements of the Euripidean drama, the romantic or religious legend which is taken for base and the story of common

life which is built upon it, stand indeed not seldom
in the sharpest and, it may be, the crudest opposition. But this very contrast gives to the reality
of what is real a strange and fascinating relief. It
is often as if the figures of some quaint tapestry
were suddenly to walk and talk from the canvas.
Nor is there the least doubt that the poet knew
well what he was doing. He loves to startle his
reader with the very bareness of sheer life thrusting
itself upon the artificial scene. High art has never
forgiven him, but mankind have never given him
up and never will.

I propose for our present amusement, and on
the chance that others may turn to use an experience of many years in the great poet's peculiar
ways, to illustrate what has been said by a brief
review of his *Andromache*. This play is classified,
with all his works, as a tragedy, and some are pleased
to call it a second-rate tragedy. No Euripidean is
concerned with this nomenclature nor bound to
defend the play as a tragedy at all. It is no tragedy.
The only tragic incident lies outside of the main
action, and merely serves the poet for a piece of
brilliant narrative. In the time of Elizabeth we
might have called it a comedy; now we have no
word for it at all. But call it what we please, it is
an admirable piece of work, full of reality, and in
the central scene subtle and yet simple in the play
of character after a fashion which Euripides has to
himself.

Interested above all things in the complications

of domestic life, an interest stimulated by the great social and material improvements of his century, Euripides has centred the *Andromache* upon a problem such as our modern civilization happily does not admit. The Greeks were in one sense monogamous: that is, a man could not in Athens be married to more than one legal wife. But, as in all slave-owning communities, ambiguous relations, regular though not matrimonial, were common. And as the slave-women of Greece were often, in all respects but status, fully as fit to be the wives of their masters as the true-born burgess-ladies whom they formally wedded, there was constant temptation to risk the double household, to "marry" one for love and one for position. This situation, with all its perils, was exciting to the eye of the poet and of the philanthropist: and Euripides was both. He sought within the prescribed circle of tradition for an opportunity to place such a situation by a little adapting of the legendary data, and he found it in the legends of the house of Peleus.

After the capture of Troy the captive Andromache, formerly the wife of Hector, was assigned to Neoptolemus, son of Achilles and grandson to Peleus and the sea-goddess Thetis, by whom she became the mother of Molossus. According to another story, probably in origin quite distinct from that of Andromache, this same Neoptolemus wedded Hermione, daughter of Helen and Menelaus of Sparta, which Hermione was nevertheless bestowed as wife by yet another independent tradition upon her cousin Orestes, the son of Agamemnon, and hero in that fearful story of murder and revenge which Aeschylus has made generally known. Again, among the many legends told by the priests of Delphi in honour of Apollo, it was related that this Neoptolemus, having attempted to plunder the sacred place, was slain by the deity, and buried at Delphi, where his grave was shown. Out of these materials Euripides, using the romantic element after his habit as a background, and adjusting the social facts, if we may term them so, to his purpose, has constructed his play of *The Rivals*, for so it might have been appropriately called in the modern style. In the house of Neoptolemus Euripides establishes both Andromache and Hermione side by side—Hermione, the princess, as the rightful wife, Andromache, the slave, though princess too, as a wife in everything but name, first in the husband's love, and superior also in the possession of a son. He gives them contrasted characters— Andromache, the woman, all tenderness, Hermione, the girl, all pride ; Andromache unable not to captivate the captor whose dominion she abhors, Hermione unable to condescend even where she is desperately eager to please ; and lastly, both women all through, both jealous not so much of love as of place, and neither able to forgo the delights of a triumph, whatever pang may be paid for it.

Such is the bed which Achilles' son has made for himself. Meanwhile the distractions of the household are observed by a watchful enemy. Taking up the story which made Hermione wife to Orestes, the dramatist supposes her to have been promised to him, but given nevertheless to Neoptolemus by her father Menelaus, a weak and crafty man (here comes out the Athenian hatred of Sparta), when Orestes had compromised his position by that unfortunate matricide, and the heir of Achilles was the most desirable ally among the Greek youth. Orestes, false and crafty as Menelaus his uncle, but strong in purpose, waited his time, and aided by the self-willed folly of Neoptolemus did not wait in vain. Neoptolemus had pleased himself by taking Hermione in spite of Orestes' better right; he had pleased himself still by not putting Andromache from the home to which he brought the princess; and he pleased himself once too often by venting against Apollo his anger for the death of his father Achilles and going so far as to demand satisfaction of the deity. Reminded of his weakness by the ill success of his domestic plans, he repairs to Delphi on an errand of apology. And now his errors come home. Hermione, with the support of Menelaus whom she summons from Sparta, determines, in the absence of her husband, to be even with the slave-rival once for all. Andromache flies for refuge to the sanctuary of Thetis, but is tempted to leave it by a stratagem of Menelaus, who discovers the hiding-place of Molossus her son. Menelaus and his daughter are about to put both mother and child to death, when they are saved by the spirited interference of Peleus, the boy's great-grandfather, before whom the cowardly Spartan finds it convenient to retire "upon a sudden and a pressing cause," leaving Hermione to extricate herself as she may.

Then follows a scene of exquisite humour and force. The princess, like the spoiled child that she is, passes in a moment from the height of arrogance to the depth of terror. She tears her magnificent and priceless robes, declares that her husband will kill her, that she will never meet him alive, and struggles with contemptible despair in the arms of the attendants who soothe her and scold her like a rebel of the nursery. Here arrives Orestes, who has surveyed if not guided the whole working of the machinery which is accomplishing his ends. He, arrives pretending to know nothing of the situation. In reality his cousin has never ceased to correspond with him, and though he has politicly stood off from her appeals while there was no fair chance of success, he has been, during the last critical days, in the very neighbourhood of the house, and presents himself at this moment ready to receive her, should she throw herself, as she does, into his arms. For her husband he has already provided otherwise. Using the jealousy of the Delphians against one under suspicion of enmity to their god, he has arranged that Neoptolemus shall be assassinated (Apollo conniving and aiding!) in the sacred precinct itself. So ends all, not more unhappily than things are apt to end when foolish men choose, as they will, to act as if they might safely defy the feelings and beliefs of the world and the course of nature. Intelligent selfishness carries the day against reckless selfishness. Orestes, cold-hearted and wary, regains his native rank and promised bride, while Neoptolemus, gallant in a sort of blundering fashion, lies in his grave among the Delphians, to the "eternal opprobrium," puts in the satirist, of their cruel and revengeful deity. And the moral of it all, if the moral signifies, is that young men should be very careful how and whom they marry! This maxim Euripides, mocking with a sympathetic smile the romance of mythology, puts twice into the mouth of Peleus and illustrates lastly from the case of Peleus himself, who having allied himself so particularly well (with a goddess of the sea, no less) is rewarded by his Thetis, who appears at the close of the piece, with an everlasting home in the ocean-caves. Thence the immortal pair may now and again come up to behold their Achilles enjoying his happy days upon a mystic island far in the Euxine Main. Andromache is dismissed finally to a new husband of her own race, and left, as happy as she may be, with her boy Molossus in Molossia.

Hero or heroine the piece has none. It is proper to tragi-comedy, which is the antithesis of tragedy rather than a species of it, to avoid these elevations. But the climax is the success of Orestes, and it is to the scene between him and Hermione that the drama advances. After this it is merely wound up. Let us put ourselves then at this point of view, and look at a pair of scenes with Euripidean eyes. The first important moment is the entrance of Hermione. Her character is a piece of the crudest realism, and Euripides prepares for it in his fashion by a delicate contrast of poetic romance. An un-rivalled linguist, he had every style at command, and the beauty of this passage has won praise from the most unwilling. I must apologise, indeed, for the attempt to reproduce it.

When the play opens, Andromache is found in sanctuary. A slave, once hers, now level with her in subjection, brings her word of the new plot laid by Hermione and her father against Molossus, and is sent, the last of many messengers and the only one found faithful, to summon Peleus. Left alone, Andromache is bewailing herself in tones which echo the old, old music, older than memory, of Homer and the poets of Ionia, when she is visited by some Thessalian women of the place, led by their sympathy to steal, as they hope, a moment when the jealous vigilance of Hermione is averted, and to approach the sufferer with consolation and advice. Thus sings to herself the widow worse than married:

Death and doom it was he wedded when in Ilium's royal tower
　　Paris led his Helen to the bower.
Troy, for Helen thou art wasted; Troy, for Helen swiftly came
　　Ships a thousand fraught with sword and flame.
Aye, for her my Hector died in death dishonoured, dust-defiled
　　'Neath the chariot-wheel of Thetis' child.

Me they took from Hector's chamber, haled me to the sounding
    shore,
    Veiled in slavish weeds—a queen before.
Tear on tear I wept to leave you, Hector, with the dying town,
    Dying, Hector, all in ashes down.
Woe is me, what profit had I more of living? I, a slave
    To the Spartan! Better were a grave
Than to fly before a tyrant to these marble arms and pour
    Fountain-tears, until I waste no more!

Thus she sings, and thus in her own mood and measure answer to her the secret visitors, softly stealing in, while one after another they take up the burden of the song:

Lady, listen, where thou clingest to the goddess of the waves,
    Faithful to the shrine that saves.
Fear us not; though thou wast bred in Asia, though in Phthia we,
    Yet in love we come to thee.
      Might compassion
Something lighten of thy misery!

And here other voices put in:

Caged, alas, and with the rival cribbed, as in a narrow room,
    Must thou battle
'Gainst the bride, poor mistress, for her groom?

And here yet others again, repeating the rhythms of the first:

O advise thee, O consider of thy helpless, hopeless case!
    Wilt dispute a royal place?
Troy and Lacedaemon, slave and princess, what a match to play!
    Ah, content thee, come away!
      Let submission
Win thee respite while it may.
Why increase the certain torture, lengthen out the appointed pain?
    She is sovran,
    She will reach thee; tempt her not in vain.

Then others, with a quicker step and a livelier urgency:

Come, descend, forgo thy refuge, quit the Nereid's holy fane;
    See what thou art and where,
        Nor think it gain,
    Humble and friendless, to disdain
    The proffer of a little care.

Aye, we love thee, captive lady, pity thee, in this too wise
    That we have feared to speak.
        We feared surprise:
    Hermione hath jealous eyes,
    And queens are mighty, subjects weak.

And now the realist has laid the train for his effect. At this very moment, breaking harshly upon the spell of the sustained and soothing lyric, Hermione herself, who has watched the unsuspecting women upon their errand of mercy, and enjoyed, with what feelings may be supposed, the proverbial reward of the listener, steps out, splendid in person and apparel but mean in act and gesture, upon the astonished circle, and addresses them in words like these:

    If I am pleased to bind my brows with gold,
    And robe myself in gorgeous broideries,
    Not Peleus nor Achilles first bestowed
    Upon the Spartan bride her proper state.
    My father dowered me with the royal right,
    Purchased and richly paid, to speak my mind.
    So, you are answered, ladies! As for thee,
    Prisoner and slave and—mistress, thine intent
    Is to expel me, to usurp my place.

Thou with thy witchcraft, thou, hast made my spouse
Mislike me, cursed my womb with barrenness,
Being, like all your passionate Asian breed,
Adept in this love-magic. But I mean
To end both it and thee; nor sanctuary,
Sea-nymph or shrine, shall rescue thee from death.
Or let thine angel, for thy one last hope,
Bend thee to quit thy greatness and thy pride,
And crouch, and grovel, and fling thee at my feet,
Sprinkle my floors and sweep them (I will find
Thee gilded vessels for the menial task),
And learn the simple truth that this is Greece!
Here is no Hector and no Priam. Here
We practise not thy shameless savagery,
To woo the embrace of hands that have on them
Thy dearest blood, be mother of a child
Whose grandsire slew thy husband! But your East
Is all for such abhorred accouplements.
No cross of kin, no soul-dividing feud
Bars like from like, or farthest hate from hate.
Bring not thy fashions here. Foul sin it is
To yoke two women in one governance;
He that would 'scape a miserable home
Let him content his amorous heart with one.

Detractors might say what else they would, but could not deny that here was breathing, staring life. Neither in Aeschylus certainly nor in Sophocles (let those smile who will) is there anything like it. Even to us, on whose ears the comparison of Asia and Hellas must needs fall as something foreign and far-away, and who must use our imaginations before the household of Neoptolemus can rise before our minds as a fact, even to us (I speak at least for myself) this formidable girl gives a startling impression of real presence. I wish there were time to spend over the rest of the scene, and the admirably contrasted figure of Andromache, sorrowful and majestic, yet not less exasperating than Hermione herself, pathetic and yet dealing wounds with every appeal :

> O Youth and Self! What peril is in youth,
> In youth that nothing loves beyond herself!...
> No spell of mine procures thy husband's hate,
> But thou thyself, wanting one wifely charm,
> The magic of companionableness.

Hermione however has in her hand for the moment the strong card of force, and plays it, but loses the game, as we have seen, by the collapse of her pitiful partner, King Menelaus. And so we pass to the best scene of the play, where Orestes reaps the benefit of his calculations and meets the dishevelled beauty in the moment of attempted flight, sobbing helplessly at the gate in the arms of her duenna. The feigned surprise of the successful plotter, the vain attempt of the queen to perform with dignity the part of throwing herself on the protection of a discarded suitor and to cover the shame of her unkingly parent, the angry explosion of her repentance, which positively stops for a time the offer which is ready on Orestes' lips, the contempt of her Thessalian subjects, the prudent chivalry of Orestes himself, who is not too much in love to see his strength, and lastly the sudden reassumption of the lady's dignity when she sees that she is sure of her object—all this makes an episode which tickles the fancy at every turn.

| | |
|---|---|
| *Orestes.* | Ladies, inform me, of your courtesy, |
| | Is this the palace of Achilles' son? |
| *A Lady.* | Aye, sir.  And thou, the questioner, who art thou? |
| *Or.* | Orestes, lady, Agamemnon's son |
| | And Clytaemnestra's.  Being in pilgrimage |
| | Unto Dodona and being come so far |
| | As Phthia, I have thought to ascertain |
| | The health and happiness of my kinswoman, |
| | Hermione of Sparta, dwelling now |
| | Far from our love, but not forgotten— |
| *Hermione.* | Saved! |
| | A haven, a haven!  O Orestes, see— |
| | See where I kneel, and answer for thyself |
| | Thy loving question of my happiness. |
| | Thus with mine arms I bind me to thy feet, |
| | And clasp mine altar.  Pity me! |
| *Or.* | Gracious Powers! |
| | Do I mistake, or do I see indeed |
| | The princess' self? |
| *Herm.* | Menelaus' daughter, sole |
| | Born of his queen, of Helen: doubt it not. |
| *Or.* | Then heaven be merciful and mend thy woes! |
| | But what, but what?  Come they from heaven at all |
| | Or fault of man? |
| *Herm.* | By fault of man, of him |
| | Who is my lord, and yet from heaven, from all. |
| *Or.* | Thou hast no children, and thou art aggrieved! |
| | Shrewdly I doubt where lies the jealous grief? |
| *Herm.* | Well doubted; there it lies. |
| *Or.* | Thy lord hath ta'en |
| | Some other to his bosom. |
| *Herm.* | Her who being |
| | The wife of Hector fell to be a slave. |
| *Or.* | It is a wrong indeed. |
| *Herm.* | It was a wrong! |
| | And therefore did I try to right myself. |
| *Or.* | By woman's vengeance on a woman? |

*Herm.*                                    Aye,
On her and on her bastard, by their deaths:
But—

*Or.*                Reached them not? Who balked thee of thy
will?

*Herm.*   Peleus was pleased to lend his gravity
Unto the baser cause.

*Or.*                    But thou, thou hadst
No helper?

*Herm.*               Aye, my father: he had come
Express from Sparta.

*Or.*                 But was overpowered
By the old grandsire, was he?

*Herm.*                     Over-awed
He was, and left me, left me here behind.

*Or.*   I take thee; thou art fearful of thy husband,
Seeing what has passed.

*Herm.*               Thou hast read my fear indeed.
Why, he will take my life; and wherefore not?
Now, for the dear sake of our cousinhood,
Take me away; farthest from here is best;
Take me to my father's. For indeed I think
The very palace cries me to be gone,
And the land loathes my presence. If my lord
Return from Delphi hither ere I go,
I die a death of shame, or live to serve
The slave, his mistress, that I ruled before.
"Why was I such a fool?" Because of fools
That had free access to me, tongues of women,
Prompting me still with fool suggestions. "So!
You have the patience to endure a slave,
Free of the house, free of the bed! I' faith,
Madam, let me say, if bed and house were mine,
The interceptress soon would lack her eyes!"
I heard the siren voices, listened to
The reckless gossip, learned the subtle cant,
And swelled with sentiment.—What need had I

To be my husband's jailer? Did I want?
Had I not wealth in plenty, queenly state,
Children, if I should bear them, noble lords
Of the base issue from the rival couch?
Ah never, say I, never I say again,
Will reasonable men, wedded to wives,
Suffer the spouse to entertain at home
Women! The women it is who teach the harm.
For one will serve temptation for a bribe,
And one, being fallen, to bring her sister down,
And more for wantonness. Thus house from house
Takes the infection. Therefore lock your doors,
Bolt them, and bar them up, and set a watch
To keep the women out, whose visiting
Is purely profitless and mischievous!

*A Lady.*   This is too loose a libel on the sex,
In thee excusable, though woman's part
Is more to gloss the frailties of her kind.

*Or.*   It was a wise advice that someone gave
To be a listener and let others speak.—
I was apprised of the domestic war
Between the Trojan rival and thyself,
And lay in truth watching the chance. Belike,
Sooner than fray it out thou wouldst retire,
Quitting possession to the doughty slave,
And though I came without a call to come,
Wouldst license me (and so thou hast) to offer
My convoy hence. Thou wast already mine
When thy false father wedded thee away.
His plighted word, before the siege of Troy,
Gave me that hand, which afterwards, to buy
Thy husband's aid therein, he pledged to him,
To Achilles' heir. I, at their coming home,
Sparing thy father, begged the son preferred
To yield thee, pleading my unhappy state
And how, an exile and for such a cause,
Failing to wed the daughter of my kin,

I scarce might hope to win a wife at all.
Whereon he scorned me for a matricide,
Haunted (what fault of mine?) by bloody fiends.
I bowed my head (the sorrows of my house
Had humbled me) but did not feel the less,
Because compelled, the losing of thy hand.
And now the wheel hath turned, now thou art fallen
Hapless and helpless, I will be thy guide
Hence to thy sire in safety. Cousinship
Is a mysterious bond, and at a need
Where should one lean but on a kinsman's arm?

*Herm.* How I should marry, till my father have
Reflected on it, lies not in my choice.
Only make haste for our departing, lest
My lord step in upon me ere I go,
Or Peleus learn that I am fled the house
And charioted pursue us.

*Or.*                            Fear him not;
He is old; and Neoptolemus, fear not him.
This hand, which owes him for his insolence,
Hath knotted him a sure and deadly snare
And set the same—but I anticipate;
Time will reveal the sequel, in the doing,
To Delphi, where, unless my Delphian friends
Fail to perform their oaths, "the matricide"
Will read my lord a lesson on the risk
Of wedding my betrothed. He shall abide
The wrath of Phoebus, whom he called to account
For slain Achilles, nor shall save himself
By his repentance and submission now.
The god will be his death, and I, his foe,
Have laid a train of rumour thereunto.
Fate in a quarrel lets the advantage poise
Alternate, for the chastisement of pride. [*Exeunt.*

Such or such-like is the chief scene in the
*Andromache* of Euripides. By what scholastic

name the work should be ticketed is not a pressing question. But if it is not admirable work, so clever in conception, so delicate and humorous in detail, if it is not first-rate work, then by all means let us have second-rate, and be thankful. Tragedy is good and so is tragi-comedy. There remains, I think, of Euripides, but one single work (the *Bacchae*) which the Muse of Tragedy should acknowledge or claim as exclusively her own. All the rest have been marred or mended by her sisters named and nameless, and all their gifts we may have without cavil or contention. Indeed it is an ill use of eternal literature to dispute over it ; and therefore, lest the reader should disagree after all with my estimate of such scenes as the foregoing, I will ask leave to try once more with a piece about which there is, I believe, no difference. That Euripides could tell a story with spirit is granted by those who like him least, and it happens that the *Andromache* contains one of his best, the death of Neoptolemus at Delphi, related to Peleus by one of the servants who bring home the body. The narrator witnessed the scene, but was prevented with his companions from bearing a hand in it by the ritual practices of the place. It will be seen that Neoptolemus at the critical moment was divided from his defenders, as the enemy foresaw and intended, by the impassable wall of the sacred close. From the high ground outside they saw what was done, but could not help. The archaeological interest of the story, enacted upon one of the most famous sites in the world, is very

great; but except in the points noticed it will
sufficiently explain itself. So I give it without
more preface.

Arrived at Phoebus' far-renowned see,
We spent the golden hours of three full days
In feasting with the show our curious eyes,
And stirring (innocently) suspicion so.
This grew and gathered, while from knot to knot
Orestes wandering whispered to the folk
His fell suggestions: "See him, how he goes
With careful survey through your treasure-close
Rich with the whole world's wealth. 'Tis the old grudge
To Phoebus brings him here this second time
For plunder." So he whispered, they believed,
Until the chartered keepers of the store,
After due conferences had and held,
Set private watch about the pillared courts.

At length, of all this coil unconscious, we
Took victims, petted on Parnassian lawns,
And waited at the high gate solemnly
With Delphians to present us and direct.
Then said the questioner, "Your purpose, sir?
What is the prayer that we shall make for you
To Phoebus?" Said my lord, "To be forgiven;
To make amends that for my father slain
I sinned so far to ask amends of him."

And now was seen to what malign effect
Orestes had possessed them with the fraud
Of our ill meaning. When my lord had passed
Within the boundary to address his prayer
In the oracular presence, there were set
Swordsmen in ambush, covered by the bays,
With the arch-plotter, Clytaemnestra's son.
And while my lord, intent upon the rite,

Faced toward the god communing, even then
They stabbed my brave lord in the open back,
But not to death. He wrenched the dagger out,
Backed to the colonnade, and snatched therefrom
The hanging armour, clad himself, and stood
Tremendous on the stair. "And why," he cried,
"Slay ye a pious pilgrim, Delphians? Why?
Tell me the charge that I must die upon."
Whereto from all their numbers never one
Made answer but with hail of stones, that beat
Upon him furiously, the while his shield
With ineffective ward to right and left
Made shift against the shower, now arrows, now
Knives, javelins, creases, all an armoury,
Growing to a heap of steel about his feet,
Which kept a dance, you never saw the like,
So strange and horrible, to escape the fall.

But when the crowded ring began to close
Towards him, respiteless, and taxed his breath,
Down from the altar-step the gallant knight
Leaped, as he leaped upon the foe in Troy,
The victim turned assailant. And they turned,
Like doves that see a hawk, they turned and fled.
And many fell, pierced in the coward back
Or jostled in the strait and cumbered port,
Rending the silence of the sanctuary
With yells that echoed from the cliffs.

                          My lord
Shone in his harness for a passing while,
An orb disclouded.

                  Then from the unapproachable
And holiest a mysterious thrilling call
Rallied the fliers; and my noble lord,
Struck through the body by a Delphian,
Whom with a many more of them he slew,

Fell; and thereon, when he was down, oh, then
Was ne'er a hand but had a hack at him,
Stoned him or stabbed, until his comely form
Was utterly disgraced with ghastly wounds.
Then, lest the nearness of the corpse offend,
They flung it o'er the censer-sacred pale.
We, on our shoulders lifting it with haste,
Have borne it hither, my lord, my father, to thee
For grace of tears and honour of the grave.
   But oh! the Teacher of the world, the Judge
Of all mankind, so foully to abuse
The fair submission of Achilles' son!
This unforgiving malice, base in man,
Doth it consist with goodness in the god?

Long ago the injured mortal has had his revenge of the false deity. The pen of the poet was writing against Apollo the irrevocable sentence even then. The spade of the explorer, when it turns the soil of Castri, will scarce find the tomb of Neoptolemus, and of Phoebus never a ghost. Let us part from them all in peace.

# LOVE AND LAW

"It makes a man despair of history."—R. BROWNING

IF Macaulay was right, as he obviously was, in insisting on the historical importance of the mutual relations between the sexes, there is no age for which these relations are of greater moment, or perhaps so great, as for the cardinal period of European development, in which the original Roman Empire of the West was formed and transformed, and in which the dominant religion of Europe took its rise. The successful enterprise of Augustus is the basis upon which political and social Europe was built. And if there is any limited proposition which, in the complication of causes, we can make with practical truth as to the cause of any one event, it is that Augustus succeeded because he professed and really aspired to be the regenerator of Roman society, the purifier and protector of the Roman family. This is indeed a familiar and even a commonplace truth. The interdependence of cause and effect is here no matter of subtle analysis or calculation ; it lies before us upon the record, material and palpable. The military forces, with which Augustus conquered, all but failed him in the crisis of his fate from the vulgar want of money. They would actually have failed him but for the direct support in cash of the better classes in Italy. And the support given then, and given in other forms before and afterwards, was tendered upon the ground put forward repeatedly by the Emperor himself and by his literary inter-preters—that morality must be rescued; that the family, as the source of population and strength, must be reconstituted; and in particular that the institution of marriage must be restored to its primitive honour and power.

By what means it was attempted to redeem these promises, how inadequate was the conception both of the evil and of the remedy, and how it befell that civilization actually died of its distemper, hastened fearfully in the close by external violence, is partly known, and may be better known by the labour of our historians present and to come. It need hardly be said that I do not now propose to follow the story. My present concern is merely with the time of Augustus and the attitude of his supporters towards this particular problem; and our considera-tion will be further limited to a certain part of the literary evidence, the more important to us as the total evidence available is miserably inadequate.

Primarily, we must observe, it is not, and it was not in the Roman world, by libertinism, as that word is commonly understood, that the framework and efficiency of the family were brought into danger, and the whole foundation of popular strength de-stroyed. Against mere libertinism, mischievous as it is, the forces of society fight, I believe, at least on fair terms, if not with advantage. Far more insidious and far stronger are those adversaries which fight against family life with weapons imitated, if not borrowed, from its own armoury. It was the *faux ménage* (to borrow a term from the sinister vocabulary of our neighbours) which honeycombed the ancient nations of the Mediterranean. The facility of ambiguous connexions, quasi-permanent and quasi-licit, must in the ancient world have been something difficult to conceive under the wide-extending and regular administration of our great modern states. The purely Roman law of burgess-marriage was in itself a model of various uncertainty, while in the Roman dominions at large there existed no general law at all, but a vast complication of what we should call "international" regulations between the hundreds of municipal atoms out of which the Graeco-Roman nation was produced. A lawyer of the provinces in the time of Augustus would probably have been puzzled to say with regard to many a couple whether they were married or not, and if so, from the point of view of what law; and if the matter were to be judged not by strict law but from social sufferance and convention, the doubt would have been still greater. Most curious indications in this direction, so far as relates to the centuries preceding the Roman revolution, are to be found in Graeco-Roman comedy; but these must wait for another time. We turn to the Augustan age, and to the special character of the Augustan literature.

The poets of the official circle which was formed around Maecenas were scarcely less a part of the Emperor's government than the ministers and other political personages themselves. They were spokesmen of the Imperialist ideals to the people, and of the enthusiasm of the people towards the Imperial office. They are represented to us by three great names, those of Virgil, Horace, and Propertius—Horace chiefly in his *Odes*, which were for his own age by far the most important part of his work. In the case of the first two poets the effect produced upon their writings by the Imperialist programme is justly represented in common estimation, though as to Horace there are misconceptions still to be removed, especially as to the matter of which we are now speaking. But with regard to Propertius the prevalent estimate is less satisfactory. For want of sympathy with the ideas of the time, and under the vast traditional prejudice piled up in ages when Propertius and his contemporaries were thought of chiefly as " heathen," the meaning of the poet has been misrepresented in a vital matter. The error has practically broken into confusing fragments one of the most interesting and best-constructed books of antiquity, and has entirely destroyed its value, which is not small, as a piece of historic evidence.

The problem which I am going to propose belongs, it will be inferred, to a class which it is usual, and usually right, to leave in the hands of professional scholars. It is, however, most desirable that now and then the light of our common

understanding should be let into these places, and that
questions habitually studied under the pre-occupa-
tions of grammatical detail should be disengaged for
a moment for the consideration of our less erudite
faculties. I do not at all despair of interesting the
most "general" reader, if he will indulge me with a
little patience. Indeed, in this "learned age" we
are all of us dabblers in criticism more or less.

In a preceding essay in this volume[1] is sketched
an outline of the story told by Propertius in the one
work which, so far as we know, he ever completed,
the poem (in three parts) of *Cynthia*. The story,
of which the poet himself is the supposed hero,
represents the beginning, the disasters, and, after
many struggles, the end of a disreputable connexion.
There is reason to suppose that the present scheme
of the poem was to some extent an after-thought.
The First Part, published before the poet became
connected with the Imperial court, shows no trace
(except in the prologue, which we may reasonably
regard as having been added or modified later) of
the subsequent development. The First Part alone
merely represents, in lively fashion, the somewhat
stormy happiness of a very young man, who in the
hallucination of passion believes, or tries to believe,
in the fidelity and affection of a vicious woman by
whom he has been enslaved.

But the Second and Third Parts, which carry on
the story over a period of five years, exhibit both
the hero and his fortunes in quite another aspect.

---

[1] "An Old Love Story," p. 27.

The Second Part, one of the most striking works of antiquity, shows him to us in all the varied miseries of a disenchanted slavery; while the Third represents his self-rescue, achieved partly through the call made upon his nobler nature by honest ambition, and the desire to do some service to his country as a national poet, partly by the prudent resolution, to which under this stimulus he manages to bring himself, of improving his chances by absence from the seat of danger. His final "restoration to sanity," in his own words, is effected by a voyage among the distracting wonders of Greece and Asia. The two latter parts of the poem are avowedly written under the official inspiration of the Emperor's minister and his literary adjutants.

Now, although I was not there writing, any more than here, for Latin scholars as such, it did not seem right to conceal what was indicated therefore in a foot-note, that this account of the book *Cynthia* was not altogether supported, or rather in its main outline not supported at all, by received authority. In the works of the best writers on the subject, the construction and plot of the book are so far from being made principal or prominent that the book is scarcely treated as one poem at all, or regarded as having a plan. We find in our "Propertius" the three books of *Cynthia* printed, without distinction, side by side with an appendix of fragments, for the most part wholly unconnected with it. And within the *Cynthia* itself no notice is commonly taken of any interdependence between the separate poems of

which the books are composed. They are read as
mere units without any thread, save that most of
them relate in some way to the poet's love.

Now, seeing that the three parts of *Cynthia*[1]
are beyond all question in their general character
respectively such as I have described them in the
former essay and here, it may be thought, and it is,
remarkable that their mutual relations should be
thus set aside as not important to the reader. For
this however there has been one single, simple, and
sufficient cause. There is one poem of the series
which, *interpreted as it is*, destroys altogether the
scheme of the work, and makes it impossible to see
in it any plan or series whatever. It is upon this
poem, interesting and beautiful in itself, that I now
propose to fix our attention.

> What of thy features can his memory keep
> Who left thee, having won, to sail the deep?
> Oh, cold of heart, to weigh his love with gain,
> These tears with all the wealth of all the Main!
> He lies belike in other arms; and thou
> Dreamest the while, too fond, of oath and vow.
> Brave beauty, chaste accomplishment, a name
> Gilt by thy grandsire with a scholar's fame—
> All these thou hast, and wealth. Thy missing part
> Of bliss, oh, find it here, a loyal heart!

> My night is near, my first. Retard thy pace
> Swift moon, for that first night, and give it space.
> Thou sun, that wheelest wide thy summer way,
> Abridge thy circle and defer the day.

[1] Propertius, Books I, II, and III. See Professor Palmer's
edition.

Time I must have to seal, to sign, to draw
Love's new indenture in his forms of law,
Which Love himself shall certify beneath,
As witness Ariadne's starry wreath.
What hours of parley I must interpose,
What long assay before we fairly close!
Love without such preamble, full and clear,
Lacks power to castigate his mutineer.
Fancy binds quick, breaks quickly. Slow and sure
Let love begin between us and endure.

Then if the plighted spouse, forsworn and vile,
The altar of his faith should dare defile,
All plagues be his that ever love hath bred:
Let hissing scandal pelt upon his head!
Wild at his lady's window let him yearn,
In utter darkness, lost beyond return!

With due deference to the correction of any
Latinist in details, I will venture to say that this
translation represents with accuracy in all material
points the 20th poem of the Third Book of Propertius. If the reader is not familiar with the
commentaries on the poet, he will, I think, hear
with a shock of surprise that this poem is commonly
supposed to be addressed to a scandalous personage of notorious ill-fame, and to commemorate the
beginning of a degraded attachment, which has
previously been deplored in every key of repentance
by the self-confessing author of the book in which it
is found.

Now it would seem that, if this is really so,
Roman society was the strangest institution, and
Latin the oddest vocabulary, that ever was known
among men. That law and that language were, it

appears, utterly indifferent to the most vital distinction in human affairs. They had no fixed and ascertained expressions which marked beyond mistake what we know as an honourable love and a legitimate union. For if the language of Propertius here does not mean this, there were no words which did. A husband in Rome could be called nothing better than *maritus*, nor the ritual by which he became such anything more august than *sacra marita*, nor the religious altar which sanctioned his troth by any term more sacred than *ara*. If the engagements of undisciplined caprice were not stigmatised by the word *libido*, there was no way in Rome by which the reproach could be expressed. If the image of a legal covenant, "drawn, signed, and sealed," did not then express real solemnity and obligation, those ideas were beyond the range of Roman thought. If this poem were written about any society of which we have a present conception, as of a real human fact, any one who tried to persuade us that such language as Propertius here uses really meant nothing definite, and that though the poet talked in the forms of matrimony, he never dreamed of being so understood, would be laughed at. Surely these presumptions are as good for the Romans as for any other people. Surely no society in which they were not true could possibly have held together at all. If this poem was accepted by Augustan readers as a natural address to such a person as "Cynthia," it is hard to see whither, below where it had already fallen, the Roman Empire

could possibly decline. If it was so, history ought
to reckon with the fact.

But it was not so. To interpret this poem as
addressed to Cynthia not only makes the poem
itself inconceivable, but also ruins the sequence, and
with it half the interest, of the book. We find it
close to the end of the story, surrounded by other
poems which describe the last determined effort of
Cynthia's lover to escape from his thraldom. A
little before (III 18) he is trying, very unsuccess-
fully, to drink himself free. Immediately afterwards
(III 21) he declares that, having now tried *every*
means of escape (many have been enumerated
before), *every* means consistent with remaining in
Rome, he will take the one remaining hope of a
distant journey. This occupies two poems. The
author comes home completely cured; Cynthia is
dismissed with scorn; and the story comes rapidly
to the due and respectable conclusion.

All, therefore—the poem itself and the place
where we find it—points to the natural conclusion,
that it represents *the marriage* of the hero, or at
least his immediate intention and expectation of
marriage. This he thought proper to try as one
of his remedies. But with some judgement and
humour, Propertius leaves it to our imagination to
fill up the details of the story. Whether the proposing husband really married, but the marriage was
a failure, as under the circumstances it well might
be; or whether, after all, the engagement (for it is
clearly an engagement) was broken off, which also

it might be, on either part, without violence to probability, we are to determine as we please. The poem is addressed to a lady of position and good family. All her virtues and social advantages—her fortune, literary grandfather, and all the rest—are usually transferred and handed over to Cynthia, and this in the teeth of the whole book, which tells us that Cynthia had not a known relation, except a mother, in the world, and paints her always in colours with which the addition of "chaste accomplishment" will on no terms combine. Whether the too commercial admirer by whom the lady had been deserted, was a husband already or a favoured suitor, is not exactly determined, nor does it matter. If the lady was married to him, release under the circumstances would not have been difficult.

If nothing were here at stake but the meaning of this single poem, it would scarcely be worth while to say so much of the matter. But the truth (whichever way it lies) is of importance to the whole purport of that Augustan literature upon which many of us, willy-nilly, spend not a little of our time, and from which are imbibed, for good or ill, more notions than are expressed by schoolmasters or put down in examination-papers. *Cynthia* is self-advertised as an official book, appearing under ministerial and practically under Imperial sanction. Both Augustus and his ministers wrote very disreputable verses, and sometimes omitted to burn them. The practice was common then and at no time altogether unknown. But it is a total misconception, as it seems to me, to infer from this and like facts that a poet of the ministerial circle would have pushed his court by producing a book really dedicated to Cynthia, or dealing with Cynthia at all otherwise than as a delusion and a snare to the well-intentioned young Roman. At the opening of the Second Book, the hero, then still in his bondage, deliberately and ostentatiously defies the new legis-lation in favour of marriage, which the Emperor, with the best designs but under much mistake as to means, was straining his powers to carry and to enforce. " Not Caesar," he says, "shall tear him from Cynthia." Was this defiance real, and not atoned for ? Are we to understand that while Horace, at the command of Maecenas, was de-ploring the decay of the Roman family and was celebrating the matrimonial happiness which the new *régime* would make universal among succeeding generations, Propertius, by the like command and with the same sanction, was filling with Cynthia a whole book, unredeemed in official eyes by any compensating moral? The truth is that *Cynthia*, such as the book became by the addition of Parts II and III, is a poetic manifesto against all Cynthias, a novel, as we may almost call it, with a purpose.

It is true that in this case, as in many others, the purpose has not very much to do with the merit of the work. The interest of it as a work of art lies primarily in the picture of man and of human feeling, much of which remains unaltered if we erase or ignore the moral altogether. But as a historical document the book of *Cynthia* is totally changed, and, as I think, totally distorted, by a reading which conceals the purpose and dissolves the connexion of it.

One little question, historical in a certain sense, though not important, we may dismiss. Did the marriage, or proposal of marriage, represented in our poem really take place in the life of the real Propertius? It is impossible to say, nor does it signify. It was open to him, having made himself the hero of his book, to coin for himself what adventures he pleased. Our modern feelings might suggest various arguments for or against the reality of the circumstances. But then we cannot be sure how far they are a safe guide.

Much more interesting and more instructive is the light thrown by the poem upon the position of literature at the court of Augustus, especially in the early years of his reign. The Second and Third Parts of *Cynthia* were written to make good the position of the author in the ministerial circle. They answer in the work of Propertius to the Imperial *Odes* in the work of Horace, more exactly, perhaps, to the Fourth and strictly Imperial Book of *Odes*, which Horace added under the Emperor's command and compulsion; only with this difference, that Propertius seems to have executed himself with a good will. He may indeed have intended from the first to make of his *Cynthia* a "Lover's Progress" and an example to youth, though, as I have said, this does not actually appear in the first and originally

sole part of the work. At any rate as an adherent
of Maecenas he plainly felt that this was his cue and
his text, and to much edification does he preach
upon it. His crowning sermon is contained in the
22nd poem of the Third Part. The 21st (the next
after the marriage) takes him, flying from the sight
of Cynthia, to the far East. In the 22nd he meets,
at Cyzicus, in Asia Minor, an old friend and mentor,
who had been accustomed in early days to lecture
him on his aberration. In the confidence of his
recovery he now repays the lecture, and scolds
Tullus, in his turn, for so long neglecting the duty
of a Roman to fill his place in Rome or Italy and to
carry on his family.

> What! couldst thou thus content, my Tullus, bide
> These many years by cold Propontis' side?...
> If storied Helle's strait have charm for thee,
> Charm to beguile regret for such as me,...
> If fancy tempt thee still to follow back
> To Colchis Argo's legendary track,...
> What marvels hath the world, however far,
> To rival those on Roman earth that are?
> Her legends raise no blush; her soil is made
> To breed nought baser than the soldier's blade.
> Not here Andromeda was chained, not here
> Was Pentheus chased, Thyestes fed not here.
> She is thy mother, Tullus, and thy home;
> The honours thou art heir to seek in Rome,
> Speak Latin to thy peers, and give thy life
> To the dear babes of some sweet Roman wife.

This very brilliant and charming piece (of which
I have given here but an outline, reproducing closely
only the conclusion to which it all leads) loses half

its beauty and all its substantial meaning if it be made to follow close on a rapturous proposal to Cynthia. But this is the way we sometimes deal with the literature of old times, upon which we have chosen to put the general stigma of a presumed indecency.

These and other lines we may follow another time, or the reader at once, if he has patience. I hope I have not tired him so far. The theme at least deserves the hour. Charity and candour are a duty between age and age, not less than between man and man.

# A VILLA AT TIVOLI

Brown Lycoris, hearing Tibur's air
Turns the brownest ivory (so they swear)
    FAIR,
Tried the breezy climate.  But alack,
Very shortly came Lycoris back
    BLACK!

THE unlucky brunette of Martial's epigram is one of the few recorded persons in ancient or modern times who have had reason to disparage the boasted attractions of Tivoli. From the time when Catullus noted it as a mark of distinction between his friend and his enemy, that the one called his dubiously situated villa Tiburtine, while the other "would bet anything that it was Sabine," from that time, and from long before, even to the present day, no haunt of pleasure has had a wider and steadier reputation. The very tea-gardens of our own suburbs will recommend their ponds and their gravel and their shrubless bowers by inscribing themselves with the name of Tivoli. To the Roman the sound was sweetness. The clime of Tibur signified a celestial region, a symbol of peace and white purity. The towers of Tivoli

beckoned, says the poet, through the night with
a singular whiteness, and the graves of the beloved
dead who slept in Tivoli, seemed to speak more
than other graves of Elysian happiness, of wrong
forgiven and stains for ever taken away.

I do not here propose to detain the reader with
any long description of the place. Innumerable
writers and painters have made known the site,
lying upon the front of the Sabine hills in full
view of Rome, and have told how the Anio or
Teverone, forcing its desperate way out of the
mountains behind, plunges into the gorge which
half encircles the town ; how, not content with its
main channels, both natural and tunnelled by man,
it breaks under and through the mass of the fortress,
and flows back into its main self by a thousand
miniature falls, making of the hillside an orchard
"fruitful with shifting streams." We, out of the
wealth of poetry which the Latin poets by their
lives and writings have bequeathed to Tivoli, will
but take at random a few pieces for the minute's
amusement, choosing them so as to illustrate both
the charm and the pathos which for different reasons attached to the town in Roman remembrance.
Tibur was to the Romans the place of retreat, in
all times, earlier and later, republican and imperial,
the place of chosen retreat, the land of delightful
homes, but in republican times also the place of
enforced retreat, the place of exile and of half-
consoled regrets. We shall see it in both these
colours, but chiefly in that which it oftenest and

longest wore, as a city and country full of delightful homes. Such it was, above all, in the not yet fading prime of the empire victorious and at peace.

Of the moderate Roman villa, no palace but a house of some dignity, as it was to be found in Tivoli when Roman society had come to its full splendour, we have one fairly complete and highly interesting picture from the hand of Statius. It is one of his poetic *Studies* (*Silvae*), and is found in the same book with that upon the *Saturnalia*, of which some account has been given in a previous essay entitled *The Feast of Saturn*. The owner of the house bore the name of Vopiscus, to English ears not happy in sound, though to a Roman poetic and pathetic enough, if, as they say, it signified properly the survivor of twin babes, the one left when the other was taken. Nothing whatever is known of him now, nor does the poet, who was not the man to hide under a bushel the glories of himself or his friends, say anything to suggest that Vopiscus was a man of uncommon mark. He was not even, and this is noticeable, a man of extraordinary wealth, but merely an independent gentleman, with a taste for literature and literary society, and able to indulge his taste by collecting about him the sort of people that he liked. All the more significant is the tone of splendour "in the air" with which the verses of Statius are filled and suffused.

The piece was apparently the offspring of

genuine gratitude on the part of the writer, not
for any mercenary service, but for a boon more
precious than money.   Like Maecenas in that
summer when Horace reminded him with remon-
strance that

> The untilted cask of mellow wine,
> And roses in thy hair to twine,

had long been ready for him in the Sabine hills,
Statius had been kept by the claims of society on
a subordinate man of fashion far into full summer
at sweltering Rome.   In the gorge of the Anio,
an easy stage from the capital, he enjoyed a brief
breathing, and begins to record it in a rapture of
regret.

> With eloquent Vopiscus have ye been,
> Where as the caverned ice his bower is cool
> In Tibur with the Anio rolling through?
> Or seen his chambers, that from bank to bank
> Answer each other and dispute their lord?
> Oh then, though Sirius howled, ye did not feel
> His dog-star hot, nor suffered, though the whelp
> Of Nemea's forest glared.   The frost within
> Is obstinate against the powerless sun,
> And still in Pisa's month the halls are fresh.

Thoroughly Roman, and pleasing in its way
to an acquired taste, is this enthusiastic pedantry.
What is "Pisa's month"?   Without any shame a
man might give it up, and probably some of the
company who were with Vopiscus at the first recitation looked it out privately in the library, and
got into trouble with their dictionary over the

resemblance between *Pisa* and the much better
known *Pisae*. As a fact, this Pisa was the place
of the Olympian festival; and as this festival was
held just after the summer solstice, to say "the
month of Pisa," when you mean "July," is as
natural and obvious as to put the "whelp of
Nemea," or Nemean lion, for the corresponding
sign of the zodiac! To Statius at least all this
erudition was alive with poetic suggestion, as he
very quickly proceeds to prove.

> 'Tis said that Pleasure drew with softest touch
> The ground-plan; Venus touched the battlements
> With perfume of Idalia from her hair,
> Which trailing on them left so sweet a trace,
> The sparrows bred thereon will never quit.

Any one who has dabbled in mortar knows that
the coping-stone must be "wetted" with something,
commonly beer; but champagne of course is better,
and scent of ambrosial Cyprus in some ways better
still. For the same reason, whatever it may be,
the bottle of champagne is broken on the prow of
a ship at the launching. It is pleasant, when you
pay the bricklayer for "drinking your health," to
remember these sparrows of Statius, which surely
are treated with an exquisite feeling. Very like,
and yet with a deep difference, is that martlet, the
"guest of summer," which commends the pleasant
castle of Macbeth, and

does approve

> By his loved mansionry that the heaven's breath
> Smells wooingly here.

9—2

Indeed the writer of Banquo's speech should have furnished our translation. As it is, we must get on as we can.

> Oh memorable hours, oh pleasant thoughts
> Which I have brought away! My eyes are tired
> With marvels. What advantage in the ground,
> How artfully improved! Not anywhere
> Has nature been more liberal to her taste.
> Over the rapid stream the high woods stoop,
> Reflected leaf for leaf; the water seems
> A moving avenue. Fierce, full of rocks
> Above and lower, Anio here is calm,
> Nor foams nor murmurs, as in fear to break
> Vopiscus' days, given to the quiet muse,
> His dreams, poetic with remembered song.

*Habentes carmina somnos*, "sleep retaining song," says the poet more exactly, but I find it necessary to sacrifice his terseness.

> Both shores alike are home;—

That the house was in two parts, one on each bank, we have already seen in the opening description. Whether this fanciful arrangement increased its convenience may be doubted, particularly as there seems to have been no bridge; but it is certainly striking to the imagination, and the painter makes more than the most of it.

> Both shores alike are home; the gentle stream
> Seems no division, and the fronting towers
> Feel themselves one, despite the flood between.
> How poor a pride was his who passed, they tell,
> By dolphins drawn across the Sestian strait!
> Here is eternal calm, all storm forbid

To chafe the waters. Eye to eye may speak
Across, or voices join, or almost hands.
So small a barrier Euripus is
To Chalcis, or the sea that sunders off
Pelorus from the gaze of Bruttian coasts.

Here we have, half in burlesque, and plainly
so intended, that ancient and specially Roman
pomposity of decoration, huge comparisons and
thundering names, which so deeply affected the
ear of Milton. The most famous waters of the
old world, and the greatest figures in old history,
Hellespont and Messina, Agamemnon, Xerxes, and
Hannibal, all serving to illustrate a bit of garden!
It is a style which easily passes into the tawdry,
and among the innumerable writers of the three
last centuries who have tried to catch the trick of
it from the Romans, very few have quite succeeded.
However, upon these heroic stilts the poet rises
to the height of his subject and in a like rapture
continues :

Where should my song begin, what progress take,
And to what close? The gilded architrave?
The Moorish piers?

that is to say, pillars of the coveted stone " hewn
in the heart of Africa," which Horace condemns
for an insolent luxury ; so rapid was the progress
of wealth between the first of the twelve Caesars
and the last.

The Moorish piers? The polished marbles veined
With lace? Or should I praise the founts that flow
In every room?

To the modern ear this seems a transition fit only
for the " Treatise on the Bathos." Water laid on
to all parts of the premises ! What a noble idea !
But here is just the lesson to the historic imagination. The comforts of the splendid Roman were
in some ways extremely modest ; the water-supply
of Vopiscus, though by no means remarkable, so far
as we can see, if judged by the present standard,
seems to have passed for a wonder of completeness,
and Statius will conduct us to the pipes more than
once in the course of his survey.

> Distracting beauties call
> My thoughts, my roving eyes ; the reverend trees ;
> The court which overlooks the stream below ;
> Or that which looks toward the quiet woods,
> Where your repose is safe, no tempests vex
> The silent night, and so much sound there is
> As whispers you to sleep.—What of the bath ?

What indeed ! We are prepared for a special effort
on the part of the poet, when he comes to this
all-important adjunct to the Roman establishment.
The bath, properly and permanently warmed, is
the one thing about the Roman residence, which
in the midst of much that served rather for display
than for real satisfaction of life, the dweller in our
English homes may notice with envy. The reader
expects to hear something particular of the bath and
of the rock in which it will be cut ; but assuredly
he does not expect what he will find, a piece of
coarse and grotesque vulgarity, standing in sharp

contrast with the delicate lines upon the night and
quiet bedchamber.

> What of the bath,
> That steams in a green basin, where the fire
> So heats the cold rock of the river bank,
> That Anio, neighbour to the furnaces,
> With laughter sees the water-fairies pant!

Here is the Roman mind in another phase, the
native grossness and crudeness breaking suddenly
through the Hellenistic surface, as it does now and
then in the Odes of Horace.    Put this amazing
piece by the side of that about Venus and the
nesting birds, and we have a remarkable lesson
in the history of taste.    However the house of
Vopiscus was after all a Hellenistic house, full of
laborious culture, and the poet, almost as if conscious of his lapse, hastens from the bath to the
galleries.

> There too is wondrous work of ancient hands,
> Metal of various mould—it were a toil
> To tell the list, the gold, the ivories,
> The gems fit for the finger, chisel-work
> In silver or in bronze, on lesser scale
> Practised at first, and thence essayed in size
> Transcending human.

Here again we might feel envious, when we
think what glorious figures, now lost for ever,
were doubtless reproduced for the decoration of
these rooms, and how, if one or two of these imitations could now be found, the capitals of Europe
would quarrel for the possession, and copies would

go out everywhere into palace and cottage. But we are soon reminded again of our compensations.

> While my lifted eyes
> Strayed over all, my feet on wealth below
> Were treading heedless, till from overhead
> Poured through translucent panes the blaze of day
> And pointed to the floor, the ground whereof
> Was rich and gay with such invented maze
> Of pattern on it that I feared to step.

If our busts and our statuettes are inferior, we can at least see without difficulty such ornaments as we have; we need not make our passages nearly dark in order to keep out the weather, and do not start with astonishment at the brilliant apparition of a skylight. And be it remembered once more that this was a great mansion.

> Rooms of unbroken space there are, and rooms
> Parted in triple aisle. And midst of all,
> Above the roofs, among the pillars, soars
> Into the bright air, reverently spared
> (Another would have cut it down), a tree,
> Which there shall live until with kindly close
> The native genius ends its peaceful days.

Here the modern mind echoes readily to the poet's feeling, to his delicate sympathy with nature, which is not the less true and direct because, speaking the language of his age and school, he figured the indwelling spirit under a multiplicity of bodily forms. A Wordsworthian would prefer to present to his imagination the life of the tree without the interposition of a Naiad or a Hamadryad; but this is pure matter of form, and we know that

Wordsworth himself sighed sometimes for the help of "a creed outworn" and the audible music of "old Triton."

> Two mounds with tables set alternately,
> Pools of white water and deep-flowing springs,
> These might have mention,—

It would be more convenient for us if they had had a little more, for as it is, we are much puzzled to say what is meant. The "white pool" was probably filled from sulphur-springs; and the "mounds" would seem to have been connected with some arrangement, symmetrical on the two banks, for taking meals in the open air.

> Or the pipe that runs
> Boldly athwart the river's self and brings
> The Marcian through the Anio. Thus the tale,
> How Elis' rivulet to Etna's coast
> Came under sea, is not unparalleled!

"The Marcian," which in this mythology plays the part of Arethusa, is of course the great aqueduct of that name, whose arches are still one of the celebrated sights of the Campagna, and remain here and there in the neighbourhood of Tivoli itself[1]. The water of it was held excellent for purposes of luxury. From the Marcian were supplied, when it was possible, the elaborate and costly grottoes affected by Roman landscape gardening and absurdly imitated in some of our own old parks. It was the Marcian which filled a splendid bath,

[1] A pretty view through one of these arches will be found on p. 11 of Burn's *Rome and the Campagna*.

described by Martial, with water not less wonderful than the precious stones,

> So clear, that you would boldly swear,
> Seeing the slabs below, that there
> Nought intervened but empty air.

To be supplied from the Marcian was a coveted privilege, for which Martial in another place petitions the emperor :

> Sweet, sire, and rich it were to me,
> Thy gift, as founts of Castaly,
> Or raining Jove to Danäe.

Not therefore without purpose are we informed that the privilege had been secured at some trouble by Vopiscus, who, having got his " Marcian," used it naturally among other purposes for such garden grottoes as we have mentioned above. The taste of the Romans for this kind of luxury is one which we can with difficulty feel to the full. It is not merely a question of climate ; to the Roman, under the influence of Alexandrian arts derived from the *Museum* of the Ptolemies, the pleasure of the grotto was tinged with intellectual associations now hardly to be comprehended. The persistence of the metaphor, by which spiritual influences of all kinds were likened to fountains and the source of inspiration set among the rocks, created, after the habit of all familiar language, a sort of reality corresponding to itself. Nothing in Roman literature is more curious than the elegiac poet's[1] description of the Muses'

---

[1] Propertius, III (IV) 2 (3), *Visus eram*, etc.

cave, gemmed with precious spar and carved with quaint *rococo* decoration in the native rock—a fit dwelling-place for the genius of Alexandria. We should have it in mind as we read the description that follows in Statius, which, pretty as it is itself, conveys also in familiar allegory the compliment of the poet to the scholar:

> Grottoes there are, for which the god himself,
> Anio, will quit his streams; in secret night
> Stripped of his vesture blue he leans his breast
> Upon the yielding moss, or flings his bulk
> Into the pools and beats the liquid glass
> Swimming. The god of Tiber in the shade
> Lies there, and Albula is pleased to bathe
> Her sulphur-laden hair.

The presence of Albula is more, we may suppose, than a fancy, for this medicinal spring was at no great distance, and its water, widely distributed for sanitary purposes, probably went to whiten the mysterious pools of which we were previously informed.

> Here is a hall
> To tempt fair Phoebe from Egeria's grove,
> To bring the Dryads hither, one and all,
> From cool Taÿgetus, to summon Pan
> From groves Lycaean. Nay, if the oracle
> Of the Tirynthian here would but agree,
> The very Sisters of Praeneste might
> Remove to Tibur!

A flirt of the sceptic pen is this, warning us in time that we must not be too gravely religious with these half-symbolic divinities. The temple of the

Tirynthian Hercules at Tivoli and the temple of Fortune, or rather of the *Fortunae*, at the neighbouring Palestrina or Praeneste were, together with the shrine of the Sibyl at Cumae, the most fashionable places of oracular consultation. The Roman lover complains that the carriage of his superstitious and volatile mistress is always running to one or other of these tempting resorts. To the patron deity of the burg Vopiscus doubtless paid a prudent respect, but plainly "with some private scholarly reservations," such as those of Mr Casaubon; so that his friend expects the appreciative nod when he gravely notes the difficulty of accommodating in one town two oracles whose responses were different.

And now having got a taste of his favourite mythology, the poet flings himself upon the feast.

> Here we need not praise
> Alcinous' fruit twice-harvested and boughs
> Which never were divested of their pride.
> Telegonus is beaten and the fields
> Of Turnus by Laurentum, Lucrine halls
> And shores of fell Antiphates; o'er-matched
> The enchanting hills of Circe falsely fair,
> Where howl Dulichian wolves; o'er-matched the height
> Of Anxur, and the home which he of Troy
> Bestowed upon the gentle dame his nurse;
> O'er-matched is Antium, which will tempt you back
> When days are short and skies with winter dim!

Here the Englishman, even if fairly read in his classics, begins to gasp a little, and to fumble for his *Gradus ad Parnassum*. The reader would hardly thank me for so long a commentary as would be wanted to make all clear. If in this catalogue he has managed to recognize the towns of Tusculum and Formiae, Circeii and Caieta, and if he knows, without stopping to think, who the Dulichian wolves were and where they came from—why then he could graduate *in artibus* with considerable credit. In the first century A.D., and in "society" at and about Rome, these things were in all the primers.

It is only natural that now we should not know them, but it is perhaps worth asking why it is that our own language and literature is so poor in all such mechanism of pleasant remembrances. We may come back to this again in this paper, or hereafter. Even Statius for the moment has had legend enough, and with good effect becomes suddenly serious in a Roman strain of admiration and friendship.

> Such is the study, where that righteous soul
> Solves duty's problem ; such his garden-plot,
> Planted with virtues, frownless gravity
> And sober elegance, and neatness not
> Luxurious overmuch ; a soil for which
> Gargettus' moralist[1] would fain have left
> His own Athenian *Garden*. 'Tis a port
> From every wind and under every star.
> Better seek safety here, than run the ship
> Around the Cape of Storms or through the Race.
> Why do our eyes esteem a pleasure less
> Because the hand may reach it ?

[1] Epicurus.

Vopiscus appears to have missed or neglected the road of ambition even in literature, practising it only, after the fashion of all Roman gentlemen, for himself and his friends.

> Here the Fauns
> Enjoy thy music, and Alcides' self,
> Catillus too, theme of a greater lyre;
> Whether courageously thou dost assay
> To strike the string with Pindar, or to rise
> High as the feats of Epic, or to put
> The smirching tint on Satire, or to smooth
> The bright Epistle with an equal care.
> The wealth of Midas, Croesus, Persian Kings
> Thou dost deserve; the better wealth of soul
> Thou hast. The Hermus, gilding where he flows,
> Or Tagus' bullion clay were well bestowed
> Upon thy peaceful meads. Hereafter still
> People, as now, thy haunts with learning; still
> As now (I pray to heaven) with cloudless heart
> Live on beyond the term of Nestor's years.

Excellent work this is of its kind, though the fashion of it is gone, not so very long ago, out of date. Whether it ever will or should come back is an open question; but one thing is not open to question, that modern literature loses greatly in power, as compared with ancient, from the fact that readers have now scarcely any common *mythology*, any general stock of associations, to which poetry can appeal, and in particular scarcely any local associations well enough known to be serviceable. For Scotland something in this way has been done and has been made public, mainly by Walter Scott, whose verses, without any other great merit, and in

spite of many obvious defects, hold and will hold
the common ear by this one delightful spell of association alone. A Scottish catalogue not unworthy
to compare with the brilliant Latin catalogue of
Statius, might be without much difficulty composed
by an able hand. But where are the local legends
of Southern England? Who but an antiquary
knows them or cares for them? Could any one,
however able, adorn an English "epistle" with
a catalogue after the manner of Statius, which
should not seem to most of us a piece of tiresome
pedantry? Such it might actually be; but where
these things cannot be done, there one Muse, and
not the unsweetest sister, is silent. Since the
Reformation *religio loci* has had a hard time, and
in no way has the anti-catholic movement cost more
to the arts than in this. Catholicism, at least before
the Reformation, was for this purpose thoroughly
pagan; the spirit of Chaucer's Prologue—

> And specially, from every schires ende
> Of Engelond, to Canturbury they wende,
> The holy blisful martir for to seeke
> That hem hath holpen whan that they were seke.—

the spirit of these lines is exactly the same for poetic
purposes, with a change of names and symbols, as
that of Statius—

> Hic tua Tiburtes Faunos chelys et iuvat ipsum
> Alciden dictumque lyra maiore Catillum.

"Catillus too, theme of a greater lyre." Among all
the merits which English poetry has and Latin has

not, one beauty in which Latin is rich we cannot
count, and we shall not, until (which doubtless will
be long first) we can believe or feign belief in such
fancies as those of Catillus and Tiberinus.

The Argive hero Cătillus, or Cātillus, or Cātĭlus
(for the "great lyres" of Rome who harped upon
him could not quite agree how he should be called)
was, under Hercules, of whose divine blood he came,
the accredited founder and patron of Tibur.   That
such an actual person of mysterious lineage did
actually lead a wandering band of Greeks to the
stream-encircled fortress on the Sabine hills, was no
doubt believed by Statius, and is quite credible.
That his spirit did and does veritably haunt his
beloved towers, the servants of Vopiscus' household and the hinds upon his farms would have
asserted even more positively. Vopiscus himself
would probably have said that it was in no way
disprovable, nay, on some grounds likely enough,
and anyhow a pleasant thing to suppose—and who
is prepared to go further, or to show any very
good reason for not going so far ?   To this name
of Catillus, and that of Coras his brother, faith and
genius had linked such glories that the very sound
of it was delightful.   They rode, says Virgil, at the
head of the Argive chivalry

> Like unto Centaurs twain, sons of the cloud,
> Down shooting from the snowy mountain-top
> Of Homole or Othrys: from their path
> The great trees break away, and the under woods
> Part with a mighty crash.

At great moments in the *Aeneid,* as at that supreme moment of all when the Trojans are pouring across the hills and the last plan of battle is concerted between Turnus and Camilla, it is on the horsemen of Tibur, on Coras and his brother, that the Italian prince relies[1]. Catillus was in fact a sort of St George for the Latins, one of many such champions (for each burg had its own patron), but known as well as Virgil to every one who read. What figure of like interest, half poetic and half religious, could one of our own writers have introduced as sharing from local attachment the simple social pleasures of an English country town? Indeed what like presence has been seen in English affairs at all, since Milton, in his earlier and halfcatholic mood, saw St Peter and the deity of the river Cam come in procession to the mourning of Mr Edward King? Somewhere about that time a certain element of the poetic spirit evaporated from our world; nor is it clear, however modern poetry may flatter itself upon its depth and height, that any sufficient balance or equivalent (of course in a merely poetic point of view) has been found for that loss, or will be.

It will be noticed, and the point is vital to the lover of poetry, that though to Statius the spiritual significance of these religious and legendary figures has doubtless become very thin and shadowy, it is not altogether gone, and what is left of it is essential to his conception. Venus is not a mere abstraction of

[1] Virg. *Aen.* XI 464, 519.

beauty, who as such makes beautiful an architectural design: she is still truly the life of the world, and the memory of her presence is linked as cause and effect with this solid natural fact, that the living birds do veritably love to breed upon the fabric. The Fauns and the god Tiberinus are not so utterly banished into the realm of mere story, that they cannot in imagination mix with the living society of the music-loving Vopiscus. If any one indeed were to observe that Milton could bring Camus into company with his own self, and with the "Pilot of the Galilean lake," and that yet the spirit of the Cam was to Milton a mere fiction, I could only answer that of this last point I am not at all sure, and on the other hand am very sure indeed of this: a mind which cannot for one moment suppose that there is an angel of an English river just as real as any saint in the Calendar, had much better let *Lycidas* alone, and with it most of the better poetry written before the eighteenth century.

There is indeed fiction of the ancient world which may be enjoyed without any faith, mere story-telling, excellent in its way, but without heart. The prince of this poetry is Ovid; an exquisite writer but a most contemptible and mischievous man, who has trained the ear of many a great composer, but in matters of feeling can teach us only to despise him.

It happens that Ovid himself has given us in one of his *Amores*[1] a legend of Tiberinus, one of

[1] III 6.

the divine company who haunted the nights of Statius at the villa. The figure of Tiberinus had to the Roman populace of the Augustan age a spiritual significance especially profound. To this deity was espoused in her distress, after the birth of the founders of Rome, the Vestal Ilia, and it was believed that the horrible floods of the Tiber by which Rome in the early days of the empire was repeatedly devastated, were a penalty for the sin committed in the murder of Julius, the descendant of Ilia herself. The vengeance of the " uxorious " river is commemorated by Horace in a passage which is not indeed of his happiest. This is the figure, and this the story, which Ovid chooses as the adornment of a trivial adventure in which he supposes himself, the accident of his being delayed by a stream in flood in the course of a journey. He tells the story exquisitely, and I am much more afraid to put my imitation into his mouth than into that of Statius. Nevertheless I will say that in any fairly faithful version it may soon be seen that Statius has the root of high poetry in him, and that Ovid has not. Here is the legend of Ilia and Tiberinus, which I shall give without further remark :—

There as she wandered barefoot in the wild
  Mourning her blasted fame, her cruel wrong,
The god himself to woo her she beguiled
  And heard the pleading murmur of his song.

"Daughter of Ida, why so woeful? Why
  Beside me strayest thou so all forlorn,
So mean-attired, and no protection nigh,
  Of all thy sacred glory shent and shorn?

"Why mar the beauty of thine eyes with tears
　And beat thy bosom bare, a foul disgrace?
Stern is his spirit, steel the heart he bears,
　Who softens not for tears on such a face.

"Oh Ilia, fear no more, oh fear no more!
　Mine hall shall welcome thee, the queen of waves:
And all the hundred nymphs, that do adore
　My river's royalty, shall be thy slaves.

"Daughter of Troy, do thou but deign consent,
　My gifts beyond my promise shall appear."
But still her shamefast eyes were downward bent
　And still upon her vesture fell the tear.

Thrice she essayed to fly; thrice rose the flood;
　Her terror-palsied feet refused to run.
At length she plucked her hair in deadly mood,
　Compelled her quivering lips, and thus begun:

"Oh, had they buried me, a maiden yet!
　How should I wed, or pledge a Vestal's faith?
Full on my face the brand of sin is set;
　They point at me and hiss. Oh hide me, Death!"

With that her straining eyes she covered o'er
　And plunged. The god, to save her desperate life,
Upon his loving hands her bosom bore
　And, for his mercy, won her to his wife.

Such were the fancies and such the pictures
commonly associated with Tivoli in the Roman
imagination. It was a place of refuge, of calm
retreat and soothing beauty. But as in all shade
there is darkness, so had this place of refuge its
darker memories and more grave associations. More
especially to the strenuous Roman was it natural to
think of retreat, however delightful, with a certain
melancholy and aversion. It is for his last days

and failing powers that Horace desires "the city of the Argive immigrant"; the same conception enters deeply into the allusions both of Horace elsewhere and of other poets, nor in any notice, however slight, of Tibur as it appears in literature, can we properly pass over this characteristic phase.

The beginning of it lay far in prehistoric times, when Tibur was the independent neighbour of infant Rome. In the ancient world of little burgs, when government was but feeble to control the powerful man, and when on the other hand the most powerful man and the wealthiest, if compelled to change his habitation and go out into a land of "the enemy," suffered loss and danger scarcely conceivable in our society, it was a common practice to compromise with the strong criminal by sparing other penalty on condition of his departure into exile. The acceptance of this practice, which has sometimes an almost absurd appearance to minds familiar with our "extradition," was really not so unreasonable. As things then were, the expelling government gained much more and the expelled offender suffered infinitely more than would be the case with a first-class delinquent who took train for Venice or the Riviera. The Roman exile of the old Republic, whatever comforts of climate or situation he might find in the cities of the Sabine hills, was nevertheless a broken man, much less than nothing, without status or legal existence, without any certain protection for his goods or even for his person. Indeed the tradition of Roman lawyers preserved

the memory of times when even nearer to Rome
than the Sabine hills lay land that was not Roman,
where the Roman man was already in exile. Under
the Imperial Government, when exile was meant to
be inflicted as a severe penalty, the shores of the
Black Sea did not to the eye of justice seem too
distant. And Ovid, who received and, so far as can
be judged, had well deserved such a sentence, in
one of the lamentations which he wrote from his
Scythian retreat, contrasts with point the old and
the new doctrines as to the proper limit of deporta-
tion :

> So mild our fathers were in banishment,
> Their furthest cruelty to Tibur sent.

This conception of Tibur as a sort of asylum
lasted on like other such, with lessening reason, till
it was a mere abuse; so that the name of the
beautiful town is coupled with some of the darkest
tales in Roman history. Thither, when the Republic
was struggling to be full-born, retired the worst
instrument of that Appius Claudius, whose half-
legendary cruelty is now proclaimed to all English-
speaking children in the brilliant ballad of Macaulay;
thither, when the Republic was agonizing between
desperate disease and desperate remedies, protection
for the moment from the fury of the Caesarean
populace was sought by some of those who had
dipped their daggers in the blood of Julius. There,
in many a miserable abode of luxury, after the final
fall of the senatorial party, the remnant of the
nobility brooded over a world ill lost. It is to one

of the most splendid and the most dangerous of
their number that Horace addresses himself, when
with his fine touch of grave gaiety he bids inopportune remembrance to lose itself in such enjoyment
as the time affords.

> Whether amid the shining pomps of war
>   Thy lot is laid,
> Or shall be hid from these afar
>   In Tibur's private shade.

I was the more anxious to touch, before ending,
upon this aspect of Roman Tivoli, because it will
give me a chance of making some restitution to
Ovid, whose merits in his own kind I am not so
foolish as to deny. In general the stories which
relate to it as a place of exile and fallen greatness
are naturally sad. Many a native and many a
foreign victim of Roman pride there found an in-
glorious close. The death of the Numidian king
Syphax, a prisoner awaiting the final degradation
of the Roman triumph, is tragedy itself; and even
the cloister of Zenobia, once empress of the East
and rival of Rome, would not be a theme for light-
ness and laughing. But among the stories of Roman
exile there is one for which no pen could be too
merry; and Ovid, who is always light in season and
out of season, had never a better subject than the
tale of the pipers which makes an episode in his
poem on the "Calendar," and which now shall serve
us for a conclusion.

The pipers or flute-players, a privileged company
of foreign artists, whose services were of no small
importance to the ceremonies of state and religion,

came somehow into collision with the jealous authorities of the republic. Whether they were expelled in anger, or whether they withdrew in anger, is a historic doubt; but exiled at any rate they were, and to Tibur as exiles they went. But the glory and independence of art were nobly revenged upon the tasteless minions of office who had procured their departure; and when there had been time for them to be well missed, an involuntary resident in Tibur, who for some little misfortune in his previous career had undergone a period of slavery, procured their restoration (and probably his own at the same time) by an appropriate feat of diplomacy, which as Ovid relates it in Latin, either Chaucer or Dryden chaucerizing would best have related in English.

The banished *troupe* their way to Tibur went
(For Tibur counted then as banishment).
The stage, the altar missed their usual cheer,
And dirgeless to the burial went the bier.
There was a quondam slave in Tibur, free
By lapse of time, as he deserved to be;
He to a banquet in the country bade
The artists; they the artful call obeyed.
'Twas dark, the guests were flustered, when a post
By pre-arrangement came to warn the host:
"Your master (he that was)" he said "is near;
Break up the feast, or he will catch you here."
They stumbled up, but doubted in dismay
Whether their feet would carry them away.
"Nay, go you must" exclaimed the host "for sure!"
And popped them in the cart which brought manure.
Night, drink, and motion aiding, soon they dreamed,
And travelled on to Tibur, as it seemed.
So dreaming still they passed, ere morning broke,
The gates of Rome, and in the Forum woke.

# "TO FOLLOW THE FISHERMAN": A HISTORICAL PROBLEM IN DANTE

IT was a natural, perhaps a necessary incident, in such a personal progress through Purgatory as is related by Dante in the Second Part of the *Divina Commedia*, that once at least we should witness the actual release of a soul, the discharge of one who has completed his purgation and ascends to the place of everlasting bliss. The choice of a person to be so discharged, involving as it did the exact appraisement of delinquency and equation of penalty, was delicate enough to tax the courage even of a Dante ; nor is it surprising that he has made such a choice as to extend the supposed period of punishment to the possible maximum. The sinner released in the year 1300 is one who, *if he was a Christian at all*, and as such capable of purgation, belonged to the very earliest generation of the Roman Church. To prove his Christianity was an affair of evidence, as Dante, a strict historian according to his lights, well knew and admits. The manner in which the poet has treated the question vividly illuminates, not only the quality and limitations of his own passionate intelligence, but the general mind of that most remarkable age.

Statius, the most successful among the imitators of Virgil, was living at the date of the Neronian persecution and martyrdom of the Apostles, and during the alleged persecution of Domitian ; in the last quarter of the first century A.D. he was the fashionable poet of Roman society. Down to a recent date, until in fact Latin ceased to be general reading, he might be called fashionable still. Though his poems, as we know, were not in stock at St Ronan's Well, it could still be supposed, in the time of the Peninsular War, that a lady at a watering-place might want them. Vogue of this sort he will hardly recover ; but references, allusions, and imitations in half the writers of Europe will long preserve to him a certain interest. For Dante and his contemporaries he was perhaps, after Virgil, the most interesting figure in literature. His works, as then known, consisted of two legendary narratives, the *Thebais*, complete in twelve books, upon the famous expedition of the Seven against Thebes, and the *Achilleis*, or story of Achilles, a fragment. The collection of fugitive pieces, or *Silvae*, since discovered, was evidently and fortunately not known to the author of the *Purgatorio* ; it would have embarrassed his charity not a little. Each of the two epics comprises a small portion giving personal information about Statius : the *Thebais* an introduction and an *envoi*, the *Achilleis* an introduction. To these Dante, as we shall see, refers explicitly and minutely. He also refers us indirectly to the satirist Juvenal as an authority on the subject of Statius; for he makes Virgil, the companion of his journey through Purgatory, claim to have heard of Statius from Juvenal himself, when Juvenal came after death to that Limbo of the lower region where the pagan poets habitually dwelt. What can obviously and certainly be learnt from these sources, what has been here stated, is fully and accurately stated, even to such a detail as that the *Achilleis* is unfinished, in the autobiography which Statius is made to give[1]. One particular is added, which we now know to be false : Statius calls himself a native of Toulouse, whereas in fact he was born near Naples. The origin of this error is not positively known, though it has been plausibly conjectured ; all that need now be said of it is that Dante, who makes no use of the allegation, certainly did not invent it.

But it is otherwise with the large and surprising revelations which Statius makes about his moral character and spiritual history. He was converted, Dante informs us, to Christianity, and at some time before the completion of the *Thebais* was actually baptized, though he had not the courage to acknowledge his new faith, which remained always a secret —a circumstance which naturally whets the curiosity of the reader as to the source of the relator's information. The conversion was begun by suggestive passages in the works of Virgil himself, notably the

[1] *Purg.* XXI and XXII.

prophecies of Christ in the Fourth *Eclogue*, and completed by admiration of the martyrs and confessors who suffered under Domitian. Besides the cowardice of thus concealing his opinions, Statius attributes to himself a sin so subtle that he has some trouble in defining it, a sin of which he justly says that it is apt to escape notice; it is a kind of prodigality, yet by no means that which is ordinarily so called, but rather a sort of defect in avarice, an insufficient estimate of wealth, a want of attention (such appears to be the meaning) to proper economy as the necessary basis of independence and the upright conduct of life. Upon these allegations, for which no warrant whatever appears *prima facie* in the documents proffered by Dante, depends nevertheless the whole position of Statius in Dante's narrative: the conversion admitted him to Purgatory, the cowardice and the neglect of economy have confined him there, and determined his place, for the greater part of the twelve centuries intervening.

What then is the base of these allegations? Did Dante invent them, or did he draw them from some source to us unknown and other than those documents which he elaborately specifies, or thirdly, did he by some process of construction extract them from those very documents? It is proposed to show that this third supposition is, upon Dante's own statement of the matter, alone entertainable; and further that there is no difficulty in following, up to a certain point, the process by which he was convinced. The question has an interest more than curious, for the light which it throws upon the state of literature and upon the poet's mind, a mind not less loyal to truth than fertile in legitimate imagination. He boasts of his accuracy in matters of fact, and not without reason. Passionately eager to know, he could make much, too much, of his data, but could not pretend, like a historical novelist, to have data where in fact he had none. What he alleges about Statius he could not have found, unless he had sought it with singular determination ; but find it he did. That Statius was a bad economist and compromised his independence, this Dante got, or perhaps pressed, out of Juvenal[1]. So much has been seen and proved before, and nothing will be said of it here. The fact that Statius became a Christian, and the history of his conversion, he inferred from the introduction to the *Achilleis*, to which, as his authority, he has actually directed his readers. And right it was that he should.

For the truth is, Dante in this matter has taken a position which, unless evidence, solid evidence, for the " concealed Christianity " of Statius had been in his opinion extant and ascertainable, would be absurd. The account which Statius gives of his conversion is elicited by a question, or rather a critical objection, put into the mouth of Virgil. Statius has already implied, as indeed his purgation

---

[1] Juv. *Sat.* VII 82—92. The facts stated really do imply what Dante asserts, though to notice it was not the purpose of the satirist.

of itself implies, that he was of the true faith. Whereupon Virgil very pertinently observes that the introduction to the *Thebais* (he marks the precise passage which he has in view) does not exhibit the writer as a Christian[1]. It does not; in fact it shows, as Virgil himself, under the polite form of his negative, intimates plainly enough, that the writer was at that time not a Christian of any sort, professed or concealed. But why this distinction of the *Thebais*? Dante alleges Statius to have been a Christian. He indicates correctly what were in his time the sources of trustworthy information about Statius and his opinions. He then insists on pointing out that a part, a comparatively large part, of that evidence, so far as it goes, disallows and contradicts his allegation. Why does he do this, or rather, how dares he do it, if no evidence equally good were producible and produced in favour of his allegation? Such a proceeding would be absurd and unintelligible.

That the affirmative document is the later poem of Statius, the *Achilleis*, we must suppose; if there were no other reason, because Dante had no other relevant document, and shows that he had none. But this reference is actually given by the form and wording of Virgil's question: "Now when thou didst sing the bloody war of Jocasta's twofold sorrow, it appears not, by that touch of the string in which Clio there joins with thee, that thou hadst yet been

[1] *Purg.* XXII 55; Stat. *Theb.* I 1—40, especially 22—31.

made believer by that faith, without which good
works are not enough. If this be so, what sun or
what candles so dispelled thy darkness, that *thou
didst thereafter set thy sails to follow the Fisherman* ?" The "war" is that of Jocasta's sons, the
theme of the *Thebais*. The invocation of the Muse
"Clio" marks the conclusion of the prelude to the
*Thebais* and the commencement of the narrative[1].
The "touch" or tuning of the lyre[2] is the prelude
itself, and especially the latter part of it, which is, as
shall presently be shown, essentially anti-Christian.
"The Fisherman" is St Peter, founder, bishop,
martyr, and patron of the Church of Rome, whose
ship (in a certain sense) Statius followed when he
entered that Church. But why this metaphor of a
voyage? Why should the converted Statius "set
his sails"? Nothing prepares us for this figure,
nor is it commonly appropriated to such religious
experiences. But the readers of Dante were ready
for the figure, and knew what it meant; for they
were all readers of Statius. The sailings of Statius
are his two poems. At the conclusion of the *Thebais*,
a pretty verse[3], once familiar to all, and still represented by many imitations (for example, that of
Spenser at the end of the First Book of the *Faerie
Queene*) compares the vast poem to a laborious
voyage; his ship is now in port. That ship set sail

---

[1] Stat. *Theb.* I 41.

[2] *Theb.* I 33 "tendo chelyn."

[3] *Theb.* XII 809 "et mea iam longo meruit ratis aequore
portum."

again when he commenced another story ; and the question of Virgil, construed as it would be by those versed in the literature of the subject, means not " How did you become a Christian ? " but, " How came you to write as a Christian ? " Seeing that the prelude to the *Thebais* is pagan, how came it to pass that the prelude to the *Achilleis* is not ? That there is Christianity there, a " concealed " Christianity, Dante assumes as notorious. Notorious however his construction of the passage no longer is ; but it should be, one would suppose, not beyond the reach of discovery.

But first, what sort of evidence shall we expect ? The prelude to the *Thebais* is not Christian, is anti-Christian. Why ? The question is answered at a glance. Because Statius there acknowledges and proclaims the essentially anti-Christian doctrine, the test of orthodox paganism, as it perhaps already was in those days and certainly soon afterwards became—*the deity of the Roman Emperor*. To Dante, with his cardinal tenet of the distinction between the temporal and the spiritual powers, this doctrine was abominable for personal reasons, as well as on Catholic grounds ; and he has noted it, in the case of Virgil himself, as decisively damnatory. Not he, says Virgil sorrowfully, may conduct Dante into Paradise; "the Imperator (*Imperador*) who reigns above permits it not, because I was dis-obedient to his laws[1]." The sting of the reproach

[1] *Inf.* I 124.

is pointed by the use of the political term. It was another Emperor whom Virgil, to the best of his power, exalted to heaven; and the plain fact is, whatever moral or religious reprobation may justly be attached to it, that no one did more than Virgil to spread and fortify the strange new worship of the Augustus. He foresaw (so Dante thought) the religion of Christ; but he preached the religion of Christ's adversary. What Dante could not think pardonable even in Virgil, he would still less have forgiven, if unrepented and not retracted, to Statius, who, in addressing the *Thebais* to the Emperor Domitian, declares the divinity of his patron in the amplest and plainest terms[1]. For this reason, and for no other, the preluding of Statius and his Clio is noted as not the work of a Christian. It is, for a Christian, blasphemous.

And now let us hear the later utterance of his Muse. The comparison is easy, for the two preludes are parallel, and that of the *Achilleis*, though much briefer than the other, concludes also with an address to the Emperor. It is in these terms: " O Thou, whose high primacy astonishes all excellence alike of Italy and of Greece, in whose praise contend both laurels, the Poets' wreath and the Captains' (long doth the one of them grieve to be surpassed); grant me Thy pardon, and, because of my fear, suffer me yet awhile to sweat in this labour of dust. To Thee, preparing long and not trusting yet, my labour

---

[1] *Theb.* I 22—31. Domitian is entreated to remain upon earth, and leave heaven for the present to Jupiter.

tends, and the praise of Achilles is the prelude to Thine[1]."

Now this is a reverent address, and a flattering address, but blasphemous it is not. From a theological point of view it is unexceptionable; it attributes to Domitian nothing not proper to man, nothing which has not often been attributed to Christian princes by Christian divines. From the scandal of the Christians, the deity of the Augustus, it is absolutely free. Let it be put beside the address in the _Thebais_, or the many addresses of Martial and other contemporary writers, and the broad difference will be instantly perceived.

This difference, change, omission, the modern critic, applying coolly the laws of scientific interpretation, will attribute to haste, weariness, want of finish, study of variety, to accident, or to some cause, at all events, other than scruple and intention. Let this opinion be right. But it is not demonstrably right. Very plausible reasons might be advanced against it, reasons of a kind with which Dante and the Latinists of his day were familiar. To omit the _Deity_ from a public and formal address to Domitian, is a thing which might have been done by chance, but was not at all likely to be so done. As easily

---

[1] Stat. _Achill._ I 14:

"At tu, quem longe primum stupet Itala virtus
Graiaque, cui geminae florent vatumque ducumque
Certatim laurus (olim dolet altera vinci),
Da veniam, et trepidum patere hoc sudare parumper
Pulvere: te longo necdum fidente paratu
Molimur, magnusque tibi praeludit Achilles."

would the framer of an address to one of the Tudor princes have omitted or inserted by chance the description " Head of the Church," or a modern composer forget the designation " His Majesty." Domitian was punctilious in this matter beyond all his predecessors and many of his successors; nor was he a man with whose rules it was safe to trifle. His very secretaries headed their despatches " From His Deity our Master[1] "; nor without some such form, we are told, was anyone permitted to approach him. This is from a hostile source[2], and is probably an exaggeration, but the usage of the time supports it as true in the main. It is not therefore extravagant, or unreasonable, or improbable at all to suppose, especially if we approach the subject, like Dante, with an affectionate interest in Statius and his character, that his omission of *Deity* was not accidental but scrupulous. Dante, or the expositor whom he followed, did so suppose, and drew the necessary inference, that between the *Thebais* and the *Achilleis* Statius had undergone a change of feeling and opinion for which, in the circumstances of the time, no explanation would be so likely as a conversion to Christianity. There were Christians about the court of Domitian; his own cousin seems to have been something like one; many doubtless were "concealed Christians," and among these Dante, upon the evidence of the *Achilleis*, would include Statius.

[1] " Dominus Deusque noster."
[2] Suetonius,

But out of this bare fact, even if established, Dante would not have made the circumstantial narrative which we read in the *Purgatorio*. At least such is not his practice. His history, though not scientific, is honest; and since he tells us positively that Statius was convinced by the testimony and courage of the martyrs, he must have found evidence, or what he took for such, of this admiration. And so he did. He got it from this same passage of the *Achilleis*, by a process which (given the first step, that the language of Statius here betrays the mind of a Christian) would not be illegitimate, or would not appear so to one passionately anxious to read the beloved poet in a saving sense. Once initiated, a comparison between the dedicatory addresses in the two epics of Statius will soon reveal another difference, scarcely less remarkable than their disagreement about the deity of the Augustus. The address in the *Thebais*, like other such compositions, declares for whom it is meant. No one but the Roman sovereign, and no other person but Domitian, the brother of Titus, "defender of the Capitol," "conqueror of the North, the Rhine, and the Danube," would satisfy the terms of the description[1]. The address in the *Achilleis* contains no such terms, nor any terms of personal appropriation whatsoever. The Man, admired by all that is excellent in the world, the summit of all virtue in mind or in action, warfare or poetry—this *may* be the Roman sovereign, and Domitian, to judge by

[1] *Theb.* I 17—24.

the date, was meant to appropriate it ; but after all, he must take it himself, and the dedicator is not committed. This is not usual. Nor is it usual that an artist, even for the purpose of turning a compliment, should depreciate his work by such expressions of disgust as Statius here employs, and describe himself as "sweating in this labour of dust." Moreover his language is obscure. "Both laurels, the Poets' wreath and the Captains' (*long hath the one of them grieved to be surpassed*)"—scholars will explain ; and the reader doubtless knows what, as addressed to Domitian, this parenthesis means ; but a phrase more ambiguous it would be hard to make.

Now surely from all this, if we suppose ourselves already to know that the words we read are those of a concealed Christian, rendering, or pretending to render, unwilling homage to a persecutor of the Church, we might not unreasonably conceive the suspicion of a latent intention, a meaning other than at first appears. "Here," we should say to ourselves, "is what purports to be a courtier's compliment to a certain prince. It neither names nor describes him. It offends by omission against a stringent rule of etiquette, a rule which the same writer upon a previous occasion has zealously observed. It is in one part strangely worded, in another part obscurely. In short, with the supposed application, it cannot be satisfactorily explained. Why then do we not seek another application ? It is the work of a Christian. Should it not then be susceptible of a Christian sense ?"

And it is susceptible of a Christian sense. The meaning of its terms, as they would, on that hypothesis, be interpreted by Dante, can be ascertained from Dante himself, and leads directly to the inference which he states. Statius will be thinking, not of the earthly Rome, the City of the Seven Hills, but of "that Rome" (as Dante pregnantly calls it) "whereof Christ is a Roman"—the Christian Church. The *Imperator* addressed will be He against whose laws Virgil was rebellious when he gave his worship to the first Augustus, and Statius had been rebellious, but was now rebellious no longer. Christ's, not Domitian's, will be the Virtue, which astonishes all that, in mind or act, is excellent in the world, the Goodness which surpasses praise. The conception of Christ as the true spiritual Sovereign, which we shall thus attribute to Statius, is no casual fancy : it is the essential conception upon which the Church Catholic, Apostolic, and Roman, was actually built, and which was for Dante the corner-stone of theology and politics. The whole *Commedia*, the *Paradiso* especially, is based on it.

It is the praise of Christ then, which will be celebrated in rivalry by the Christian laureates of both kinds, by poets and by soldiers alike. But let us observe that of these symbols one will have a new and a totally different meaning. The Prince, whose kingdom is not of this world, is praised by the same poets as other princes are, and "the laurel of poetry" means in the court of Christ (if we may use without offence the characteristic language of the *Paradiso*)[1] just what it meant in the court of Caesar. Nor was the thing, for Dante, a metaphor at all, but a familiar reality. It was for "the laurel,". an actual, visible wreath, that he laboured in his vocation as a Christian poet upon the *Divina Commedia*. He won the wreath and wore it, and hoped, but in vain, to receive it some day, with far happier glory, in and from his beloved Florence, as we shall presently read in a passage intimately connected with our subject. For Statius then also, speaking as a Christian, "the laurel of the Poets" would have the same meaning as for a pagan; it is still an emblem of his own art, however differently he might conceive his poetic duty, when it was to be paid to so different a Prince. But it is otherwise with the laurel of the soldier. Not by such soldiers, as serve the princes of this world, is served the Imperator, the Supreme Commander, of the Church Militant. What is meant by "a soldier of Christ" is known to all who know anything of Christianity; though the correlative conception of Christ Himself, as a military sovereign, is no longer very familiar to a large part of the Christian world, and even to those of the Roman communion is perhaps not quite so familiar as it was to Dante, or as it was in those primitive times when it was formed, when the Church was, in more literal truth than she has been

---

[1] See especially *Par.* xxv, where the parallel is pursued to the utmost detail: St James is a "Baron," and speaks of Dante's introduction to the "secret chamber" of the "Emperor" and to His "Counts."

since, a militant power, warring against the world
to win her place.  So deep in her literature, her
liturgy, her most sacred formularies, was this
thought engraved, that it has passed to heirs who
scarcely know their inheritance.  Millions are aware
that their baptism was an enlistment, the taking of
a soldier's service, and that they were signed with
the sign of the Cross " in token that thereafter they
should not be ashamed manfully to fight under
Christ's banner," who, if they were asked to explain
why this was so done, would give an answer not
historically adequate.  Millions more, who never
heard the formulary, shape their religious thoughts
by that figure, and this not only, as they may
suppose, because it may be used by St Paul, but because it was adopted by the Vatican.  The soldiers
of Christ are the Christians, and His "laurel" is the
emblem of the Christian warfare.

    And if it should be said that the metaphorical
soldiership of the Christian is not parallel to the
literal bardship of the poet, and that, though each
separately may have its laurel, we could not properly
speak of them as "the two laurels," nor couple the
substance of one thing to the shadow or simile of
another ; it will be answered that so we may think,
but so did not think Dante.  For he not only makes
the conjunction himself, but uses it as if it were in
itself natural and obvious, intelligible and familiar,
founding upon it a peculiarly impressive utterance
of his inner feelings and personal aspirations.  In
Paradise he figures himself, as a first step towards

his participation in the highest mysteries, to be
catechised upon his faith by St Peter, who finally
approves his answers by crowning him thrice[1].
What is the reflexion which this act suggests to
him? Any modern, not already informed, might
guess in vain for ever. It reminds him of the hopes
which he may entertain from the success of his
poem, the *Divina Commedia* : admiration of his
work may possibly procure at Florence the repeal of
his exile, and he may be re-admitted, as an approved
poet, to the city of his youth. And what then?
What conceivable connexion is there between this
patriotic desire and his celestial graduation (the
figure is Dante's own) by the Apostolic Examiner?
Because *then*, as a sign of his triumph, he will
receive and put on " the wreath," the poet's laurel ;
and this ceremony will be performed at the church
of his baptism, " because into the Faith, which
maketh souls known of God, 'twas there I entered,
and afterwards Peter, for that faith, did so encircle
my brow." The literary career and the Christian
profession, art and churchmanship, poetry and
baptism, these are ideas which an average man of
the modern type could not easily connect if he
would, nor perhaps would if he could. But to
Dante, nursed in the two great traditions of Rome,
the Catholic tradition and the Classic, those ideas
are, as it were, two aspects of one thing, so that he

---

[1] " Tre volte cinse me " *Par.* XXIV 152, but more precisely
*"sì mi girò la fronte"* in the subsequent allusion, *Par.* XXV
12.

turns from one to the other almost without sense of transition. And the link is a laurel wreath. His art and his faith, his poem and his baptism, each promises and confers "a laurel"; this the laurel of Christian scholarship and inspiration, and that the laurel of Christian warfare and triumph. Branches of one service, duties to one Master, they bring the like, or rather the same, reward. And he presumes as of course that Statius, when he had become a Christian and a Catholic, must have thought in the same terms.

Since then the military laurel signifies for Statius the crown of the faithful Christian, what is "the laurel of the Captains" or "Leaders" (*duces*)? For it is of this specially that he speaks. The soldiery of Christ being, as Dante says again and again, the Church Militant and Triumphant, who in that host are the leaders? And in particular, who would be so regarded and described by a Roman Christian, writing towards the close of the first century A.D.? Who else but that "noble army" of martyrs and confessors, who at that very time were inaugurating by their triumphant sufferings the Sacred City of Christendom? Who else but "that soldiery who followed Peter," the companions and successors of the Martyr-Apostles, they of whom "the Vatican and other the elect parts of Rome are the burial-place[1]," the victims of the persecution commenced by Nero and continued, as Dante believed, by

---

[1] *Par.* IX 139.

Domitian? These events, for the Roman Church
historically important beyond all others save that
of Calvary, fill such a place in the mind of Dante
himself, that he can actually designate St Peter,
upon this ground simply, as " the high Centurion,"
"the great Leader of the File" (*l' alto primipilo*) ;
and indeed the *Commedia*, especially the *Paradiso*,
everywhere illustrates them and the conceptions of
which they were the base. How should they not
have been all-important to a Christian contemporary, such as Statius, or how should he speak
of them otherwise than as Dante himself had been
taught?

And if Statius, having thus naturally brought
together the laurel of the Poets and the laurel of the
Martyrs, goes on to say that of these two " one hath
long grieved to be surpassed," do we not easily
understand him? Well might a great poet who
was also a concealed Christian, writing in the last
days of Domitian, thirty years after " Peter and his
beloved brother had put Rome on the right track,"
describe the laurel of Christian poetry as ashamed
of her representative, and grieving to be so long
and so far behind the sister wreath, the laurel of
Christian soldiership. Well might such a Statius as
Dante figured, eager and yet afraid to confess his
faith, and to devote his talents to the service of his
spiritual Prince, grieve while he set himself wearily
to celebrate a mere Achilles, while he postponed to
this poor task the noble theme of Christ and His
triumphant Church, while he cautiously trimmed the

ambiguous phrases which, under the disguise of a
compliment to the anti-Christian persecutor, should
express and yet hide his ineffectual remorse.   Well
might he grieve to compare himself with the victors
of the arena, the Captains of the Host, who sealed
with their lives the testimony by which he had been
convinced.   "Grant me Thy pardon, and *because
of my fear*, suffer me yet awhile to sweat *in this
labour of dust*.   To Thee, preparing long and *not
trusting yet*, my labour tends, and the praise of
Achilles is the prelude to Thine."   It may be and
is a strange effect of chance, but it is none the less
fact, that these words are far more appropriate to
the secondary sense put upon them by Dante, than
to the primary and sole sense for which they were
really written.   Domitian, if he read them, must
have read with a sneer.   The *Thebais* opens with
similar excuses: the exploits of Domitian are a
theme for which Statius is not yet fit; let him
practise first upon Thebes, and then he will venture.
Twelve books of practice, published successively in
about as many years, had followed this declaration ;
and now "he dares not yet," but starts instead, by
way of further preparation, upon an unlimited story
of Achilles.   The insincerity is so transparent, the
uneasy emphasis so plainly false, that silence, one
would think, might have better pleased.   But the
Christian interpretation makes all simple.   Between
the times of the two compositions, suppose the poet
converted to the Christian faith ; and then his second
plea, as addressed to the neglected Majesty of his

secret homage, becomes a real thing, new, natural, and expressive.

In brief then the matter stands thus. If Dante had been in the situation which in *Purgatorio* he attributes to Statius; if Dante had been living in Rome about the year 90 A.D., a poet baptized but unprofessed, a proselyte of the martyrs, but a proselyte silent and ashamed; if he had designed to relieve his oppressed feelings by uttering them in the form of symbol and enigma, a form which he loved for its own sake, as a species of art, and uses constantly in his own work; then he would naturally have written in just such words as Statius actually employs. Therefore he did not hesitate to infer the situation from the words. This argument was indeed fallacious; because the notion of one Catholic way of thinking and one Catholic language, the same in all ages and for all persons, in the first century and the thirteenth, is not sound; because there is such a thing as evolution. The precise coincidence and conformity upon which Dante founded his conclusion, really disproved it. Statius, if he had had Dante's thought, would doubtless have expressed it otherwise. But if Dante had been capable of seeing such an objection as this, he would not have made the *Divina Commedia*. According to such laws of interpretation and proof as he had learnt, the authority upon which he went was perfect; and there is no reason to think that he has broken his general rule by putting forth as history what he did not believe to be demonstrable.

When he makes Statius say that, even after his conversion and baptism,

> *"per paura* chiuso Cristian fu' mi,
> *Lungamente* mostrando paganesmo:[1]"

*"through fear* I concealed my Christianity and *tediously* pretended paganism," he is translating the *trepidum* ("in my fear") and the *olim dolet* ("long have I grieved") of the *Achilleis*. The *trepidum* indeed he has translated twice; for the sound of it, or perhaps an alternative reading *tepidum*, has suggested the next words,

> "E questa *tiepidezza* il quarto cerchio
> Cerchiar mi fe' più ch'al quarto centesmo."

This lukewarmness cost the sinner more than four centuries of purgation.

Two facts Dante alleges, for which if he had express authority, we have still to find it: that Statius was disposed to Christianity by the prophetic hints which he found in the *Bucolics* of Virgil; and that he was baptized. Both facts, the Christianity itself being once established, might fairly be presumed. To Dante, himself accustomed to regard the Fourth *Eclogue* as a Messianic prediction not less clear and scarcely less sacred than those of the Bible, it was impossible that, in the situation supposed, the true sense could escape Statius; and it was inconceivable that the penitent of the *Achilleis* should neglect the rite necessary to salvation. But

---

[1] *Purg.* XXII 90.

in each allegation there is a particularity of circumstance, an exactness of detail, which points to
something more than presumption. Dante will tell
us *what words* in the Fourth *Eclogue* Statius laid to
heart; he knows *when* Statius was baptized, that is
to say, how much of the *Thebais* had been written
when the rite was performed.

"Before I brought the Argives in my poem to
the rivers of Thebes, I myself had received baptism[1]."
What does this mean? "Before I described the
expedition of the Seven," before the composition of
the *Thebais* as a whole? Impossible. Dante has
just said and proved that Statius, when he began
the *Thebais*, was a pagan. "Before the poem was
finished"? Impossible. The story, which Dante
knew minutely, is so far from ending with the
arrival of the expedition at Theban waters, that
there rather, after too many preliminaries, it may be
said to begin. The point, fixed by a reference quite
explicit and almost reproducing the words of Statius,
is the entrance of the invaders upon the territory of
the hostile city[2]. And the assertion is, that what
follows from this point, the latter half of the story,
which takes place at Thebes, was written after the
author's admission to the Church, but the preliminary
portion before it. Are we then to suppose that
Dante invented this? Were he liberal of spurious
history as any Dumas, this statement, from its very

[1] *Purg.* XXII 88.
[2] Boeotaque ventum flumina, Stat. *Theb.* VII 424; a' fiumi di
Tebe, Dante, *Purg.* XXII 88.

nature, he could not have made, except as a scholar and upon documentary evidence.

Evidence for this, to him satisfactory, he must have found, and probably also for the Christian studies of Statius in Virgil's Fourth *Eclogue*; though it by no means follows that his researches are now traceable by us.

Yet as to Virgil and his prophecy the evidence is obvious, in that same preface to the *Achilleis*, and in the first lines of the poem. The poet's address to his Emperor (that is, to Christ), is preceded by a brief passage in which he declares his theme, appeals for inspiration in the conventional form, as Dante himself and his Christian brethren did, to Apollo, and claims favour as the author of the *Thebais*. "Tell, Muse," he begins, "of the great-hearted Achilles, *and of that Offspring whom the Thunderer feared and would not suffer to inherit his native heaven.*"

> "Magnanimum Aeaciden, *formidatamque Tonanti*
> *Progeniem et patrio vetitam succedere caelo,*
> Diva, refer."

Now the Virgilian words which Dante makes Statius quote for Christian are the famous

> "ab integro saeclorum nascitur ordo,...
> Iam nova progenies caelo demittitur alto[1]."

"Now comes the birthday of ages new...and *from high heaven a new Offspring is sent down.*" These

---

[1] Virg. *Ecl.* IV 7 ; Dante, *Purg.* XXII 72, "e progenie discende dal ciel nuova."

words, out of much else similarly interpreted, Dante might no doubt have chosen for their celebrity, and by conjecture only. But not so. Statius, he thought, alludes to them. How should he think otherwise, when he found Statius presently saying to Christ : " To Thee my labour and preparation tends, and the praise of Achilles is the prelude to Thine "? How should he not think that Statius saw an analogy between the prelude and the sequel, saw in Achilles a type of the Christ to be, and suggested this connexion in such terms as a student of Virgil naturally would ? We of the North do not habitually think of Christ as the enemy, the terror, and the dethroner of Jupiter, as the Prince whom the devil-deities of the pagan Empire imprisoned and fain would have kept in Hell, whom, even after He had ascended to His Father's heaven, they excluded long from His lawful prerogative. All this never had much hold, even as a figure, upon our exotic Romanism ; and now, when we meet reflexions of it in our imitators of the Italians, it has a foreign and not very congenial air. But to a mediaeval Italian, loyal both to the Holy Empire and the Holy See, this was reality, the chief reality ; was history, and the very core of it. Nor is it now natural to seek Christian parables in pagan legend, or to celebrate the Saviour of mankind as a greater, a victorious Achilles. The world has unlearnt that language, and we Teutons the faster, as we had some pains in learning it. Jupiter never reigned here, and Achilles is not our compatriot. But to an

Italian Latinist of the thirteenth century this was the native voice of religious imagination, the Catholic speech as it had been spoken always, or should have been spoken, since the new birthday of Time. How then should Dante not suppose that the Christian Statius, who joins in one project the themes of Achilles and Christ, remembered Virgil's prophecy of "the Offspring from heaven sent down," when he wrote of "the Offspring whom Jove would not suffer to inherit His Father's heaven"?

Much more difficult, and probably not now answerable, is the question why the latter part of the *Thebais*, the Theban part, is alleged to be Christian work. The evidence should lie in the *Thebais* itself, in some change of tone, some allusions to Christian thought, language, rites or symbols, appearing at or after the point of division. But the field of search is wide, and the object vague; I have found nothing which seems worth notice[1]. That Dante was more successful we need not doubt, and meanwhile we can see what put him on the track. In the prelude to the *Achilleis* Statius says that this beginning of a new poem is not his beginning in poetry: "this brow has worn the wreath before, as witness *the land of Thebes*." We have seen how closely in the mind of Dante his office as a Christian poet is connected with his baptism, two gifts of the Spirit joined by the common symbol of the laurel crown. With such feelings he would find it only proper that a poet

[1 But see the next essay, written five years later.]

speaking as a convert to Christianity, should date his true beginning in poetry from his birth to God. Now Statius here associates his previous work with *the land*, or more exactly, with *the territory of Thebes* (*Dircaeus ager*)[1]. By this limitation he doubtless means nothing particular; he is no precisian in words: "the territory of Thebes" is "Thebes," and "Thebes" means generally the *Thebais*. But Dante, one of the most precise writers that ever was, if he had used such a limitation, would probably have meant what he said, and would have referred only to that part of the poem which really is connected with Theban soil. Here was enough, not indeed to prove that Statius was a Christian "before he brought the Greeks to the rivers of Thebes," but to prompt the search for proof; and a search conducted with such good will as Dante brought, was not likely to be disappointed.

Not that this or any part of the investigation must have been made for the first time by Dante. The contrary is to be supposed from the way in which he uses the results, treating them, and the process by which they were attained, as known and accepted. He went over the ground for himself, we see; and so always, to the best of his power, he did. But the lines must have been laid before, probably by some one of the ardent Latinists who were his friends or teachers. Like almost all contemporary work of this kind, the speculation, if ever it was put into written form (which is by no means

[1] *Achil.* I 12.

presumable), has doubtless long ago irretrievably disappeared.    Dante took the proof for granted. The earliest commentators on Dante were concerned, naturally and reasonably, with other things, which they supposed to be more perishable, and perhaps more interesting.    But this has an interest too.

# DANTE ON THE BAPTISM
## OF STATIUS

ALL readers of Dante will remember his strange problem concerning the position in Purgatory assigned to the poet Statius, and the historical explanation, elaborate and confident, by which that position is justified and defended[1]. Statius, one of the most successful and celebrated among the followers of Virgil, lived and wrote in the second half of the first century A.D., chiefly under the Emperor Domitian. According to Dante, his soul, for various offences, had continued in Purgatory from his death to the year 1300, the date of Dante's journey through the three worlds, and was at that very time released,—the sole example of such an event which the poet of the *Purgatorio* exhibits. Now, to be qualified for Purgatory, it was of course necessary that Statius should have been a Christian. This he might possibly have been ; but of the fact there is not the least record, nor any trace of a tradition to that effect. On the other hand, the work of Statius, or at least his principal work, the *Thebaid*, contains unquestionable evidence that the author was

---

[1] *Purgatorio* XXI and XXII, especially XXII 55 foll.

not a Christian, and (most remarkable of all) this fact, apparently fatal to Dante's assumption, is clearly and emphatically indicated by Dante himself. It is an inevitable and an interesting question, upon what grounds Dante thought himself justified in over-ruling this evidence, what answer he made, or supposed himself able to make, to the initial objection which he has raised against his own narrative.

This question has been discussed fully in the immediately preceding essay[1]. It was there shown that, as we might fairly expect, the evidence upon which Dante relied as favourable to the Christianity of Statius, was evidence of the same character, and, if valid, of the same authenticity, as that which he has himself adduced on the other side. It was evidence from the work of Statius himself. The argument, which is sufficiently indicated by Dante in the *Purgatorio*, and fortified by references to the relevant passages, turns upon the difference between the poetical prefaces prefixed by Statius to his earlier and complete poem, the *Thebaid*, and to the later and incomplete *Achilleid*. Both these prefaces comprise, according to the fashion of the day, a complimentary address to the reigning Emperor, Domitian. The custom of the time demanded that the Roman Emperor, who claimed a divine character, should be recognized in this character by those who addressed him : he must be addressed as a " god." In the preface to the *Thebaid* Statius complies with

[1] *To follow the Fisherman*, p. 153.

this requirement fully, and with apparent enthusiasm. In the preface to the *Achilleid* there is not the least reference to this aspect of the monarch, and the address, though respectful, contains nothing which might not be said by a Christian. Dante, or the authorities whom he followed, assumed that this change of tone and style was not (as it probably is) accidental, but deliberate. If it were so, it would indeed go far to show that the author, before he wrote the second address, had adopted the Christian view upon this vital question, the test-question, as will be remembered, by which Christianity, under the pagan Empire, was commonly proved. The assumption of deliberate change, and the argument from it, though not justified by sound criticism, is by no means absurd ; and it is not strange that Dante, for whose poetical purpose in the *Purgatorio* a Christian Statius was extremely and uniquely suitable, should have found the theory convincing.

For the details of the supposed proof, which are curiously illustrative of the scholarship and methods of thinking prevalent in Dante's time, and can be pursued far by the indications of his text, the reader is referred to the preceding essay. Our present purpose is to elucidate a point which was then left in some doubt,—upon what grounds Dante held himself warranted in his strangely precise statement respecting the baptism of the supposed convert. For this purpose we shall assume from the previous discussion only the main results, that the Christianity of Statius, according to Dante, is demonstrable and demonstrated by reference, chapter and verse, to the works of Statius himself, and in particular to the prefaces of his earlier poem, the *Thebaid*, and of his later, the *Achilleid*; the first of which prefaces is, as Dante admits, the composition of a pagan, but the second, as he implies, is the composition of a Christian.

The subject of the *Thebaid*—this also it will be convenient to recall—is the invasion of Thebes by a body of confederates, chiefly Argives, who support the claims of Polynices against the alleged usurpation of his brother Eteocles.   The contest is the theme of the *Seven against Thebes* of Aeschylus, and, chiefly through Statius, became the subject of frequent allusions in modern literatures, as in our own from Chaucer downwards.   With these preliminaries, we may come to our special point.

Having established, to his own satisfaction, that Statius was a Christian when he wrote the commencement of the *Achilleid*, Dante might well assume, without further proof, that, before that time, the convert had actually joined the Church, and had privately received the initiatory rite, which could not without deadly peril be deferred.   He might even perhaps assume, though the evidence did not go quite so far, that the conversion and the baptism were accomplished at some time during the twelve years which, as Statius himself tells us, were occupied by the composition of the *Thebaid*.   And if Dante were content so to limit his statement about the performance of the rite, if he merely said that

Statius received baptism during the composition of the *Thebaid*, there would be, on this head, no particular observation to make.

But as a matter of fact, Dante goes far beyond this. He has the audacity—that is the word which naturally presents itself—to date the event, the baptism, by a particular passage, a definite point in the *Thebaid*, which no one, familiar with the poem, could fail to recognize. " I had received baptism," so he makes Statius say, "before, as a poet, I had brought the Greeks to the rivers of Thebes."

It is not surprising that the expositors of Dante have tried to relieve their author of responsibility for this startling precision, and to persuade themselves and others, that by "the bringing of the Greeks to the rivers of Thebes" Dante describes the whole story of the *Thebaid*, and means no more than that, at some time during the relation of this story, the baptism took place. But this interpretation, however well meant, could not for a moment impose on any one familiar with the *Thebaid*. The arrival of the Greeks (that is to say, of the Argive invaders) at the rivers of Thebes is not a conceivable phrase with which to mark the close of the *Thebaid* or to sum up the story. To one who knew the poem at all—and Dante knew it well—such a description could not possibly occur. The arrival is a conspicuous and cardinal point in the middle of the poem, dividing it into two nearly equal parts, which differ broadly in contents and theme. The preceding portion contains the preliminaries to the war (together with much else of doubtful relevance); the sequel, more continuous and coherent, relates the war itself and the fates of the Argive leaders, concluding of course with the internecine duel of the rival brothers. With as much, or as little, propriety might Milton be made to describe the whole story of *Paradise Lost* as "the bringing of Satan through Chaos," or Scott to mark the end of *Guy Mannering* by the phrase "before I had brought my hero to the landing-place at Ellangowan." "Before Sophia Western reached London,"—"before I had got Mr Pickwick into prison,"—"before Jeanie Deans arrived at Richmond,"—"before Queen Guinevere fled from the court to Almesbury": these phrases mark conspicuous points within the respective stories, and could not possibly be otherwise meant or understood. The last example illustrates the phrase of Dante in this significant detail, that it marks the intended point by reference to the very words of the narrator—

"Queen Guinevere had fled the court..."

So also Dante; for in his words "to the *rivers* of Thebes," "a' *fiumi* di Tebe," the noticeable plural is a literal, rather too literal, reproduction of Statius, who writes, at the place indicated[1]—

"Iam ripas, Asope, tuas Boeotaque ventum flumina."

And further, the necessity of a definite reference, the impossibility of a loose and vague interpretation,

[1] Statius, *Thebaid*, VII 424.

is much stronger in the phrase of Dante than in any of the various parallels above suggested. For the arrival at the rivers, so far from being the close and sum of Statius' story, is much rather the beginning of it, the point at which, after long, too long, postponement, he takes up at last the narrative of the war, the subject announced in the opening. This defect of construction, the extension of the preliminaries by episodes more or less irrelevant, until they actually cover one-half of the entire composition, is a conspicuous feature of the *Thebaid*; and the phrase of Dante "before I had brought the Greeks to the rivers of Thebes" recalls, and must be intended to recall, not only the point fixed, but the tardiness, the excessive tardiness, of the narrator in reaching that point. We may illustrate this also by an appropriate parallel. In R. L. Stevenson's story of *The Wrecker*, the subject proper, the dealings of the hero with a wreck, emerges late, and is deferred, like the Theban portion of the *Thebaid*, by episodes for which Stevenson, like Statius, might perhaps have made a defence, but for which he, like Statius, admits that a defence might be required : they contributed, he tells us, with humorous self-criticism, to build up "the story of the Wrecker—a gentleman whose appearance may be presently expected." Similarly Statius, after devoting two large books and more, in his "Story of Thebes," to the foundation and performance of the Nemean Games, informs us at the beginning of Book VII, that the delay of the Argive army in commencing operations has provoked the impatience of Jupiter. It has certainly tried, if not exhausted, the patience of the reader, a reflexion so obvious that it cannot have escaped the author. He had probably received hints to proceed without further delay— possibly from the Imperial critic, Domitian himself; for when a writer of that age speaks of " Jupiter," it is always legitimate to consider whether it is not the earthly " Jupiter " whom he has in his eye,—but at all events from some quarter; and he excuses himself, like Stevenson, by a side-stroke of self-criticism. When therefore Statius is made to speak of the time " before I brought the Greeks, in my poem, to the rivers of Thebes," it is inevitable for us, if we know the poem, to subjoin the tacit remark, "where, as you very well know, you would have done better to bring them sooner." We shall see presently that this aspect of the matter is material, and indeed vital, to the meaning of Dante. For the moment we will merely note that it enforces, with special stringency, the true and only possible interpretation of the phrase, as a reference, not to the *Thebaid* generally, but to the particular passage, the arrival at the Asopus, which Dante signifies and actually cites.

The question then arises, Upon what evidence does Dante build? Manifestly it must be evidence in the *Thebaid.* Here perhaps most plainly we see what, for any one familiar with the poems of Statius, is plain enough throughout the whole account which Dante gives of him. Whatever hint for it Dante may have found in tradition—we know nothing of any such hint, but it is of course possible,—the substance of the account is not based on tradition, but on the supposed evidence of the documents, the poems of Statius themselves. The repeated and specific references to the words of Statius prove this; and most of all, perhaps, this particular reference. The statement of Dante here is such as could not, from its nature, be made otherwise than upon the evidence, real or supposed, of the *Thebaid.*

Nor would any evidence be sufficient, which did not at all events include an inference from the particular passage to which Dante directs us. It would not be enough, even if it were true, that in the subsequent half of the poem there were traces of Christian knowledge or sentiment, such as do not appear in the preceding half. I have actually tried this track, but with no success; nor did I enter it with much hope, because, after all, no such collective inference would really satisfy the language of Dante. He states precisely, that the baptism of Statius preceded the composition of a certain passage, definitely marked by reference to the wording of its first sentence. Manifestly, if we consider, nothing could prove this, except the assurance of Statius given in the passage itself. Dante supposed, he must have supposed, that *in this place* Statius alludes to his baptism; that he *here* uses language which, coming from a person known to have been a Christian not very long afterwards (that is to say, at the commencement of the *Achilleid*), implies that he had received the initiatory rite. And he must also have supposed that, to the readers whom he contemplated, the grounds for this supposition were either known or sufficiently indicated by himself. Nothing short of this, it seems, could account for his statement at all. It by no means follows that the indications are sufficient for us. But the thing must be there; and it is worth our while, if only as matter of curiosity, to look for it.

And our first step should be, to examine minutely the context of the statement in Dante, on the chance that the exact sense of it, or some part of it, may have escaped us. The agreement, says Statius, between the Christian preachers and the prophetic language of Virgil in the Fourth *Eclogue*, so far impressed him that he began to visit them. The rest, his conversion, was the work of their virtues :

" They then became so holy in my sight, that, when Domitian persecuted them, their wailings were not without tears of mine. And while by me yon world was trod, I succoured them, and their righteous lives made me despise all other sects; and ere in my poem I had brought the Greeks to Thebes' rivers, I received baptism ; but through fear I was a secret Christian, long time pretending paganism."

> " Vennermi poi parendo tanto santi,
>     che, quando Domizian li perseguette
>     senza mio lagrimar non fur lor pianti.
> " E mentre che di là per me si stette,
>     io li sovvenni, e lor dritti costumi
>     fer dispregiare a me tutte altre sette ;
> " e pria ch' io conducessi i Greci a' fiumi
>     di Tebe poetando, ebb' io battesmo ;
>     ma per paura chiuso Cristian fu' mi,
> " lungamente mostrando paganesmo."
>
> *Purg.* XXII 82—91.

So the passage is presented in the faithful prose of the Temple Classics. And here is a portion of it, the piece with which we are specially concerned, in the version, even more close, of Mr A. J. Butler: "And whilst there was a station for me in that world, I aided them, and their upright fashions made me hold all other sects of small price. And before I brought the Greeks to the rivers of Thebes in my poem had I baptism, but through fear" etc.

Now both versions assume, and it appears to be universally assumed, that in the words *mentre che di là per me si stette*, that is, literally, *while I stood* (or *stayed*) *on the other side*, the description *di là, on the other side*, means "the other side of the earth," the world of living men, as regarded from the Mount of Purgatory, situated, according to Dante, at the Antipodes; so that "while I stayed on the other side" means "while I lived" or "before my death." The assumption is natural, for *di là* is not only so used in the *Purgatorio* constantly, but occurs twice, with that sense, in speeches of Statius.

Nevertheless there is more than one reason for doubting whether that sense is admissible here. The first reason is a point of language, a doubt whether, in the Italian of Dante, *per me si stette*, or *per me* with any impersonal verb, could be applied, as the current interpretation here assumes, to a fact or circumstance, in which the speaker of the *per me* was purely passive, in which he exercised neither will nor even permission. Such a fact—if we disregard the irrelevant case of suicide—is the

standing or staying of a man in this life. He stays
while he is left, and goes when he is taken. How
then can it be said that the staying happens "by"
or rather "along of" him? In Latin, at all events,
such a use would seem to be impossible: *per me
stabatur, per me statum est*, must imply that the
speaker was at least permissive, not passive, in the
matter. In both the versions above cited will be
noticed a desire to modify the language in this
respect: in "while by me yon world was *trod*" the
sense of *stette* is a little forced, and in "whilst there
was a station *for* me in that world" we might demur
to the rendering of *per*. This scruple can perhaps
be removed by illustrations from Dante or elsewhere. Meanwhile it may count with graver and
more conclusive objections, which are founded upon
the whole context.

For let us suppose that *mentre che di là per me
si stette* may, so far as the words go, mean "while
I lived," "before I died." Statius is then made to
say this: "Before I died, I had conceived, from the
good morals of the Christians, a disesteem for all
opinions except theirs. And before my *Thebaid*
had reached [a certain place in Book VII], I had
joined the Christian Church." Is it possible that
the story should be told so preposterously and per-
versely, with such disregard of progress and order?
If Statius actually sought baptism, in spite of his
fears, before he wrote the seventh book of the
*Thebaid's* twelve, and at a time which, upon the
evidence of the *Thebaid* itself, must have been

years, six years and more, before his death, what
need is there to tell us, as a preliminary to this
information, that, all those years after his baptism,
he had come so far on the road to Christianity as
to conceive a distaste for paganism ? Can any other
passage be produced, in which Dante is guilty of such
an inversion ?

And further, the context not only excludes the
interpretation of "while I stayed on the other side"
by "while I lived," but imposes another interpretation—namely, "while I abstained from joining the
Church and receiving baptism." Let us illustrate
the matter by an example from familiar English.
The phrase "while he remained at the bar" is in
itself ambiguous. But it is not ambiguous in the
following : "While he remained at the bar, he had
become weary of the excessive labour, and before
1908 he accepted a place on the Bench." Nor again
in the following : "While he remained at the bar,
his head had begun to feel very uncomfortable, and
before ten o'clock he left the hotel and went to bed."
In each case the commencement is interpreted by
the conclusion. Exactly similar is the relation of
the clauses in Dante : "While I *stayed on the other
side*, I had come to dislike paganism; and before [a
given date] I *was baptised and entered the Christian
Church.*" The last words relate to the words before,
and require them to mean "before I entered the
Church."

The question then arises, by what thought or
metaphor Dante is led to describe the delay or

hesitation of the convert, his abstention from the decisive step of receiving initiation, as a staying "on the other side." On the other side of what? The context again furnishes the answer, about which indeed we could hardly doubt, even if we were left to conjecture. The comparison of baptism to a river is, for obvious reasons, so well established and familiar, that in this connexion it would be almost sufficiently signified by "on the other side" itself. But Dante explicitly gives us the "river"—

> "e pria ch' io conducessi i Greci a' fiumi
> di Tebe poetando, ebb' io battesmo:"

"And before, as a poet, I brought the Greeks to the rivers *of Thebes*, I had *myself* received baptism." The emphasis on *of Thebes*, given by the position of the words in the verse, and on *myself*, given by the inversion "ebb' io," imply an antithesis or comparison between Statius and the Greeks of the poem, between the "rivers" to which they came and that to which he came, the *river*, according to the familiar figure, *of baptism*. This river he long hesitated to pass; he "halted on the other side," as a man who was no hero might, when to be baptised was to be in danger of death,—though, as he tells us, the delay cost him centuries of expiation upon the purgatorial mountain. But before he brought his Argives to the Asopus, he himself had made his passage.

Now if this be the true meaning of Dante's words, plainly then it is, or should be, no hard matter to discover, in the place to which he refers us, the grounds of his inference, or, at all events, the interpretation which he adopted. He has told us implicitly what we are to look for, precisely as he implies, in the same canto, where we are to go for the proof that Statius did in fact hold the opinions of a Christian. We are to find, he says, in the immediate context of the words *Boeotaque ventum flumina,* "they arrived at the Boeotian *rivers,*" an illustration of Statius' own position in reference to Christianity, so exact that we must suppose it intentional, and such as to imply that, before composing it, he had taken the decisive step and had undergone the initiatory rite.

Let us then read on from the words marked: "Now see them come to the banks of Asopus, to the rivers of Boeotia." There was a halt there. The unfriendly stream, we are told, then chanced to be swollen by a formidable flood, and the Argive horsemen hesitated to pass.

"Then the daring Hippomedon forced down the bank his shrinking steed, a great piece of earth rolling beneath them, and dashing on to the mid water, called, as he hung between bridle and shield, to those behind: 'Gallants, come on! As here I show you the way, so will I at the wall, and will break you a passage through the rampart of Thebes.' *Then plunged they all into the river, ashamed to be not the first.* So, when a herdsman would drive his herd through a stream they do not know, *the beasts dismayed will hesitate.* How far the other side, how broad is the terror between! So doubt they all. But when a leading bull goes in, when he has made a ford, *then gentler seems the flood, the leaps not difficult, and the banks less distant than before.*"

"The beasts dismayed will hesitate" : *stat triste pecus.* Dante, in his "per me si *stette*," is transcribing the actual word of the Latin poet, and marks, beyond mistake, the analogy which he read in the whole incident, and especially in the concluding simile. Nor would this reading be unreasonable, if we could believe, as Dante believed and implies in the same canto, that the Christianity of Statius, and the fact that he was shamed into Christianity by admiration of the martyrs, is demonstrable from the exordium of the *Achilleid.* On this supposition, the suspicion of an autobiographical reference in the passing of the Asopus would be legitimate, from the aptness of the parallel, even if there were no external indication that the Argive soldiery here stand, by allegory, for the soldiery of Christ.

But such an indication there is ; or at least Dante, with his general views, would be likely to think so. The arrival at the Asopus is preceded by a hasty and violent march upon Boeotia—the poet being apparently determined to show that he has done with digressing, and means to quicken the pace. The movement excites a desperate protest from the oracles of the gods, which are against the Argive enterprise,—although, let us observe, it is promoted and stimulated by Jove. The oracles then protest, not articulately, but by desperate disorder; and the

chief of them all, the oracle of Delphi, protests by
silence, by ceasing to speak—

"tunc et Apollineae tacuere oracula Cirrhae."

But the failure of the oracles, and in particular the
silence of Delphi, was universally held to have been
among the signs by which decadent paganism protested, and protested in vain, against the victory of
Christ and of Christianity. Milton has made the
thought familiar to Englishmen in his Hymn on the
Nativity—"The oracles are dumb;...Apollo from his
shrine can now no more divine."

With these ideas, it is at least not unnatural to
see a symbol of the Christian army in an army which
is thwarted by the silence of Delphi, and urged to
advance by that "Jove" whose name Dante actually
uses as a synonym for the crucified God.

It should however be observed, that Dante draws
a distinction between his reading of this place in the
*Thebaid* and his preceding inferences from the *Achilleid*, from the definitely Christian language (as Dante
held it to be) which Statius there uses, and from his
supposed reference to the Messianic prophecy of
Virgil. The passage of Dante now before us, the
passage which cites for authority the fording of the
Asopus, is introduced by these words : " That thou
mayst better see that which I outline," says Statius to
Virgil, "*I will stretch my hand to put in the colours*"—

"a colorar distenderò la mano."

It is but fair to suppose that this distinction is significant. Dante means that his interpretation of the

*Thebaid* is an imaginative interpretation, which might be ventured without indiscretion, upon the assumption that the "outline" of the history, the main fact of Statius' Christianity, is, as he held it to be, established.

So far then for the general meaning and main purpose of the connexion which Dante makes, between the fording of the Asopus and the baptism of the poet who describes it. But we have by no means yet exhausted the significance, for Dante, of the words "mentre che di là per me si stette," *while I stayed on the other side.* We have already observed that the arrival at the Theban river is, merely from a literary point of view and in its relation to the story, the end of a long, a too long, halting on the part of Statius. Whatever may have been the history of his opinions and his conduct as a man, it is certain and obvious that, as composer of the *Thebaid,* he comes too late to the Theban river, and stays too long on the wrong side of it. No one, as we said, who is familiar with the *Thebaid,* could read the words of Dante, without perceiving this personal application to the Latin poet's "conduct" of his story.

And since this is so, since the "staying" of Statius is represented by Dante as doubly characteristic, both of the composer and of the man, and since Dante is at the pains to mark this trait by the very word of Statius himself, one can hardly escape the suspicion that Dante supposed a special and personal connexion between Statius and this particular word—*stat.*

It is certain that Dante did suppose such a connexion. He held, and clearly implies, that the name of the Latin poet, or rather the name by which he was commonly known, was not a proper name but a nickname, significant, and derived from *stare* in the sense of "standing" or "staying." He implies this necessarily, when he makes the Latin poet say of himself: "*Statius* I am still called by the folk on the other side [of the world]"—

"Stazio la gente ancor di là mi noma."

It is surely unnatural, not to say impossible, that a man should so speak of his proper and only name. With no propriety, with no sense, could the spirit of Shakespeare be made to say: "*Shakespeare* I am *still* called." Why should the name have been changed, and what other name could have been substituted? Such a way of speaking implies that the name in question might, or even should, have been dropped: that there is another, and this other more strictly appropriate. Just so the author of *Middlemarch* might properly and significantly say: " By the living world I am *still* called *George Eliot*," meaning that her literary reputation persists, and that, in this connexion, her literary name is *still* preferred to designations personally more proper.

And the same thing is implied when Statius speaks of a "more honourable" and "more durable" name which, by a certain date, he bore. At the time of the destruction of Jerusalem, in A.D. 70, he was, he says, "with the name which more lasts and

more honours, famous enough." The name, say the
expositors of Dante, is that of "poet"; and this is
so far true, that it must be a note or mark of the
poet as such. But whether the mere word *poet* could
properly be so indicated, one may well doubt; and
when we compare the subsequent and more explicit
reference to the name "Statius," we must conclude
that this, and not merely "poet," is the name by
which he was "famous enough." This last expression, *famoso assai*, is noticeable, since it suggests at
once, by its colour, that the name in question was
not an unqualified compliment, but was at least
susceptible of an interpretation not laudatory. And
this accords well with the obvious fact that Dante,
though he admired Statius, did not over-rate him:
"Without the *Aeneid*," he makes Statius say, "I
should not have weighed a drachm." This is a
strong, perhaps too strong, acknowledgement of the
later poet's imitative dependence; and we might
presume therefore, and we have seen, that Dante
was not blind to what else may be alleged against
him, and in particular to his *longueurs*, the marked
tendency of the *Thebaid*, especially in the earlier
part, to be "halting" and dilatory. He connected
this quality, we have seen, with the word *stare*, and
would naturally connect with it the name *Statius*,
on the assumption that this was a literary nickname.

But what in the world, it may be asked, should
lead Dante, or those whom he followed, to suppose
that *Statius* was in fact such a name,—that it was

not the poet's proper name? Let us not however
be impatient. Like every other part of the theory
respecting Statius and his history, which the scholars
of the thirteenth century seem to have extracted
from their data, this conjecture about his name,
though not true, was by no means without plausible
grounds. It is even true, in a certain way, that
"Statius" was *not* the name of the poet, not in that
sense which might most readily be supposed. If
the present reader were only a little less learned
than he doubtless is, one might easily prove this
point. The name *Statius* has the form and appearance of a Roman family-name, a name like *Vergilius*,
*Horatius*, *Propertius*, *Terentius*, *Livius*. We ourselves at this day, if we did not know the contrary,
should certainly assume that *Statius* was such a name,
the poet's family-name. It is even not unlikely that
some persons who hear it do so suppose. Yet in
fact, we know, this is not the case. The poet's
family-name was *Papinius*; and his full name, *P.
Papinius Statius*, has the unusual appearance of
containing *two* family-names, and no personal name,
or *cognomen*, at all. As a matter of fact, *Statius*
was, it seems, one of the very few names of this
form (names in *-ius*), which were used, even from
early times of Roman history, in place of a *cognomen*.
But of this the scholars of the thirteenth century,
without disgrace, might not be aware. It was not,
then, by any means an absurd conjecture, that the
name *Statius* was a fiction, an artist-name or poet-
name of the sort familiar to Italians, which in

common currency had replaced the proper name *Papinius.*

As for the significance of the name, if it were fictitious and therefore significant, about this there could be no doubt. The author of the *Thebaid* himself, in his brief epilogue, dwells upon the enormous time over which the production had extended —twelve books in twelve years—the consequence of his slow and scrupulous habit of work. He himself there betrays some doubt whether this laborious and dilatory method had been altogether favourable to his art. When we take with this the fact that the story so told is marked, more deeply perhaps than any composition of equal fame, with the fault of suspensory interludes and deferred progression, it is obvious to suppose that the name *Statius,* if it were bestowed upon him for his literary quality, referred to his *stationes* or *halts.* It marked the impatience with which the eager and admiring audiences of Papinius attended upon the too leisurely progress of their favourite epic. The eagerness of the Roman audiences is noticed by Dante, who cites for it, by a verbal allusion[1], the solitary passage where Statius is mentioned by Juvenal,—the only sound material for the life of Statius, except the *Thebaid* and *Achilleid,* which the thirteenth century would appear to have possessed. Even the impatience might not unfairly be inferred from the same passage, since we are told by Juvenal that Roman

---

[1] *Purg.* XXI 88, *dolce...vocale spirto,* compared with Juvenal vii 82 *vocem iucundam.*

society "ran" to the delights of the *Thebaid*, "when *Statius* had promised a day." With all this, if it were once assumed that the name of *Statius* or "Stayer" was a literary nickname, bestowed upon the poet in the quizzical familiarity of fondness, no one could doubt what it meant; and this obvious interpretation is what Dante has in view when he contrasts the time, during which Statius stood, stayed, or halted, with the moment when, at last, he brought his Greeks to the river of Thebes. If the name of *Stayer*, and the disposition to be hesitating and dilatory, were also appropriate, as Dante implies, to the moral character of a man who, after he had become in opinions a Christian, abstained long, for want of courage, from the reception of baptism, and who deferred the actual confession of his new religion until death made confession impossible,—then all the more justifiable and the more interesting was it to insist upon the history of the name, and to make it, as Dante does in fact make it, the main pivot of the poet's autobiography.

# THE BIRTH OF VIRGIL

## (DANTE, *Inferno* I 70)

Nacqui *sub Julio*, ancor che fosse tardi,
e vissi a Roma sotto 'l buono Augusto,
al tempo degli Dei falsi e bugiardi.

"I was born *under Julius*, though it was late;
and lived at Rome under the good Augustus, at
the time of the false and lying gods."—With these
words the shade of the great Mantuan poet, the
founder of the Roman Imperial literature, introduces
himself to Dante at the outset of his journey through
Hell, Purgatory, and Paradise, as the guide destined
to accompany and direct him through so much of
his journey as was terrestrial, and lay within or upon
this earth. For the first two stages, for the passage
through the Underworld, and for the ascent of the
Mount of Purgatory at the Antipodes, Virgil, as
he announces, will be a sufficient and authorised
director; but for Heaven another and worthier guide
will be provided; "for that Emperor, who reigns
above, because I was rebellious to His law, wills
not that entrance into His city should be made by
means of me."

The symbolic purpose of this distinction between the present and the promised guide, is transparent and universally recognised ; and equally transparent is the propriety, from Dante's point of view, of the function assigned to Virgil. Truth is attained partly by human intelligence, but the highest truth only by divine grace and revelation. Virgil, the inheritor and consummator of the intellectual efforts which preceded the Christian revelation—Virgil, who gave a final form and a new beginning to that language and poetry of the Roman Empire which was for Dante the eternal language and poetry of the world—Virgil, who forefelt, indeed, and foreshowed (as Dante believed) the coming of Christ, yet was himself the first and most powerful preacher not of Christ but of Anti-Christ, the first to salute effectively that new deity of the Roman Caesar which, embodied in the successors of Julius and Augustus, fought successfully for three centuries against the accession of the Messiah to His rightful sovereignty upon earth—Virgil, both by his achievements and his limits, represented exactly, for Dante, the culmination and the defects of Man not yet enlightened by the self-revelation of God.

The brief biographical particulars by which Virgil is made to disclose his identity, have, in all respects but one, that close and precise relevance to the purpose, which is perhaps the most remarkable feature of Dante's style and way of thinking. We are told, *first*, that he was an Italian, a full-born native of the Imperial state ; *secondly*, that he celebrated the "coming of Aeneas," that is to say, the foundation of Rome, and more particularly, the foundation of Rome as a spiritual state, the seat prepared for the Vicar of Christ. This significance of Aeneas' enterprise, though not here stated by Virgil, is expressly and fully set forth by Dante in the following discourse between the two poets ; and we are correctly referred for it to the Sixth *Aeneid* in particular, the account of Aeneas' journey to the Underworld, and the revelations there made to him, "the causes of his victory and of the Papal Mantle[1]." We are thus shown precisely in what respect the *Divina Commedia* depends historically and poetically upon the *Aeneid*, and why Virgil, and no other, should hold in the later poem, in the *Aeneid* of a better Rome, that large but limited place which he actually does. *Thirdly*, we are told that the life of Virgil coincided with "the time of the false and lying gods," that is to say, with the establishment under Augustus of the Imperial pretensions to deity. And *lastly*, Virgil informs us that he was himself a rebel against the true and heavenly "Emperor"; that is to say, he recognized, acclaimed, and promoted those false pretensions of deified men, by which the spiritual Governor of the World, the veritable God-Man, and his appointed representatives, the Pontiffs, were unlawfully debarred from their terrestrial throne. All this is perfectly true and exactly appropriate ; the biographical statement could not possibly be

---

[1] *Inf.* II 13—27.

improved, with regard to its intention, by any omission or addition whatsoever.

But with these statements Dante, to the amazement of his expositors from earliest to latest, combines one assertion which, taken in the *prima facie* sense, is not only false, but would, if it were true, destroy the very basis of all the rest. " I was born," says Virgil, "under *Julius*, although it was late," "Nacqui *sub Julio*, ancor che fosse tardi." This is held, not unnaturally, if we take the sentence alone, to mean that Virgil was born when Julius Caesar was monarch (48–44 B.C.), but very near the end of his life and reign, that is to say, in or not earlier than the year 45 B.C.

Now in the first place, this date is enormously wrong, too late by twenty-five years or something near a generation, the true date being 70 B.C. And further, if the alleged date were right, the rest of the biography, though it might be in some sort true, manifestly could not bear the significance which Dante here and elsewhere assigns to it. On both grounds, error and incongruity, the statement would be surprising if found in Dante anywhere, and is especially surprising in this place.

On the mere question of error, the probability or improbability that Dante should be wrong by twenty-five years respecting one of the chief dates in the first century before Christ, we need not dwell at any length. Among his expositors, one of the most positive in pronouncing the error, merely as an error, impossible, is one of the nearest to the poet's own time, and the best qualified, so far, to estimate his general equipment. Nor is it easy to refute Benvenuto upon this point. The age which witnessed the establishment of the Roman Empire was more interesting to Dante than any except (if we should except) his own. He possessed, and claims and proves himself to have deeply studied, books which gave a general outline of that age, sufficient to exclude utterly a statement so absurd as that the birth of Virgil nearly coincided with the death of Julius Caesar. Nor, so far as I am aware, has any error of his, comparable in matter and gravity, ever been cited by way of illustration. It would require us, for instance, to suppose that Dante had not got the faintest notion, even at second-hand, of the contents and historical bearing of Virgil's Fifth *Eclogue*. The supposition is perhaps not disprovable by chapter and verse, but few readers of Dante will venture to call it likely. And even if we assume the possibility of the error, there would still remain the incongruity, the irrelevance, and worse than irrelevance, of the statement in this particular place. The whole account of Virgil here given comes briefly to this, that he was the originator, the founder, of Roman Imperial literature, the leader in the production of poetry framed and governed by the conception of the Roman Empire as a sacred world-state,—the first of the Augustans. This is fact; and all that Dante here says of Virgil, and the whole propriety of the place assigned to Virgil in the *Divina Commedia*, depends upon the fact.

" Art thou then that Virgil, and that *fountain* which pours abroad so rich a stream of speech? O glory *and light* of other poets!...." Such is the salutation with which Dante, blushing with humility and delight, receives the Great Leader's description of his career. What is signified by these figures of *fountain* and *light* is plain enough here in their context, and is made still plainer in the Fourth Canto. There we see Virgil (and Dante with him) rejoining his compeers, the group of Roman and Imperial poets with whom, in the Limbo of the Underworld, is his eternal abode. Homer is included in the group, to represent the preparatory work of Greece; Dante himself is adopted into it, to represent heirs and successors. The rest are the *Augustan* poets in the large and political meaning of the word, the Latin poets of the Empire—arranged, we may note, correctly in order of date—Horace, Ovid, and Lucan. Approaching these, Virgil is none the less saluted as *the highest Poet* (*l'altissimo poeta*)[1]. He is the chief, the leader, the prince of human language and thought, as estimated by the standard of a Christian Imperialist, by Dante, a true and loyal subject of the Holy Roman Empire. All this is intelligible and true, if we assume the true date of Virgil and his work, its true relation in time to that cardinal change of Roman ideas and of the Latin language which bears the name of Augustus. It is not true, unless we assume, as the fact is, that the decisive operation of Virgil *preceded* the whole Imperialist

[1] *Inf.* IV 80.

movement in literature, and set the pattern of it;
that all the work of Ovid, and all the vitally
significant work of Horace, is subsequent to the
decisive entrance of Virgil; that all the body of
Augustan poetry is later than the *Bucolics* and
*Georgics*, most of it later than the *Aeneid*; that it is
all in various ways not only Augustan but Virgilian,
and could not have been what it is, if Virgil, first
and long before, had not sounded his new and
inaugurating note.

But how is this conceivable, if, as Dante is
understood to say, Virgil was but just born when
Julius Caesar fell, if Virgil was an infant at the time
when Augustus achieved power? If this was so,
then one of two things—either Virgil, as a poet,
instead of being the leader of the Augustan age,
must have been one of its latest products; or else,
if the Augustan movement in thought and language
really began with Virgil, then all the Augustans
were junior by a generation to Augustus himself,
and some of them, Ovid for instance, would be
junior by two generations.

Such is the palpable absurdity, the plain contradiction, of which Dante is guilty at the very
outset and foundation of his systematic poem, if,
when he made Virgil say—

Nacqui *sub Julio*, ancor che fosse tardi,

he meant that the birth of Virgil preceded indeed,
but barely preceded, the death of the first Roman
Emperor. The offence would be aggravated, we

may remark, by the ostentation of exactness. We are particularly asked to note, as if it were not only true but specially important, that though the birth of the poet *did* precede the death of the sovereign, it was not by much—and this although what follows cannot be properly appreciated, unless we know and realise that Virgil, as an adult and accomplished poet, was *the first* who proclaimed effectively to the world the deity of the deceased Julius, and asserted the devolution of that sacred character to the inheritor of his name and power.

To call this hypothesis impossible would be perhaps too much. In the way of human error, nothing perhaps is strictly impossible. But more improbable no hypothesis could be, and as a basis of interpretation it is inadmissible. Any supposition must be preferable, or in default of any, none—the abandonment of the verse as hopelessly obscure. And to try first the positive and more comfortable way, we should consider exhaustively, what are the conditions to be satisfied by an interpretation really acceptable.

Three things such an interpretation must do, none of which the primary interpretation does. First, it must show some significant and interesting connexion between the birth of Virgil and the person of the first Emperor in his character as a pretended god. For this, and this only, is the aspect in which Julius is here introduced: he was one, and the first, of the "false and lying gods." We have hitherto assumed, without remark, that this description signifies the Roman Emperors, and especially the two who are mentioned, the founders of the cult, Julius and Augustus. But as commentaries on Dante seem to be generally silent about this, it should perhaps be further explained. There is nothing, except the Roman Emperors, to which the description, "false and lying gods," can be here referred, if we duly regard the context and the opinions of Dante. He could not so describe, for instance, the gods of Roman mythology, Jupiter and the other Olympians. Milton might have so described Jupiter, and indeed does use very similar language about him; because Milton held the view that the pagan gods were really devils, who deceived their worshippers into accepting them for deities. But Dante held the view, totally different and at least equally defensible, that the figure of Jupiter was an imperfect adumbration, a human and partly erroneous conception, of the true Deity, God himself. He actually speaks of Christ as the *crucified Jove* (*Giove crocifisso*); and this way of looking at the matter is not only well-founded in history, but absolutely necessary to Roman Catholicism as apprehended by Dante. Moreover, even if Jupiter and the rest had been, for Dante, "lying gods," it would still be pointless to distinguish the time of Virgil as the time of those gods—who were worshipped for centuries after Virgil exactly as they had been for ages before. The worship of the Augustus, on the other hand, was the essential and characteristic novelty of Virgil's time. To this therefore clearly

Dante here refers, borrowing his sarcasm upon the Imperial pretensions from such authors as his favourite Lucan, who, in his treatment of the subject, fluctuates between pompous flattery and scathing contempt. Lucan's "dead gods of Rome" (*Romanorum manes deorum*) signifies the same thing as Dante's *bugiardi Dei*, and puts it much more strongly. Moral distinctions between different Emperors may of course be admitted—and Dante does admit them by making Virgil call his patron "the *good* Augustus"—without prejudice to the condemnation of all the Emperors, in respect of their claim to deity, as liars. As a deity, then, a pretended deity, Julius is here brought in ; and the first problem for our interpretation is to find some real and interesting connexion between Julius, in this character, and the date of the birth of Virgil.

Further, a satisfactory explanation of the words " I was born *sub Julio* " must show why " under Julius" should be expressed not in Italian but in Latin. Latin is little used by Dante in his Italian poetry, and when it is, there is commonly an obvious reason or necessity for the licence. A Latin psalm, hymn, prayer must of course be indicated by its proper words—*Te Deum, Veni Creator, In exitu Israel*; and a poetical quotation, if sufficiently important, may be similarly distinguished—*manibus date lilia plenis*. But no literary offence is more displeasing to a delicate taste than gratuitous polyglot, an alien idiom inserted arbitrarily or to save the trouble of speaking correctly. If, then, Dante means no more than that Virgil was born in the reign of Julius, why does he not say it in the vernacular?

Lastly, and above all, we should require some real justification for the strange and enigmatical words *ancor che fosse tardi*, " though it was late." " I was born *sub Julio*, though it was late," is no proper way to express the sense hitherto assumed, " I was born late in the time of Julius." So clumsy and pointless a periphrasis is not fairly attributable to the composer of the *Divina Commedia*.

Let us, then, start again without prejudice; and since the supposition of Dante's ignorance or carelessness has proved so unfruitful, let us start by supposing on the contrary his complete knowledge and profound study of the subject. For really this is, in the present matter, the more natural supposition. All the material which we have for the life of Virgil, with insignificant exceptions, was extant in the time of Dante, and might naturally be open to his investigation. What historical documents he had, he studied, and so did his contemporaries, with a passionate and scrupulous thoroughness which no age has surpassed. Let us suppose, then, that he knew and had considered all that there is to know about the birth of Virgil; that the learned readers, whom he desired to satisfy[1], knew it all too; that

---

[1] This should always be carefully borne in mind in considering a problem in Dante. He assumes learning in his readers, all the learning of his time, and makes no attempt to meet the popular intelligence.

he assumes their knowledge, and might naturally write whatever such readers could interpret. And let us then ask, what is known or knowable about the date of the birth of Virgil?

Tradition places it in the year 684 of Rome (70 B.C. by our era), in the month of October, and on the Ides or 15th day of the month. From the year (as has been only too completely ascertained) we can deduce nothing which throws any light upon Dante. The year had no special association whatever with the name or the fortunes of the first Emperor. Let us, then, next try the month. At first sight this looks equally unpromising: the Emperor is not, and never was, associated with the month of October. He has, indeed, a month of his own—a month which, bearing his name, has eternalised (so far as it is possible for man) the memory of his unique and almost superhuman greatness. But it is the month of *July*. And it is scarcely too much to say that, if any event is to be associated through its date with the name of Julius, it is through the month of Quintilis, converted into *Julius* in honour of his deity, that the link of association must be sought.

In this embarrassment we go back to Dante; and we may now observe, not without hope, that he appends to his *sub Julio* the exception or qualification, "although it was late." What was late? We have assumed hitherto that the subject of this remark is the birth of Virgil. But Dante does not say so; he says that *something* was late, and so far as the words go, may perfectly well mean that it was the date, that is to say, the month, and not the infant that was belated. And this, as a matter of fact, it certainly was. In 70 B.C. all the true months—the months of the natural year—were, and long had been, in consequence of accumulating error, behind the nominal calendar. The accumulated error amounted to almost exactly three months, and persisted, as all the world knows, until Julius Caesar, in 46 B.C., rectified it by inserting ninety days (three months) in a single year, and took means to prevent the error in future; whereby it came to pass that his name, as that of a deity, was given to the month in which he was born.

Consequently, a child whose birth was recorded, in the year 684 of Rome, as occurring in the middle of October, was really born in the seventh (not the tenth) month of the true year, in the height of summer, not in the autumn; and if the birth had been properly recorded, according to the true calendar as afterwards established by the Emperor, would have been described, and should now properly be described, as born *sub Julio*, in the month and under the auspices of Julius. But the true and proper name of the month was then "late," "lagging," "behindhand," by a whole quarter: *Quintilis*, or *Julius*, which should have been present, lay nominally three months in arrear; and Virgil therefore figures in history, though falsely, as born in the middle of October.

This, then, I venture to think, is what Dante

means by his terse but correct observation. Deeply interested as he was in astronomical and calendric studies, and in the history of the age which witnessed the foundation of Imperial Rome, he might very naturally have observed the error respecting the season and true character of the time, which presumably lies in the statement that Virgil was born on the Ides of October. Nor would he think it pedantic or irrelevant, as perhaps we might, to introduce a notice of this error, and of the fact as corrected, into his poetical biography of the Augustan poet. It is irrelevant only upon the assumption that there cannot be any real significance in the true fact, the birth of the first Imperial poet in that portion of the year which was to bear the name of the first Emperor. But Dante of course would not have admitted this. As a sound astrologer, he would have maintained, on the contrary, that the fact was, or probably might be, a sign of destiny; and more than a sign, an actual element in the natural and spiritual influences which contributed to mould the nascent soul of the Imperial poet and prophet, and to fit him for his appointed work of revealing and worthily celebrating the evolution of the Roman world-state, from the beginning by Aeneas to the new beginning by Julius and Augustus,—the building of Imperial Rome, of a throne for the Vicar of Christ.

It is true, as Dante sadly acknowledges, that Virgil did not perceive (and perhaps, when we consider how much was revealed to him in his

Fourth *Eclogue*, was guilty of rebellion in refusing to perceive) that the throne of Rome, the spiritual throne, was not really destined, and could not lawfully be given, to the head of the political Empire. In making Julius and Augustus into gods, in annexing the spiritual headship to the political, the poet did the very same wrong which was done reversely by those of the Popes who strove to annex the political supremacy to the spiritual—the error and crime against which the whole *Divina Commedia* is designed to protest. But it was none the less true that Virgil, by the will and providence of the Almighty, powerfully aided to build the throne. For this reason chiefly he holds his place in the story and symbolism of Dante; and for this reason Dante thought fit to introduce him with the statement that he "was born *sub Julio*"—Italian could not give the point—"*sub Julio* (though *Julius* was belated), and lived at Rome under the good Augustus, at the time of the false and lying gods."

# THE ALTAR OF MERCY

WHEN Gibbon, preparing the foundations of his history[1], distributed the views of religion which prevailed in the Roman Empire before it was invaded by Christianity, under the triple division of the magistrates, the philosophers, and the people— defined respectively as those to whom all religions were equally useful, equally false, and equally true— how did it not occur to him that his enumeration was singularly defective ? He repeats his epigram in various forms again and again, and bases his whole account of the conditions with which the invading doctrines had to deal, upon the assumption that the action of the State, the speculations of theorists, and the practices of the populace, include between them all those aspects of religion with which the historian is concerned. It is not surprising that the outcome of this procedure is to represent the evolution of the Graeco-Roman world into its Christian shape as a sort of cataclysmic puzzle. A rival epigrammatist might say, with at least equal truth, that the historian's catalogue of

---

[1] Chapter II.

mankind omits just all the "people" whose feelings
are most important.   And similarly, in the neatly
numbered list of causes by which the enigmatic
phenomenon is to be explained[1], we note that the
preparations and approaches upon the pagan side
count apparently for little or nothing.   It hardly
seems to be thought worth mentioning that, in
various ways, that vast and influential part of
society which is neither official, nor scientific, nor
superstitious, had been long in training, when the
new preachers came, to receive just such a gift
as they brought.

   This exaggerated sharpness of division between
Christians and Pagans is characteristic of historical
study in the times which follow the rupture of the
Catholic world in the seventeenth century; and it
attained its height in the eighteenth.   The tendency
is not confined to the sceptical side.   Johnson, who
roundly asserts that Horace, when he says—

> parcus deorum cultor et infrequens
> insanientis dum sapientiae
>    consultus erro, nunc retrorsum
>       vela dare atque iterare cursus
> cogor relictos :

is merely playing with the idea of an awakened
conscience, was as little disposed as Gibbon, his
adversary in the Literary Club, to recognize that
between "religion" and "the classics" there could
be any material connexion or affinity.   It is strange
to go back five centuries, to an age of comparative

[1] Chapter xv.

ignorance, and to see how the students of the thirteenth century, with their scanty apparatus and defective method, could nevertheless read the records of the transition to Christianity in a reasonable way, simply because it had not occurred to them that the cause of Catholicism could be either fortified or impeached by misrepresenting the manner of its growth, or by arbitrarily severing it from some of its natural and necessary antecedents. When Dante says that the poet Statius, by his studies in Virgil, had been led so far towards the coming revelation that he promptly recognized its truth, and was actually initiated by baptism into the religion which he had not the courage openly to profess, Dante asserts, no doubt, much more than is likely to be true, and his proofs (which in their general outline are not beyond the reach of a fair guess) would have been rejected, and rightly, by a better critic of documents. But he has the root of the matter. He sees what to any simple and unprejudiced mind is obvious, that the *Thebaid* of Statius is a document of the first importance to the history of European religion. It does not, indeed, represent any of Gibbon's categories: it is neither political thought, nor philosophic, nor popular. But it stands for something not less significant, as a prognostic of development, than any of these—the vague aspirations of classes disposed to think, but not disposed, or indeed able, to think with rigour. To represent such aspirations is necessarily the chief business of poetry which asks to be taken seriously and to achieve a permanent place.

In a picture of the society into which Christianity came, to leave out the *Thebaid*, or not to put the *Thebaid* well in the foreground, would be like describing the England of the eighteenth century without notice of the *Essay on Man*, or the England of the nineteenth without *In Memoriam*.

Every age has its own way of error, and we, no doubt, ours. But our way is not the Voltairian. If we do not read our *Aeneid* exactly as Dante read it, we are at least aware that, when Dante described the visions of Virgil as a main contribution to the establishment of Catholicism, when he wrote that the journey of Aeneas to Hades was "the occasion of the Papal mantle," he stated a fact, and a fact of vital significance. How we read the *Thebaid*, it were perhaps best not to inquire. One cannot read everything; and it would appear that, in the whole repertory of important European literature, no part just now lies more in the shade than the "minor" Latin epics. The *Thebaid*, indeed, does not deserve that epithet in any sense worth notice. But at present it goes with the rest; and for this reason a reminiscence, even of its main aspects, may have freshness enough to hold attention for a few minutes. If it should even convey the impression, that to read the poem continuously from beginning to end is a thing not impossible or unprofitable or unpleasant, that is no more than may be very fairly affirmed.

The immediate purpose of the poem—a purpose which it completely achieved—was to satisfy the taste of fashionable audiences at Rome during that precise period, the latter part of our first century, when the stir of the Christian movement began to be felt there. It is in form a descriptive romance, and doubtless depended upon its romantic qualities for a first hearing. But the author aspired to more than this, and believed, before his work was complete, that he might modestly expect more. In the brief epilogue, which records his ambition and forecasts the future of his enterprise, he desires for his poem a place upon the same line, at however humble a distance, as the *Aeneid* itself. To rival that "sacred" book the *Thebaid* will not pretend; but it does pretend to be of the same kind, and to have a post in the sacred procession. And in partial confirmation of this claim, the author adds that not only has his work obtained the notice of Caesar, but—what he justly estimates as more significant for his pretension—it has already made its way, like the *Aeneid* itself, into the schools: already, he says, it is an instrument of education. No mere romancer, no mere story-teller, could have ventured to use such language. We cannot conceive the *Lay of the Last Minstrel*—a poem which presents, as a romance, some actual resemblance in type and method to the work of Statius—we cannot conceive even the *Idylls of the King*, put forward by Scott or by Tennyson as following, however distantly and respectfully, in the wake and track of *Paradise Lost*. They have not the "sacred" character. This character Statius attributes of

course, as any one of that age would do, to the
*Aeneid*; and for the *Thebaid* he claims that it is
in kind the same or similar; the *Thebaid* also (to
translate his phrases into our language) is, he thinks,
or may be, in some sort a gospel.

It would have been strange if he had thought
otherwise. The *Thebaid* attempts not only to
latinize, but also to expand and deepen into larger
significance, a story which for several centuries had
held a chief place in the religious symbolism of that
Hellenic or Hellenistic world to which Statius by
birth belonged.

This story, which here we need not tell, descends
originally from a source not now open to investigation, the "Theban cycle,"—that portion of the
ancient poetry passing under the name of Homer,
which had Thebes for its centre of interest, as
another portion, the "Trojan cycle," revolved about
Troy. Whatever may have been the artistic merits
of the Theban cycle—we have no reason to suppose
them small—its moral interest seems to have been
great from the first, superior probably to that of
the Trojan. In that chapter of the epic narrative
which forms the substructure of the *Thebaid*, the
subject was the doom of unlawful war, the defeat
and condign punishment of a wicked confederacy,
resolved, in despite of warning, to prosecute an un-
holy quarrel. In the earliest version which we now
possess, the *Seven Against Thebes* of Aeschylus, the
ethical and humane sentiment is already powerful,
much more so than in the *Iliad* or even in the

*Odyssey*; nor does it seem likely that this element is entirely assignable to the Athenian dramatist.

But into these early developments we need not enter, because in the fifth century B.C., and in the latter part of it, later (that is to say) than Aeschylus, a totally new colour was given to the story by the establishment, if not the first invention, of a sequel, devised in honour of Athens, and representing the spirit of that new humanism of which Athens became the accepted centre and guardian.

In the original version, the wicked and defeated warriors incurred, as part of their natural punishment, the refusal of funeral rites. The poets of the cycle, like the poet of the *Iliad*, doubtless accepted this as an incident horrible indeed, but proper to war. But according to the new version, Athens, as the champion of humanity, refused to permit such an outrage, and enforced the common right of the race by forcibly rescuing the corpses from the insolent victors, and committing them solemnly to religious sepulture. The adoption of this supplement (whenever first propounded) as an article of Athenian religion can be dated with near precision. There is no trace of it in the *Seven Against Thebes*, which indeed would seem rather to exclude it. But about fifty years later it appears complete in the *Suppliants* of Euripides. In this play and in the *Children of Heracles*, by the same author, where Athens plays a somewhat similar part as the vindicator of the oppressed and a respecter even of the enemy, we see for the first time clearly the conception of Hellas, and of Athens in particular, as the guardian and champion of humanity. Then for the first time it became distinctly visible, at least to an enthusiastic few, that the human world can be imagined, and might possibly be realized in fact, as something other than the sum of many hostile and internecine clans, more or less efficiently organized for mutual destruction.

Upon the importance of this idea or sentiment, and the part which it played in the history of the Mediterranean peoples up to and including the formation of a Mediterranean state under the protection of the Caesars, we need not insist. The *Thebaid* is entirely occupied with it. The whole story, as conceived by the author, is a preparation for the final interference of Athens, an ideal Athens, which figures symbolically as the sacred city of humanism and humanity.

And now let us see precisely in what terms the essence of this Hellenistic religion is described, for the edification of " Italian youth," by Statius, a son (be it remembered) not of Italy, but of the Hellenic city of Naples.

To invoke the interference of a defender on behalf of the dead, in whom humanity is outraged, the widows of the slain repair to Athens. There, and there only as yet (we are told), the conception of Godhead had been partly dissociated from that of mere superhuman power. There and there only was to be found, among the temples consecrated to force, one place reserved for compassion.

"In the midst of the city was an Altar, pertaining not to Might nor the powers thereof, but to gentle Mercy. Mercy there had fixed her seat, and misery made it holy. Thither new suppliants came ever without fail, and found acceptance all.

"There to ask is to be heard, and dark or light, all hours give access unto One whose grace costs nothing but a complaint.

"The ritual takes no tax, accepts no incense-flame, no drench of blood, but only the dew of tears upon the stone, and the shorn hair of the mourner for a wreath above, and for drapery the cast robe which sorrow puts away.

"With trees of kindness the ground is planted about, and marked for pardon and peace with the fillet-bounden bay and the olive's suppliant bough.

"Image there is not any: to no mould of metal is trusted that Form Divine, who loves to dwell in minds and in hearts.

"Nor lacketh there perpetual assembly. For shaking fear and shivering poverty, these know that Altar well, and only happiness knoweth it not.

"The legend is, that it was the children of Hercules who founded the sanctuary, in the city whose warriors protected them when their sire had passed from the pyre to the sky.

"So the tale sayeth, but sayeth not worthily. Rather we should believe that it was those Visitants from Heaven whom Athens had ever made welcome to her soil, the same who there, in Athens, created law and the new man and the better way, they who thither brought the seed which thence descended upon the waste places of the earth—these (we will say) did in Athens likewise set apart a place of common refuge for souls that are sick, a sanctuary closed against wrath and threatening and tyrant strength, and which prosperity should not profane.

" Even in those old days that spot was known to the wide world. Thither the conquered came, and the exile, fallen power and wandering guilt. There did they meet, and prayed their peace.

" The time was near, when the grace of that hospice should vanquish even the fiends of an Oedipus, should cover the corpse of Olynthus, and take even from an Orestes the torture of his mother's ghost[1]."

Prose does of course no justice to the fine melody of the Latin ; nor is it possible for English words to convey exactly the native flavour.   But the sense of this admirable passage (if we have caught it) will sufficiently show why we should not be too impatient with the scholars of the thirteenth century, or too ready to insist on our superiority in historical and philological science, when we find Dante searching for proofs that the Roman who was expounding this religion to the society of Rome, within a few years after " the prisoner of Christ Jesus " was brought in by the Appian Way, had actually been in touch

---

[1] Statius, *Thebais*, XII 481. The legend of Olynthus (?) is apparently unknown. It probably belonged to the same Areopagitic circle as those of Oedipus and Orestes, and symbolized the same doctrine of forgiveness.

with "the new preachers," and had welcomed their message as the very word for which he was waiting. Such an error is nothing beside that of enumerating a laboured list of causes why the Christian doctrine should have rapidly made its way in the Graeco-Roman world, and omitting to specify, for one cause and the chief, that this world, so far as it had comprehended and embraced the Hellenistic culture, was more than half Christian already.

It was not on this passage in particular that Dante rested his conviction that Statius was an actual convert; for he dates the baptism of the poet by an earlier part of the *Thebaid*[1], and before Book XII was presumably written. But doubtless this description, the cardinal point of the whole poem, weighed with Dante, or with the authors of his theory, as general evidence towards their conclusion. And well it might. A Christian reader need not be either ignorant or prejudiced, to feel a shock of surprise or curiosity upon reading, in a contemporary of St Paul, and in what is manifestly intended for a declaration against paganism (as it was commonly held and understood), the allusions of Statius to the "new man" and the "seed descending upon the waste places of the earth." From the whole tone and method of Dante's comments upon the Latin poets, especially upon Virgil and Statius, we must infer that he would have cited these expressions as consciously

[1] See the Essay on *Dante and the Baptism of Statius*, above, p. 181.

Christian, as betraying that secret acquaintance with the Christian mysteries which he attributes to the author of the *Thebaid*—outwardly a courtier of Domitian, but inwardly an adherent of the Apostles. It would, of course, be unpardonable, with our present lights, to repeat this error and exaggeration. The Athenian, or rather perhaps Eleusinian, symbols to which Statius does really allude, the legendary restoration of the human race and the mystic sign of the corn-seed, were far older than Christianity, and by no means identical with the Christian signs or doctrines which they superficially resemble ; though, on the other hand, a historian who should deny all connexion between the two systems, would be going beyond proof and indeed beyond likelihood.

But upon dubious resemblances or solitary phrases there is no need to insist. What is solid and evident, what leaps to the eye, is the sentiment of the whole passage, the spirit, the general conception of religion, from which it proceeds. For this there is only one suitable word. It is exactly that sentiment to which Christianity appealed. To console the miserable and the guilty, to heal the wounds of the world and the sense of sin—these are the offices of that Altar to which Statius directs the worship of mankind. "I will have mercy and not sacrifice"; "Come unto Me, all ye that labour and are heavy-laden ";—for such inscriptions, and for such only, the shrine of his imagination is prepared.

Imaginary, visionary, an ideal rather than a fact, we must evidently consider it, although it had an historical counterpart and actual existence. There were in Athens altars to more than one " Deity " or spiritual abstraction, answering more or less to the "Clementia" of Statius—an altar of " Eleos," an altar of "Aidos." They are catalogued, as Athenian curiosities, by the antiquarian impartiality of the traveller Pausanias, whose description of Hellas dates from our second century ; and we hear of them otherwise. But it is not in the spirit of a Pausanias that Statius commemorates them. The Athens of his religion is a spiritual Athens, the imperfect symbol of that Hellenism by which he lived. The "Altar of Mercy" is not for him an object in a museum, an item in a collection of miscellaneous antiquities. He scarcely cares to place it : it was "in the midst of the city." For the venerable legend associated with it, the story of Hercules and his children, he has nothing but scorn. The Altar of his thought was *not* founded by the children of Hercules, nor in fact by any earthly hand. Like other such emblems of aspiration, it was "never built at all, and therefore built for ever."

And in the thought of the poet it stands alone. We cannot miss, nor misunderstand, the sweeping depreciation by which, in comparison with this Deity of the soul, and with the uncostly sacrifice of a broken heart, the whole art and ritual of polytheistic superstition are waved away. Such ornaments and offerings are for the patrons of power; and to these let those bring them who will. Nor can it be fairly said that there is anything in the *Thebaid* that cannot, with reasonable allowance for the use of conventional literary forms, be reconciled to the position here finally taken up. The Apollo, the Juno, and the Minerva of Statius are no more real than those of Christian poets, of Dante himself for example. We can no more reason from the use of such machinery to the opinion of the writer, than we could infer the theological convictions of Scott from the spirits which discourse upon the progress of the story in the *Lay of the Last Minstrel*. In this respect the *Thebaid* differs greatly from the *Aeneid*, where, to the advantage doubtless of the story as a picture for the fancy, but to the detriment or confusion of the significance, the traditional figures of the Olympian gods have pretensions to reality which in Statius they have lost. This difference among others was noted, we may presume, by Dante, who had his own practice and feelings, as a poet both Christian and classical, to guide him in such observations. He would naturally reckon it in favour of the opinions and theology of Statius, and attribute it to the advance, or rather the approach, of the true religion.

But in fact we may suspect that this difference between Statius and Virgil is due not so much to time as to place. It is a difference in origin and native culture. The *Thebaid* has nothing Roman

about it, or almost nothing, except the language.
Even the Latin has marked Hellenic features, and
the substance is pure Hellenism. Allusions to Italy
and things Italian, which might have been easily
introduced, had such been the purpose, are almost
entirely absent, and when they occur, are made
as a Greek might have made them. Nothing else
could be expected from a Neapolitan, from a writer
so conscious of the difference between the Hellenic
and the non-Hellenic elements in the civilization
of the Empire, that when he reviews the epics of
Rome in search of a compliment to the memory
of Lucan, he can remark that, "as a poem for
Latins" (*Latinis canens*), the *Pharsalia* might
claim a preference even to the *Aeneid*. The
work of Virgil would have been reckoned by the
Neapolitan, not to its disadvantage, as largely
Greek. Naples, described as a city still fully
Greek in the time of Augustus, retaining the Greek
constitution of society, Greek life, festivals, and culture, had presumably lost little or nothing of this
character in the brief interval which brings us to
Statius. Rather the marked patronage extended
to its festivals by succeeding emperors, and the
conspicuous imitation of them by Domitian, the
prince under whom Statius passed the time of his
maturity and production, would strengthen the
conscious pride of the Neapolitan in representing
the chief centre of Greek learning and civilization
within the bounds of Italy. It is worth noticing,
that Naples claimed to have received a colony from

Athens herself—the more worth noticing, because the historic fact is perhaps something more than doubtful. When we see what part is played by Athens, a somewhat imaginary and idealized Athens, in the *Thebaid*, we may suspect that, in the view of Statius, his pretension to an Athenian affiliation was at least as valuable as that Roman citizenship which the Neapolitans, though faithful "allies" of Rome, accepted late and with regret. The natural religion of such a person was the religion of Euripides, matured and enlarged,—Hellenistic humanism in its latest stage of rational refinement and cosmopolitan scope.

The part belonging to this type of sentiment and imagination, among the influences preparatory to the adoption of Christianity as the religion of the Empire, might doubtless be overrated, but may be underrated more easily. It is certainly not from the actual leaders of the Christian movement, that we shall learn to depreciate the importance of its relation to that species of thought whose ideal centre was the Areopagus of Athens. "Whom therefore ye ignorantly worship, Him declare I unto you." It does not belong here to consider the precise position in history which should be assigned to the *Acts of the Apostles*. But manifestly the author of that book, and those by whom it was invested with authority, did not desire to overlook or to minimise any advantage which the new religion might obtain from its claim to embrace, absorb, and satisfy that gentle doctrine of humanity which had radiated, or was at least supposed by the world to have radiated, from Mars' Hill. "Ye men of Athens, I perceive that in all things ye are exceedingly God-fearing." To an exhaustive commentary upon these words, and upon the discourse which follows them, no small contribution should be furnished by the *Thebaid*.

As we have had occasion to express the approval which, when all reserves are made, is due to the historical appreciation of Statius and his position by the scholarship of the thirteenth century as represented in Dante, we ought not perhaps to leave unnoticed the strange and somewhat disconcerting perversion by which Dante, as commonly and naturally interpreted, attributes the origin of Statius, not to Naples, but to Toulouse—

" So sweet was the breath of my voice, that I, a citizen of Tolosa, was drawn by Rome unto herself[1]."

It would no doubt be possible, without absurdity, to suppose that Statius, like Lucan, came from the far west; nor did Dante apparently possess the direct evidence which we now have to the actual fact. But even upon the documents which were certainly before him, and in view of what he himself infers and propounds, it is somewhat surprising that he should have accepted the supposed datum, and still more so that he should have thought it worthy of mention. However, it is enough here to note his error, which in any case is of little importance.

[1] *Purgatorio*, XXI 88: "che, Tolosano, Roma a se mi trasse.'

# ARISTOPHANES ON TENNYSON

THE Muse of Comedy and the Muse—if there be one—of Criticism are not sisters; they are "scarce cater-cousins." The business of Comedy is to plant a jest and get a laugh—with or without sense, reason, and justice; it is not for her to inquire. When Aristophanes, shy perhaps of politics in the delicacy of the political situation, took for his *Frogs* a subject purely literary, and faced the risk of inviting a popular audience to spend some hours upon a comparison between the fashionable tragedy of the day, as represented by the recently deceased Euripides, and that which had been admired, by command of Aeschylus two generations before, little can he have dreamed of the gravity with which some of his impudent tricks would be canvassed by the erudition of future ages. It may be worth while to illustrate the true value of one trick,—his very best, if estimated for the purpose of the comic stage,—by applying it to a poet and poetry not yet ancient enough to be, like Euripides, half-buried in misunderstanding.

Among the formal innovations of Euripides, one of the most conspicuous was that of opening the play with a compendious narrative of the antecedent facts or suppositions defining the situation, or at all events that view of the situation from which the action starts. For this practice there was good reason in the peculiar attitude of Euripides towards the subject-matter of Athenian tragedy; and Aristophanes, to do him justice, says nothing to the contrary. But of course there is in such openings a similarity of form and style, a certain dryness or simplicity of manner, which does not belong to openings directly dramatic. There are not many possible manners, or rather there is but one, of telling a story rapidly and yet completely in verse. Moreover, from the nature of the case, there is a tendency (which, as we are going to see, is almost irresistible) *to start with a statement about some personage in the story, so that the grammatical subject or nominative case of the first sentence will be a proper name.* "Samson, the mighty man, Manoah's son...," or "The shepherd David, summoned from the flock...," are obvious ways of beginning a summary account of those heroes.

Now, as a matter of fact, Euripides in his prologues avoided this ready and quite proper form of commencement with much more care than (as we shall see) could be expected or reasonably asked. But he used it sometimes. And Aristophanes perceived that, by collecting these cases, he could get the material for a good theatrical joke. He could pretend to show, in a dramatic manner, that Euripides knew but one type of sentence for a beginning. For, whenever this type occurs, you can of course surprise the audience by an interruption and a nonsensical finish. "Samson, the mighty man, Manoah's son—...Walked up a hill, and then walked down again." "The shepherd David, summoned from the flock—...Walked up a hill, and then walked down again." And since every kind of verse has, by necessity, certain habitual places of punctuation, it will often happen that, as in these instances, the same nonsensical finish will find a possible point of attachment. From a habit of the tragic metre in Greek, it chanced that the middle of the verse was the most convenient point for attaching a tag; what point you take matters nothing, provided it is always the same. Accordingly Aristophanes, having got together, out of some three-score Euripidean plays, half-a-dozen legitimate instances (and one not legitimate[1]) of opening sentences similar in this respect, that all have a personal subject and proper name, and all are punctuated at the same point, compels his pretended Euripides to quote these selected cases as typical, and assigns to his pretended Aeschylus, in the character of a critic, the part of interrupting Euripides each time at the proper point, and completing the sentence with the same nonsensical end. As a stage-trick, nothing could be better; and how

---

[1] *Frogs*, 1219. "Euripides" (see the context) cites this as an instance to the contrary; and so it is, though the tag can be botched on somehow. The only legitimate example among the nineteen extant plays (*Iphigenia in Taurica*) is cited.

effective it is, an Englishman will more promptly perceive, if we apply it to poetry and themes for which we have a natural, and not merely a cultivated affection. But as criticism, were it so meant, it would be futile, as by the same application we shall most easily show and understand.

It happens that the greatest master of narrative verse among modern English poets has really done what Aristophanes attributes to Euripides—falsely, as he well knew, and idly, had the charge been true. Tennyson, in the *Idylls of the King*, does really, and quite properly, prefer to open his stories, more than half of them, in the way which Euripides used very seldom, though often enough for the purpose of the comedian. The style of Aristophanes is not to be had at command; but any one may exhibit his impertinence.

For this purpose Tennyson shall be put, as any son of man may, whatever his dignity and glory, in the place of Euripides.

In the place of Aeschylus, the "Aeschylus" of Aristophanes, we will most certainly not put any English poet or person of credit. "Aeschylus" is a malicious fool, for whom we will borrow the name of "Gigadibs, the literary man,"—with apologies to Browning, and indeed to Gigadibs. And thirdly, to complete a parallel with the scene in the *Frogs*, we require in addition to the poet and the critic, contenders in the literary debate, a by-stander, as spectator and umpire. In Aristophanes this part is played by a sort of average Athenian ass, upon whom, as representing the patrons of the drama, is conferred the title of the "god" Dionysus, in his character as proprietor of the public theatre. We have no "Dionysus" in England, but the "Philistine" of Matthew Arnold will be good enough. These three, then, shall be the interlocutors of our comedian,—a "Tennyson," such as he chooses to manufacture, a "Gigadibs," *ditto*, and a "Philistine," such as he is:

> *Gigadibs (to the Philistine).* I say, sir, and
> repeat,—this Tennyson
> Was uninventive, dull, a mere machine
> For turning verse, and I will prove the same.
> *Philistine.* Oh come, I say!
> *Gig.* Look at his *Idylls*, then!
> *Tennyson.* Yes, look, and show them faulty, if
> you dare!
> *Gig.* I'll wipe out all your *Idylls of the King*,
> All, with a single pocket-handkerchief.
> *Tenn.* A handkerchief!
> *Gig.* A handkerchief, a towel,
> A napkin, rag, or anything that wipes.
> All's one. So poor you are in artifice,
> So stiff, mechanical, and monotonous,
> That one may fit the self-same piece of stuff
> To all your patterns.
> *Tenn.* What on earth do you mean?
> *Gig.* Just what I say. You can't begin a tale
> In any way but one. Your opening lines
> Invariably admit, invite, suggest

The same pathetic end and supplement,—
A cold in the head and pocket-handkerchief,
Proper to those afflicted with catarrh.
 *Tenn.* Nonsense! How dare you!
 *Gig.*       Very well, begin.
Begin, and I will tag you every time
With just the same conclusion, every time
Same ailment and same simple remedy,
A cold in the head, *et caetera.* Come, begin :
Quote me an Idyll, any one you please,
The opening lines.
 *Tenn.*    But really...
 *Phil.*        Pray, my lord,
If only to expose his impudence,
Oblige the gentleman.
 *Tenn.*    Oh, certainly.
Which Idyll?
 *Gig.*  Any.
 *Phil.*    "Gareth and Lynette."
 *Tenn.* (*reciting pompously*). "The last tall son
  of Lot and Bellicent,
And tallest, Gareth, in a showerful spring"——
 *Gig.* Had a bad cold, and blew his little nose.
 *Phil.* Eh?
 *Tenn.*   What? What's that?
 *Phil.*     Surprising! Had a cold?
How did he get it?
 *Gig.*    "In a showerful spring";
The poet says so. Gareth, I presume,
Walked in the rain, forgot to change his clothes,
And hence the sequel. Anyhow, the tag

Fits, as I promised.

*Tenn.*                    Pooh! An accident!
You will not do it twice.

*Phil.*                    No, that he won't;
Impossible.

*Gig.* (*to Tennyson*).   Then try me. Start again.

*Tenn.* (*beginning* "*The Last Tournament*").
 "Dagonet, the fool, whom Gawain in his
  mood
Had made mock-knight of Arthur's Table Round,
At Camelot, high above the yellowing woods,"——

*Gig.*   Had a bad cold, and blew his little nose.

*Phil.*  Goodness! I never! There it comes
  again.

*Gig.*  And very aptly.   Note the time and
  place:
"At Camelot, high above the yellowing woods,"
The autumn season, damp and treacherous,
The unsheltered situation of the town,
And carelessness of "Dagonet the fool."

*Phil.*  Hm! Rather odd!—I fear, Lord
  Tennyson,
This is another accident.

*Tenn.*                    Oh, bosh!
Listen to this, and own yourself an ass.

 (*begins* "*The Coming of Arthur*") "Leodogran,
  the King of Cameliard,
Had"——

*Gig.*   A bad cold, and blew his little nose.

*Phil.*  Why, this is worse and worse! The
  handkerchief

Pops out already in the second line.

*Gig.* Yes, 'twas a chilly climate, as we hear
Later : "the land of Cameliard was waste,
Thick with wet woods "—a most unhealthy spot.
And pray observe, the poet gives me "had":
Leodogran, according to the bard,
Had something. Well, I say he had a cold.

*Tenn.* Blasphemer!

*Phil.* Come, come, Tennyson, be calm.
The case is getting grave. Three accidents!
Three Idylls tainted with this monstrous cold!
There must be one that will not let it in;
At him again, and make a better choice.

*Tenn.* (*beginning* "*The Grail*"). "From noiseful
 arms, and acts of prowess done
In tournament or tilt, Sir Percivale "——

*Gig.* Had a bad cold...

*Phil.* Poor Percivale!

*Gig.* It came
From getting hot in tournaments and tilts.

*Tenn.* Nonsense!

*Phil.* Why so?

*Tenn.* Shut up! I will be heard ;
It all comes right directly.

*Gig.* Go ahead.

*Tenn.* (*recites*). "...In tournament or tilt, Sir
 Percivale,
Whom Arthur and his knighthood called The
 Pure,"——

*Gig.* Had a bad cold...

*Tenn.* No, no! (*shouting*) "Sir Percivale,

16—2

Whom Arthur and his knighthood called The Pure,
Had "——

 *Gig.*  A bad cold, and blew his little nose.
I knew it!

 *Tenn.* (*roaring*). But I say...

 *Phil.*       No, Alfred, no,
It will not do; Sir Percivale is doomed.
Give us "Geraint and Enid." They perhaps
May escape this influenza, though—I fear.

 *Tenn.* (*begins "Geraint and Enid"*). "The brave
  Geraint, a knight of Arthur's court,"——

 *Gig.* Had a bad——

 *Phil.*     Yes, alas! But let it pass.
We must not be too cruel, too severe.
Even in the fatal air of Camelot
It must, I think, have happened, now and then,
That people ran a risk of...you know what,
But somehow did not have it after all.
Geraint shall get the benefit of the doubt.

 *Gig.* Just as you like.

 *Phil.* (*to Tennyson*).  Go on, and let us hear.

 *Tenn.* "The brave Geraint, a knight of Arthur's
  court,
A tributary prince of Devon, one
Of that great Order of the Table Round,
Had "——

 *Gig.* A bad cold.

 *Phil.*     Oh dear!

 *Gig.*        Of course he did,
And blew his little nose. I told you so!

 *Phil.* This is too awful. Really, Tennyson,

We had better give it up.

*Tenn.* Give up! Not I!
Listen to this, and tag it if you can.
(*begins* "*Elaine*"). " Elaine "——

*Phil.* I'm certain she will have a cold.

*Tenn.* (*reciting*). " Elaine the fair, Elaine
the "——

*Phil.* Oh, beware!
Now comes the dangerous point. Take care of her.

*Tenn.* (*reciting with hesitation*). " Elaine the
fair,...Elaine...the loveable,"——

*Gig.* Had a bad cold. That's one!

*Phil.* It is, it is.

*Tenn.* Silence! I'll gag you if you interrupt.
(*beginning again, and reciting faster*). " Elaine
the fair, Elaine the loveable,
Elaine, the lily maid of Astolat,"——

*Gig.* Had a bad cold. That's two!

*Phil.* It is, it is.

*Tenn.* (*reciting at a furious pace*). " Elaine the
fair, Elaine the loveable,
Elaine, the lily maid of Astolat,
High in her chamber up a tower to the east "——

*Gig.* Had a bad cold, and blew her little nose.

*Phil.* She did, she did, she did! Three colds
she had,
At every verse a cold. Poor lily maid!

*Gig.* And well she might have in that windy
flat.

*Phil.* " High in her chamber up a tower to the
east."

*Tenn. (changing desperately to another Idyll).*
"Queen Guinevere had"——
   *Phil.*                No, my lord, no more.
We will not ask the fate of Guinevere;
She had a cold, and there's an end of it;
She had a cold, she caught it from Elaine;
Your Idylls reek with it.   And since the thing's
Infectious, and the air is getting thick,
We had best perhaps go home—and take quinine.

# THE PROSE OF WALTER SCOTT

WHEN Byron and Scott were approaching, one of them the end of his life, and the other of his prosperity, they exchanged in a monumental correspondence the princely compliments of literary diplomacy; and Byron, who, though he had then disclaimed the quarrel of "English Bards" with "Scotch Reviewers," was engaged more deeply than ever in defending the Augustan manner of Pope against the fashions which he himself had helped Scott and others to introduce,—Byron, than whom few men have been more independent of fashion and of flattery, affirmed that he found no one of whose superiority Sir Walter could reasonably be jealous, either among the living or, all things considered, among the dead. It is certain, from the principles and practice of Byron as a critic, that in this judgement he regarded form as well as substance, technical merit not less, perhaps even more, than abundance of imagination and invention; certain also, that it was upon the prose of the romances that he built his judgement, rather than upon the metrical merit, already questionable, of *Marmion* and *The Lady of the Lake*. And after the lapse of a century, when there is no more any question of living and dead, and the measure of Scott is to be taken solely by the standard of what is common to good work universally, the opinion of Byron may still stand as defensible. It is true that Scott's works show the mark of his rapidity, and that in average pieces of narrative he is not fastidious in expression or always correct. It has been said, and may perhaps be said with as much truth as is demanded from an epigram, that in average pieces of his prose "he has no style at all." But it is also true that in the great moments to which those rapid sketches are subsidiary, in the pinnacles for which the scaffolding is somewhat hazardously piled up, he displays not only a touch of hand peculiar to himself, but also perfect command of sound construction, a sure hold upon those principles of speech—call them rules, practices, or what you will—which come from the deepest parts of humanity, and are common to all that succeed in this kind. A mind not sensible to the effects of Scott, when he intends effect, would have to seek satisfaction somewhere else than in literature as it has been practised by all Europe (to take the narrowest limit) from Homer to this day. And it is to be added that even the unpretentious freedom of his ordinary manner has a value in its place by way of relief and contrast.

A signal instance of both qualities may be found in the scene which lays the corner-stone of *Guy Mannering*—the denunciation of the landowner and magistrate, Bertram of Ellangowan, by the gipsy witch,, Meg Merrilies. The little band to which she belongs, after having been protected and encouraged for many generations in a precarious settlement upon Bertram's estate, have now been expelled, in a capricious fit of reform, by the summary process of pulling down their miserable tenements. The author of this improvement, little content with his severity, absents himself on the day of execution; but as he rides home, he meets the emigrant families in painful procession upon the confines of his property. To the sufferers his act naturally appears tyrannous, a provocation of the higher powers of providential justice; nor is it beyond common reckoning to divine that, in a country and among a population not very orderly, the defiance of such enemies may lead to disaster. Of such feelings and prognostications, raised to the tone of prophecy by the ambiguous pretensions of a witch-wife, Meg Merrilies makes herself the voice. The sequel of the story turns, as will be remembered, upon the fulfilment of her prophecy, to which, in the natural course of things, she contributes a great and, in the end, a dominant influence. The conception of her character is the key to the whole design; and here, in the scene of the prophecy, is the leading note upon which the whole depends.

The chapter (VIII) containing it will throughout repay study; but for our present purpose we may begin with the two paragraphs which immediately precede the denunciation itself. The first gives the psychology of the situation, describing, without

affectation of subtlety, the uncomfortable feelings of
the magistrate, who has just undergone, from the
passing caravan, the novel experience of resentment
and hatred.

"His sensations were bitter enough. The race, it is true,
which he had thus summarily dismissed from their ancient place
of refuge, was idle and vicious; but had he endeavoured to render
them otherwise? They were not more irregular characters now
than they had been while they were admitted to consider themselves as a sort of subordinate dependents of his family....Some
means of reformation ought at least to have been tried before
sending seven families at once upon the wide world, and depriving
them of a degree of countenance which withheld them at least
from atrocious guilt. There was also a natural yearning of heart
on parting with so many known and familiar faces; and to this
feeling Godfrey Bertram was peculiarly accessible, from the limited
qualities of his mind, which sought its principal amusements
among the petty objects around him. As he was about to turn
his horse's head to pursue his journey, Meg Merrilies, who had
lagged behind the troop, unexpectedly presented herself."

Manifestly we have here no research of style,
"no style at all" in the sense which the word
"style" has for the critic or the conscious artist.
In vocabulary, phrasing, the cast and turn of
sentences, there is as little character and stamp as
the individuality of authorship may well admit. If
anything is to be praised, it is a certain plain gravity,
proceeding partly from this very absence of pose.
And there are negligences which are almost faults.
" *To render them otherwise...* ; *depriving them of a
degree of countenance...* ; *from the limited qualities
of his mind...* ; *to turn his horse's head to pursue
his journey...*"; these and other phrases might be

improved, and would not have satisfied a punctilious composer. But on the other hand, there is no hitch, nothing to stumble at, and we are put without strain in full possession of the meaning.

The next paragraph is much more important and characteristic, and, as a composition, is both better and worse. It contains what for Scott, in such a situation as this, was essentially significant— the stage-directions, so to speak, for setting the group and scene in preparation for the coming effect. Stage-directions we may well call them, for it is actually to the theatre that the author has gone, as he often did, for inspiration; and later, at the crowning moment of the scene, he refers us to the source from which he has drawn: "Margaret of Anjou" (he says), "bestowing on her triumphant foes her keen-edged malediction, could not have turned from them with a gesture more proudly contemptuous." From the mind of Scott Shakespeare was never far; and with *Henry the Sixth*, especially the final scenes, the figure of Meg Merrilies is more than once associated[1]. The particular passage to which he directs us we will presently quote, for it is even more pertinent than his words imply. But for the moment we note only, as a fact, his theatrical prepossession, and now present in this light what we are justified in calling his stage-directions:

"She was standing upon one of those high precipitous banks which, as we before noticed, overhung the road; so that she was

[1] See the motto to chapter LIV.

placed considerably higher than Ellangowan, even though he was
on horseback; and her tall figure, relieved against the clear blue
sky, seemed almost of supernatural stature. We have noticed
that there was in her general attire, or rather in her mode of
adjusting it, somewhat of a foreign costume, artfully adopted
perhaps for the purpose of adding to the effect of her spells and
predictions, or perhaps from some traditional notions respecting
the dress of her ancestors. On this occasion she had a large
piece of red cotton cloth rolled about her head in the form of a
turban, from beneath which her dark eyes flashed with uncommon
lustre. Her long and tangled black hair fell in elf-locks from the
folds of this singular head-gear. Her attitude was that of a sibyl
in frenzy, and she stretched out in her right hand a sapling bough,
which seemed just pulled."

Considering this from a practical point of view,
as a catalogue of points which the reader is to focus
as a preparation of the eye for the delivery of the
tirade that follows, we may pronounce it beyond
improvement. Nothing is neglected or slurred;
posture and colours, properties and accessories,
suggestions, duly vague, of history or literature, all
is prescribed : the least lively imagination must be
ready to work on such terms, and the *tableau* could
be set, one almost fancies that it could be painted,
by an amateur. But for style—the conscious stylist
might say again that there is none. The whole
method is the very negation of art, in so far as art
is said to lie in the concealment of the mechanical
process. Stevenson, for example, would have can-
celled a chapter, and that not once but twice or
thrice, sooner than leave such a paragraph in such
a state. He actually cited another passage of *Guy
Mannering*, and might have cited this, for proof of

his master's indifference to such scruples as consumed his own days and weeks. Scott wants, at this moment, certain details of scenery and costume ; and with perfect simplicity he now recapitulates them, or now puts them in. They ought, perhaps, to be ready beforehand ; or at least that is the more artistic way, the way of Stevenson, and of Dumas when he is on his mettle. The points might have been so touched and emphasized before, that to collect them now would be needless. But Scott will not be troubled with anything so unpractical. "Those high precipitous banks," which overhang the road, "*we before noticed*," says the author. "Banks" we may have noticed. That they should be high and steep he himself has not before seen ; but as height now proves to be necessary, he simply raises them. The "clear blue sky" is similarly imported, and without the least preparation. The red turban comes rightly enough, and, as a property, is of the best ; but it is put in with so much fumbling —*we have noticed...or rather...or perhaps...on this occasion*—that we seem to be watching a sketcher while he changes his brushes for a tint.

From these two paragraphs, taken separately or singly, no one, we suppose, could receive direct pleasure ; and if the history of literature has any lessons, assuredly no such work would, by itself, have roused the admiration of the world. The effect of it all is just to excite expectation, which, as the literary novice is warned by Horace, is a very dangerous thing to do. But Scott will have it so, and he is not even yet content. He has posed and painted his performer, and now, before she speaks, he insists on defining the effect:

"'I'll be d——d,' said the groom, 'if she has not been cutting the young ashes in the Dukit park!' The Laird made no answer, but continued to look at the figure which was thus perched above his path."

Now this is all very well, but what is to come of it? "How is this big-mouthed promise to be kept?" "Quid dignum tanto feret hic promissor hiatu?" You may protest that you have imagined something really most impressive, and may invoke in attestation the most august memories of art and religion— Delphi and Avernus, tragedy and epic, Cassandra and Deiphobe; but, given your sibyl, what will you make her say?

"'Ride your ways,' said the gipsy, 'ride your ways, Laird of Ellangowan—ride your ways, Godfrey Bertram! This day have ye quenched seven smoking hearths—see if the fire in your ain parlour burn the blither for that. Ye have riven the thack off seven cottar houses—look if your ain roof-tree stand the faster. Ye may stable your stirks in the shealings at Derncleugh—see that the hare does not couch on the hearthstane at Ellangowan. Ride your ways, Godfrey Bertram—what do ye glower after our folk for? There's thirty hearts there that wad hae wanted bread ere ye had wanted sunkets[1], and spent their life-blood ere ye had scratched your finger. Yes—there's thirty yonder, from the auld wife of an hundred to the babe that was born last week, that ye have turned out o' their bits o' bields, to sleep with the tod and the blackcock in the muirs! Ride your ways, Ellangowan! Our bairns are hinging at our weary backs—look that your braw cradle at hame be the fairer spread up; not that I am wishing ill

[1] Delicacies.

to little Harry, or to the babe that's yet to be born—God forbid
—and make them kind to the poor, and better folk than their
father!—And now, ride e'en your ways; for these are the last
words ye'll ever hear Meg Merrilies speak, and this is the last
reise[1] that I'll ever cut in the bonny woods of Ellangowan.'

"So saying, she broke the sapling she held in her hand and
flung it into the road."

What wonder if the world sat up to listen! To
praise such a composition would be superfluous
indeed, and I cite it for no such purpose. A man
who could miss or mistake the impression, would be
beyond instruction by words. But there may be
some interest and profit, especially in view of what
is said—and said truly, if rightly applied—about
Scott's neglect of style, in examining this passage
in detail, and exhibiting some part of its almost
incredible fidelity to rule. We know that *Guy
Mannering* was written at full speed, and not even
the plan of it laid out beforehand. There is no
reason, as far as I am aware, to except from this
record the present passage, or other such points of
high light, which make the whole what it is. But
after all, that only means that the true preparation
had been immeasurable. Years of training, now
among books, now in the walks of men, had wrought
the sensitive ear and brain to such consummate
readiness that, when the call came, the pen ran
headlong without a trip, and, at the utmost speed,
put in strokes which challenge the microscope.

A single instance will prove this, and may tempt

---

[1] Sapling branch.

us perhaps to look further. The substance, the kernel of the prophetic menace, is resumed in the repeated parallel between past and future. "As you have done, so it shall be done to you," says the oracle over and over again. Loss for loss, violence to the violent, your house, your family, for those that you have torn from their place. "This day have ye quenched seven smoking hearths—see if the fire in your own parlour burn the blither for that." Thrice the same parallel is repeated, hearth and fire, thatch and roof, Derncleugh and Ellangowan; thrice, but each time with a slight variation in the phrase—"*see if* the fire..." "*look if* your roof..." "*see that* the hare...." A trick to avoid monotony? Is that all? It does this indeed; but it lays the way, it provides the chance, for something far more important. "*See if,...look if,...see that...*"; the ear is left expectant, as in a rimed quatrain which should stop at the third line. Was the composer designing this? Was he aware of it? Not in his fingers, nor in the driving-wheels of his brain. But deep down, somewhere within him, was an engine or other organ which was awake and forefeeling, which knew that, in the natural harmony of passion, we must come back to this major chord, and that a place should be kept for the return. And therefore, when we do return, our composer, so negligent of style, fails not to finish the quatrain with the missing form: "Our bairns are hinging at our weary backs—*look that* your braw cradle at hame be the fairer spread up"—, achieves this exquisite precision at full stride, and leaves correction dumb.

Endless are the observations of this kind with which we may amuse ourselves if we please. There is, for one thing, the severe purity of the vocabulary, so absolutely English (or Scotch if you like, anyhow German, Teutonic) that the flavour even of French origin—as in *parlour, couch, sunkets*—is instantly noted for foreign, unhomely, and tells with the intended touch of mislike. It is here, I think, rather than in the mere gain of an extra key-board, that Scott gets advantage from his dialect.

Then again, what a feeling has Scott for the strong parts of English, the grand, long monosyllables, which are so carefully collected and placed by Milton. "*Ride your ways*," said the gipsy; and in what other tongue could she have condensed her point—luxury, pride, domination, defied and bidden go to their own end—into three such sounds as these?

Equally remarkable, perhaps even more so, if judged by the prevalent laxity of English rhetoric, is the faultless structure of the speech, the perfect attainment of that symmetry without stiffness which makes a frame organic. In this respect especially Scott surpasses the Elizabethan poet to whom, as we saw, he acknowledges his debt for a hint. The analogy to the situation of the Lancastrian Queen whose young Edward is killed in her presence by the princes of York, is but remote; but the two maledictions coincide in the fundamental idea that

cruelty to victims of tender age will be visited upon
the infants of the offender :

> "O traitors, murderers!
> "They that stabbed Caesar shed no blood at all,
> Did not offend, nor were not worthy blame,
> If this foul deed were by to equal it:
> He was a man; this, in respect, a child:
> And men ne'er spend their fury on a child.
> What's worse than murderer, that I may name it?
> No, no, my heart will burst, an if I speak,
> And I will speak, that so my heart may burst.
> Butchers and villains! bloody cannibals!
> How sweet a plant have you untimely cropped!
> You have no children, butchers! if you had,
> The thought of them would have stirred up remorse;
> *But if you ever chance to have a child,*
> *Look in his youth to have him so cut off*
> *As, deathsmen, you have rid this sweet young prince*[1] *!"*

For a tragedy-queen this is well enough, and,
regarded merely as rhetoric, it is much upon the
average level of the Elizabethan and Jacobean
theatre. Those poets were seldom careful of
structure, and their precedent has been only too
well followed by our dramatic composers since. But
the tirade so ill bears comparison with that of Meg
Merrilies that, if Scott were capable of a trick, he
might be suspected of wishing us to remark his
triumph over what passes for Shakespeare. And
the weakness of the one speech, as contrasted with
the other, lies chiefly in the want of structure, of
rhetorical frame. Here Scott's craft is supreme,
good enough for Racine, Euripides, or the Homer of

[1] *Henry VI*, III, v, 5.

the Ninth *Iliad.* Commentary upon such technique is apt to be unconvincing unless exhaustive, and if exhaustive, to be tiresome. But let one point serve for all. Take the triplet, which sets the text, as it were, to be developed : *" Ride your ways,…ride your ways, Laird of Ellangowan—ride your ways, Godfrey Bertram !"* Here we have three forms of address, one anonymous, then the territorial title, and last the personal name. Observe then, first, that exactly these three, and no more, recur as head-notes for the divisions that follow. Next observe that they recur in the reverse order : *" Ride your ways, Godfrey Bertram….Ride your ways, Ellangowan….And now, ride e'en your ways,…"* with the result, a result vital to the purpose, that we know by ear and instinct when to expect the close, and thus the thrill of the dismissal gets a reverberation from our simple pleasure in not being disappointed of our count. And observe, lastly and most carefully, that the distinction between title and name, the Laird and the man, " Ellangowan " and " Bertram," proves significant. For this we might hope ; count upon it we could not ; but we get it, and are pleased in proportion to the rareness of such fidelity to poetic promise. When the former friend of the gipsies is to be reminded that he has thrown away the affection of his dependents, he is " Godfrey Bertram "; but he is " Ellangowan," when the misery of their homelessness is to be contrasted with the pride and comfort of his house : *" Ride your ways, Ellangowan.* Our bairns are hinging at

our weary backs; *look that your braw cradle at
hame be the fairer spread up.*"

And beyond all this, deeper and more vital yet,
lie the effects of sound and of rhythm.   It is a little
matter, perhaps, that the more commonplace uses of
echo and repetition—"*burn the blither*"..."*stable
your stirks*"..."*wad hae wanted bread ere ye had
wanted*"—are used, and are forborne, with rare
economy.   But it is no little matter, it is rather the
very essence of poetry, when the paired sounds
touch, just touch without crossing, the confine of
sobs : "What do ye glower after our *folk for*?"...
"the wife and the babe, that ye have turned out o'
their *bits o' bields*"..."God...make them kind to the
poor, and better *folk than their father*." Pathos
with dignity can do no more.

From sound to rhythm is perhaps scarcely a
distinguishable transition; but it is from the rhythm
of this passage, from the melody proper, that, for
my own part, I get the greatest delight.   Here
again there is no end to the possible remarks.
Most obvious is a device which is a favourite with
Burke; though, when I say "device," I do not
mean that Burke always, or perhaps ever, thought
of it.   The consciousness of the artist is generally
an open question.   Be that as it may, the trick is
this.   Everybody who takes lessons in English
prose-composition soon gets a warning "to avoid
blank verse."   The precept is sound and important.
That rhythm, from its familiarity, easily catches the
ear; in prose it is mostly purposeless; and nothing

is more vexatious than rhythm without a purpose. But regularity is the ground of variation, and the supreme end of artistic rules is to be broken with proper effect. Here, in our speech, the blank-verse rhythm is scrupulously excluded. Not any group of words suggests it, except one, where it is strongly marked. "*Our bairns are hinging at our weary backs*" is a verse of five accents, and a good one; better, I should say, than any of Queen Margaret's in the play. And as any one may see at a glance, it is placed as it should be, where, by a slight touch of pomp, it sustains the complaint of the vagabond above the suspicion of mendicancy.

Many other like delicacies there are; indeed every clause and phrase will bear and repay examination. But the best of all is kept for the close:

"And now, ride e'en your ways; for these are the last words ye'll ever hear Meg Merrilies speak, and this is the last reise that I'll ever cut in the bonny woods of Ellangowan."

Here are two points principally to remark. It cannot escape notice that, for some reason, the introduction of the speaker's name, "Meg Merrilies," is here strangely impressive, and that the sentence seems to hinge and to swing upon it. Every one perceives this; and the cause, though less obvious, may be ascertained. We have already noted that the vocabulary of the speech, as is usual with Scott on such occasions, is extremely simple, and almost exclusively English in the strictest sense of the name. Now this vocabulary, with many merits, has, for the composer, some defects, and not least among them this—that, consisting almost wholly of monosyllables and dissyllables, it supplies hardly ever a succession of syllables, not even so much as a pair, absolutely without accent, and therefore falls naturally into an up-and-down jog, without those pleasant trisyllabic movements which in prosody are called dactylic. Introduce the elements which, in later times, our writers borrowed from Latin, and dactyls (or rather quasi-dactyls) spring up in abundance—*irregular, accessible, limited, principal, precipitous, general, singular*—these, and more, may be picked from the paragraphs, written in the common language of literature, which precede the speech of the gipsy, and have been cited above. But in the speech itself, nothing of the sort. With the vocabulary of the gipsy, the thing is hardly possible. Such combinations as *"what do ye," "wife of an," "babe that was,"* are the nearest approach; and they differ materially in rhythm from *principal* or *singular.* But in " Meg *Merrilies* " we do get an English triplet, the sole triplet of syllables within one word which the speech presents ; and Scott, with an instinct sharpened by practice, seizes upon this by-gift of his own invention to swing off the finale with the desirable roll.

Partly alike is the music of the last words, alike in this, that in the proper name " Ellangowan " we have again a valuable element seldom provided by pure English—a quadrisyllable with two equal accents, our nearest equivalent for the double trochee, such as *comprobavit*, so beloved by pupils of Cicero. It is the only such form in the speech. But here we have another thing to note. However well we may love our native tongue, we must allow that, as compared with some others, or with almost any other, its word-groups are seldom musical. You cannot have everything at once. Our fathers chose for us that we should talk mostly in monosyllables, a good way, but not musical. The collision of hard sounds must at this rate be incessant, and very harsh collisions will hardly be kept out. Scott himself, writing pure English, cannot avoid them, and wisely does not try, for the constriction of such a rule would be deadly. But the result is what it must be, a "music" bad or poor. No one, I suppose, will say that, taken as mere sound, there is any pleasure in such combinations as *quenched seven smoking hearths,...at Derncleugh,...hearthstane,...scratched,...and the blackcock,...babe that's,...* and the like everywhere. There is no help for it. But what then is the artist to do? Why, do like an artist, turn stones to stepping-stones—offer, at some chosen place, the good gift which will take more value from his very poverty. The close of the speech, the last sentence, runs almost without a trip, and the final clause, as a bit of prosody, might challenge Italian or Greek:

"And this is the last reise that I'll ever cut *in the bonny woods of Ellangowan.*"

With Scott, as with all artists in English, the contrast between the various elements in our heterogeneous lexicon, the mixture and opposition of them, is a main principle. Most often, as in the case of Meg Merrilies, he recurs for solemnity to the pure Teutonic, fashioning of course his personages accordingly. The reader will expect here the pleasure of comparing Meg's malediction with its not less admirable pendant, the gipsy's farewell to Derncleugh. I will cite it therefore, but spare my comment, which, after what has been said, will easily be conceived and supplied:

"She then moved up the brook until she came to the ruined hamlet, where, pausing with a look of peculiar and softened interest before one of the gables which was still standing, she said, in a tone less abrupt, though as solemn as before: 'Do you see that blackit and broken end of a sheeling?—There my kettle boiled for forty years—there I bore twelve buirdly sons and daughters. Where are they now?—Where are the leaves that were on that auld ash-tree at Martinmas?—the west wind has made it bare—and I'm stripped too.—Do you see that saugh-tree?—it's but a blackened, rotten stump now—I've sat under it mony a bonnie summer afternoon, when it hung its gay garlands ower the poppling water—I've sat there, and' (elevating her voice) 'I've held you on my knee, Henry Bertram, and sung ye sangs of the auld barons and their bloody wars. It will ne'er be green again, and Meg Merrilies will never sing sangs mair, be they blithe or sad. But ye'll no forget her?—and ye'll gar big up the auld wa's for her sake?—and let somebody live there that's ower guid to fear them of another world. For if ever the dead came back amang the living, I'll be seen in this glen mony a night after these crazed banes are in the mould.'"

With the imported parts of our language, imported chiefly from Latin, as well as with the primitive parts, Scott could make masterly play when he chose. An example is to be found in that incomparable story which makes a detached episode in *Redgauntlet*, under the title of "Wandering Willie's Tale." Stevenson in *Catriona* has testified his admiration of it by exerting his utmost strength to produce a parallel, and with as much success as could be hoped. One cannot mention Scott's story, even for the purpose of technical illustration, without turning aside to praise its general excellence. In its kind it has perhaps not a rival in English literature or anywhere else. To tell, and to refute in the telling, a legend of the supernatural, is an ancient and popular trick, but never perhaps has been performed with such delicate balance of gravity and humour. In substance the tale is simple. A certain landlord, Sir Robert Redgauntlet, a former persecutor of the Covenanters (the date is about 1700), has a retainer and tenant who waits upon him to pay certain arrears of rent. In the midst of the business the Laird is taken with a fit, of which he almost instantly dies; and the debtor in the confusion departs without, as he believes, having got a receipt. The money too is not to be found, and the heir demands a second payment. The honest defaulter, half mad with despair and drink, wanders at night to the grave of his late landlord; and there, after a dream in which he visits the dead man, he wakes with the receipt in his hand. Payment being thus proved, the disappearance of the money is soon traced to the theft of a monkey which was present at the time of the transaction. With singular skill and power Scott shows how, from these not wonderful incidents, has grown in the course of a generation an awful story of retribution and reward. About the true facts there is no doubt. To establish the supernatural version, it would of course be essential to show that the receipt was *got*, and not merely found, by the debtor on the night alleged, that is to say, after the death and burial of the payee. The receipt itself, the document, was so dated! So at least we are told; but the paper was immediately destroyed! Everything therefore turns on the question whether the debtor took such a paper from the room at the time of the payment, or whether, as he supposed, he did not. And most unfortunately our informant, the debtor's grandson, actually gives, though he is not in the least aware of it, two accounts of the transaction, *which differ totally at the critical point.* The thing is a delightful example of Scott's profound acquaintance with story-telling men, and the masterly use which he made of it; and the passages will serve, as well as any, for specimens of the narrator's language and style. Here is his first account of the payment:

"My gudesire, with as gude a countenance as he could put on, made a leg, and placed the bag of money on the table wi' a dash, like a man that does something clever. The Laird drew it to him hastily—'Is it all here, Steenie, man?'

"'Your honour will find it right,' said my gudesire.

"'Here, Dougal,' said the Laird, 'gie Steenie a tass of brandy downstairs, *till I count the siller and write the receipt.*'

"But they werena weel *out of the room* when Sir Robert gied a yelloch that garr'd the Castle rock. Back ran Dougal—in flew the livery-men—yell on yell gied the Laird, ilk ane mair awfu' than the ither. My gudesire knew not whether to stand or flee, but he ventured *back into the parlour*....[His] head was like to turn. He forgot baith siller and receipt, and down stairs he banged," etc.

Now upon this showing it is plain, both that the receipt could easily be written, and that the debtor could easily take it away unawares; and, given these facts, no reasonable person would doubt that the whole story should be so understood and explained. But presently we have the interview between the debtor and Sir Robert's heir (Sir John), when, of course, the circumstances of payment have to be related again, as accounting for the absence of proof. And behold, they are completely transformed! The narrator thus dramatises the dialogue:

"STEPHEN: 'Please your honour, Sir John, I paid it to your father.'

"SIR JOHN: 'Ye took a receipt, then, doubtless, Stephen; and can produce it?'

"STEPHEN: 'Indeed, *I hadna time*, an it like your honour, for nae sooner had I set doun the siller, and *just as his honour, Sir Robert, that's gaen, drew it till him to count it, and write out the receipt, he was ta'en wi' the pains that removed him.*'"

If this were the truth, or near the truth, evidently the receipt could not be written, and the debtor knew, by the witness of his own eyes, that it never was. But here, on every material fact, the latter version is contradicted by the first, though both are given, as this very discrepancy proves, in good faith. That Scott perceived the flaw, and deliberately planned it, is proved (if proof be wanted) by his providing the narrator with a plausible pretext for giving, or rather purporting to give, the second version, the erroneous and misleading, in the form of a dramatic dialogue, reported *ipsissimis verbis* :

"I have heard their communings so often tauld ower, that I almost think I was there mysell."

Accordingly he describes the interview exactly as if he had been there, and at the very point where he becomes essentially false, becomes also (as we see in the quotation) most precise and positive in form, dropping narration altogether, and acting each speaker in turn. To this change of form Scott emphatically directs attention, actually arresting the story at this point and inserting a comment, by the supposed auditor, upon the narrator's dramatic talent. At a first reading, or a second, this may appear needless or cumbrous, but presently we perceive the humour of it. The supposed precision is of course altogether illusory, and merely serves to disguise from our informant the fact that, as can be proved out of his own mouth, he is not here reporting the incident as it was originally told. Scott's own view of the facts, the rationalistic view, is implied clearly enough in the final paragraph of the story, and indeed throughout.

We have not space to compare in detail Stevenson's rival tale of the Bass Rock (in *Catriona*), though the comparison would be full of interest. In the tone of the two there is this important difference, that the allegations in Stevenson's tale

cannot possibly be resolved into common incidents
*plus* involuntary error. When we are told that at
one and the same moment several persons saw
A.B. dancing (in spirit) at one place, and a crowd
of other persons saw him lying motionless (in body)
many miles away, we are driven to suppose that
either the facts or the lies are abnormal. Our
choice will depend on our opinion of the witnesses
and our general theory of the universe. To Frederic
Myers the facts in the " Bass Rock " story, so far as
I have yet given them, seemed abnormal indeed, but
quite natural. Never shall I forget the grave and
reproachful tone in which, talking of *Catriona* soon
after its appearance, he complained of Stevenson for
disfiguring an otherwise legitimate and persuasive
piece of imagination by the "ridiculous" addition,
that when the dancing spirit is shot, the silver coin
with which the gun was loaded, is found in the
man's body, which dies at the same moment but—
several miles away. The precise boundary between
the natural and the ridiculous is sometimes not easy
to fix.

However, to return to Scott, such, in the bare
outline and in general style, is the famous tale of
Wandering Willie. But if there were no more to
say of it, if it rose nowhere above the level which
we have described, it would be good indeed, even
so perhaps best in its kind, but it would not have
the sublimity which Scott has contrived to impart.
This depends on the moral source of the legend,
the assurance of future punishment reserved for a

persecutor of the saints. The Sir Robert Redgauntlet of the story was, as we have said, an
oppressor, a cruel oppressor, of nonconformists and
recusants; and his tenant, the originator of the
legend, though no saint, was a religious man, and
had no doubt whatever of his master's destiny *post
mortem.* Accordingly, in his dream beside the
grave, it is to Hell that he goes for the receipt, a
Hell which is also and at the same time Sir Robert's
own house. There still, there again, as in this
world often, he and his wicked friends are holding
such feast as yet they may. The vision is profoundly moving and solemn, and from it is diffused
over the whole narrative a strong religious enchantment, which raises what otherwise were a trifle to
the level of Dante and Homer.

Indeed, I have such a reverence for this episode,
the Hades of the oppressors, that I have some
scruple in touching it with a philological finger.
But since I do not myself find in such remarks any
bar to emotion, but feel the poetic achievement only
the more when I seem to perceive the means, others,
I suppose, may feel the same; and the truth is, that
the effect is partly, and even principally, a matter
of vocabulary. The strolling fiddler, Wandering
Willie, who tells the tale, is by birth a peasant, and
his ordinary language is not very far, though it
differs, from that of Meg Merrilies. But he is no
gipsy. He has had the regular Presbyterian training and, from special circumstances, much irregular
education besides. He has notions of history,

theology, literature; and especially, like all good
Scots, he knows and reverences the language of the
preacher. The influence of it may be traced often,
and grows when he begins to describe his grandfather's dream. And when for a while he is fully
possessed by the moral and religious purport of the
vision, shade by shade his speech takes the learned
colours of the pulpit, French and Latin, even Greek,
points from the Pentateuch, and rhythms modelled
upon the Psalms. You will hardly find anywhere
a finer example of what can be done by economy
of art than the simple effects of this passage, the
unexpected and therefore thrilling note of such
words as *fierce, savage, dissolute, beautiful, contorted,
melancholy.* And finally, this far-away spell dies out
as it came in, and we sink back into the plainness
of the vernacular. Here is the passage, with so
much of the context as will suffice to show these
contrasts. Coming in his dream to Redgauntlet
Castle, the debtor is received there, as usual, by
Dougal MacCallum, Sir Robert's old servant, whose
death, be it remarked, has followed close on that of
his master:

"'Never fash yoursell wi' me,' said Dougal, 'but look to
yoursell; and see ye tak naething frae ony body here, neither
meat, drink, or siller, except just the receipt that is your ain.'

"So saying, he led the way out through halls and trances that
were weel kend to my gudesire, and into the auld oak parlour;
and there was as much singing of profane sangs, and birling of
red wine, and speaking blasphemy and sculduddry, as had ever
been in Redgauntlet Castle when it was at the blithest.

"But, Lord take us in keeping, what a set of ghastly revellers they were that sat around that table!—My gudesire kend mony that had long before gane to their place, for often had he piped to the most part in the hall of Redgauntlet. There was the fierce Middleton, and the dissolute Rothes, and the crafty Lauderdale; and Dalyell, with his bald head and a beard to his girdle; and Earlshall, with Cameron's blude on his hand; and wild Bonshaw, that tied blessed Mr Cargill's limbs till the blude sprung; and Dunbarton Douglas, the twice-turned traitor baith to country and king. There was the Bluidy Advocate MacKenyie, who, for his worldly wit and wisdom, had been to the rest as a god[1]. And there was Claverhouse, as beautiful as when he lived, with his long, dark, curled locks, streaming down over his laced buff-coat, and his left hand always on his right spule-blade, to hide the wound that the silver bullet had made. He sat apart from them all, and looked at them with a melancholy, haughty countenance; while the rest hallooed, and sung, and laughed, that the room rang. But their smiles were fearfully contorted from time to time; and their laugh passed into such wild sounds as made my gudesire's very nails grow blue, and chilled the marrow in his banes[1].

"They that waited at the table were just the wicked serving-men and troopers that had done their work and cruel bidding on earth. There was the Lang Lad of the Nethertown, that helped to take Argyle; and the Bishop's summoner, that they called the Deil's Rattle-bag; and the wicked guardsmen in their laced coats; and the savage Highland Amorites, that shed blood like water; and mony a proud serving-man, haughty of heart and bloody of hand, cringing to the rich, and making them wickeder than they would be; grinding the poor to powder, when the rich had broken them to fragments. And mony, many mair were coming and ganging, a' as busy in their vocation as if they had been alive."

It will of course be understood that Scott, as a manipulator of language, is not to be praised

[1] Between these points the dialectic forms almost totally disappear. In the next paragraph they gradually reappear.

without discrimination. Not only is he often careless, sometimes in place and sometimes very much out of place, but a certain class of his romances, the so-called " historic," are all debased, more or less, by a deplorable amalgam, which he compounded from cuttings of every kind of English between Chaucer and Gray, and vended as, in some sort, the style of chivalry. *Ivanhoe* and *The Talisman, Quentin Durward, Nigel* even, *Woodstock, Peveril* and others, are sown more or less liberally with this pernicious flower. It pleased the day, but it was a bad thing and, like all weeds, was fertile : it has helped to make some of the worst literature that we possess. But let us say no more of it. It has little or no part in these : *Guy Mannering, The Antiquary, The Heart of Midlothian, Old Mortality, Rob Roy, Redgauntlet, The Bride of Lammermoor, St Ronan's Well,* and within this round one may comfortably circulate without end.

*St Ronan's Well* ? Yes, assuredly, *St Ronan's Well.* It has defects ; it is not such a masterpiece as *The Bride.* The elements, comic and tragic, are not so well accommodated ; and Scott, alas! was persuaded, almost compelled, by his publisher to sacrifice the very base of his tragedy to the conciliation of the vulgar, who were not won nevertheless. But the story is fine, and the strong scenes—chapter xxiii for example, or chapter xxxv—very strong. And they will supply instances of the power and dignity which Scott, when he chooses, can put even into the artificial, super-literary English which he inherited from the eighteenth century. So here :

"'There is a Heaven above us, and THERE shall be judged our actions towards each other! You abuse a power most treacherously obtained—you break a heart that never did you wrong—you seek an alliance with a wretch who only wishes to be wedded to her grave. If my brother brings you hither, I cannot help it—and if your coming prevents bloody and unnatural violence, it is so far well. But by my consent you come *not*; and were the choice mine, I would rather be struck with life-long blindness than that my eyes should again open on your person— rather that my ears were stuffed with the earth of the grave than that they should again hear your voice.'"

Or here :

"'Oh! no—no—no!' exclaimed the terrified girl, throwing herself at his feet; 'do not kill me, brother! I have wished for death—thought of death—prayed for death—but, oh! it is frightful to think that he is near!—Oh! not a bloody death, brother, nor by your hand!'

"She held him close by the knees as she spoke, and expressed in her looks and accents the utmost terror. It was not, indeed, without reason; for the extreme solitude of the place, the violent and inflamed passions of her brother, and the desperate circumstances to which he had reduced himself, seemed all to concur to render some horrid act of violence not an improbable termination of this strange interview.

"Mowbray folded his arms, without unclenching his hands, or raising his head, while his sister continued on the floor, clasping him round the knees with all her strength, and begging piteously for her life and for mercy.

"'Fool!' he said at last, 'let me go!—Who cares for thy worthless life?—Who cares if thou live or die? Live, if thou canst—and be the hate and scorn of everyone else, as much as thou art mine.'"

*Extreme solitude, inflamed passions, improbable termination*—the movement of the narrative is cumbrous and wordy. But it is strong; and the stronger notes of the speeches are relieved against it with discretion and temperature.

In conclusion let it be said, though it is perhaps needless, that I do not here pretend to estimate, as a whole, the merits of Scott's work as a romancer. Of many aspects, and these the most important, we have said little or nothing. In *Guy Mannering* the variety and coherence of the topics, in *Old Mortality* the subtle distinction of similar idiosyncrasies, in *Rob Roy* the picturesque backgrounds, in *Redgauntlet* vigour of caricature, in the *Heart of Midlothian* a perspective of society, humour in *The Antiquary*, horror in *St Ronan's Well*, and all together in the tragedy of *Lammermoor*—these and other qualities are doubtless more vital than style. But without style they would not have achieved the end. Scott, in his way and at his hours, is a very great stylist, supreme and hardly to be surpassed. His manner of working, his profusion, the nature of his faults, give room for mistake and misrepresentation about this aspect of his genius. And for this reason it may not have been amiss to bespeak attention to the form, as well as the matter, of his prose.

# "DIANA OF THE CROSSWAYS[1]"

"Do you honestly enjoy this book, and, if so, what in it pleases you? Does your enjoyment increase as you study it, and if so, through what process of thought?" Such are perhaps the questions which the members of a reading union should ask themselves upon a work of Mr George Meredith. To presume the affirmative answers—or, worse, to force them—may in this case be to miss the best of the profit. Some art is strong in the width of its appeal, and some not in the width, but in the depth. It is a great thing to satisfy desires that are universal or common, and great also, whether more or less, to gratify intensely even one desire that is natural. Disclaiming all pretentions to dictate, and confessing, or rather insisting, that others may very well see where I am blind, I have to say for myself that my pleasure in Mr Meredith is, if not solely of one kind, yet in one kind intense beyond expression, and otherwise slight. All other things that belong to literature the English reader may find more easily, if not in better quality, elsewhere; but of one thing, in which English writers

[1] This essay forms one of a series on George Meredith's Novels and Poetry contributed by various writers to the *National Home-reading Union*.

as a class are singularly poor, he may find in Mr
Meredith such a store as was hardly ever, I verily
believe, dispensed by a single mind since writing
began. And the question to ask—once more let
us say that a true answer is not to be given with
haste—is whether we have, or wish to get, an appetite for this particular food. I can warrant it possible
for a man to read *The Egoist* with enjoyment so
often that he literally cannot read it any more, because he knows, before turning, the contents of every
page ; but to tell any one, without intimate knowledge of his constitution, that he ought to admire
*The Egoist* is, as likely as not, to say that he ought
to be a humbug. Given a person, time, and place,
we may say of certain works that by that person
they ought to be admired—at least in this sense,
that, not admiring, he shows a dangerous diverg-
ence in taste and faculty from the type of man
with whom he will have to deal. But for England
and for this age that is certainly not to be said of
Mr Meredith. What may safely and rightly be
said is that, if we do not take pains to appreciate
him so far as may be possible for us, we miss the
best chance that Englishmen have, or ever had, to
cultivate a valuable faculty which is of all least
natural to us.

This faculty is wit—*wit* in the sense which it
bore in our "Augustan" age of Pope and Prior, and
should always bear if it is to be definite enough for
utility :—wit or subtlety, on the part of the artist, in
the manipulation of meanings, and on the part of the

recipient or critic the enjoyment of such subtlety for its own sake, and as the source of a distinct intellectual pleasure.  The faculty and the pleasure, for obvious reasons, have been most highly developed in small concentrated societies.  Among large bodies of people it is difficult to bring about that uniformity of habit in language and ideas without which a speaker dares not and cannot be subtly suggestive; and among scattered bodies it is more than difficult.  Between two foreigners wit is well-nigh impossible, and for high wit not all of one nation even can be native enough to one another.  Athens in the fifth and fourth centuries before Christ, Florence in the fourteenth and fifteenth after, Paris and, to a far less degree, London in the seventeenth and eighteenth —these have been the chief homes of wit.  But it is observable, and important to the student of Mr Meredith, that though cities have been the breeding-places of the art, it is not always within the local urban limits that the urban and urbane company finds the very best ground of exercise.  To form and finish the personal atoms, the quick close life of a town is, broadly speaking, indispensable; but once formed, they may be more free to group and grapple in a cultured rustication; more especially is this so when the city has swollen to the size and complexity of modern times.  Fashion your wits in Paris, and then away to the villa!  An urban society rusticated—that is the properest situation.  Mr Meredith has himself summed up the matter, and with it a great chapter or volume in the history of human education, in the characteristic phrase (darkly splendid as wit should be) which describes the actors of *The Egoist* : "A simple-seeming word of this import is the triumph of the spiritual, and where it passes for coin of value the society has reached a high refinement—Arcadian by the aesthetic route." The preference of the author for companies in this predicament, folk of intellectual fashion, transplanted to the parks of the province, is scarcely less than that of Peacock, with his Nightmare Abbey, Crotchet Castle, and other synonyms for a scene always constantly the same. But the various ingenuity of Mr Meredith in conducting us to the favourable field is as far above the rude machinery of Peacock as the wit of Peacock, though copious for an Englishman, is below the wealth which Nature, laughing as her wont is at her own rules, has suddenly chosen to reveal in a denizen of Surrey.

It may not perhaps be said that without a Patterne Hall or a Beckley Court or a Copsley for focus of the story Mr Meredith has never achieved success ; but it is in the dining-rooms and the drawing-rooms of such mansions, and at social gatherings there, that those scenes are enacted which are most entirely and distinctively his own. Certainly the crises of the drama do not always occur when "the daughters of the Great Mel have to digest him at dinner" (*Evan Harrington*, chap. XXII), or in "animated conversation at a luncheon-table" (*The Egoist*, chap. XXXVI), or amid the cross-currents of an inopportune call, as in "the scene of Sir Willoughby's generalship" (*The Egoist*, chap. XLVI); though, when such crises do so occur, the reader who cares for Mr Meredith at all, gets something scarcely to be priced in the literary exchange.  But beyond this, the principal personages of Mr Meredith, all and always, owe so much of their characters to the experience of such meetings, that their behaviour elsewhere is scarcely to be understood until we have read long enough and widely enough in the author to know, without telling, how they would behave themselves in that sort of arena.  This is the engine that he delights to work.  Take a set of people all trained to use with facility the same medium of choice and exact speech, and all sufficiently sensitive in intellect and feeling to shrink from anything like rudeness or baldness or bluntness in manner and expression.  Place them in such relations to one another that each has much to conceal, much to reveal, and much to discover in the thoughts, desires, and generally in the nature of himself and his companions; in such relations that from interview to interview, and indeed from moment to moment, there must be changes of mutual attitude, sometimes slow and sometimes sudden, as in the pattern of a kaleidoscope turned gently.  Then have a Mr George Meredith to provide them with dialogue, and to explain the inner springs of movement when dialogue, however delicately constructed, is not explanatory enough.  And then—why, then you will see what you can see,—*Diana of the Crossways*, for example, chaps. XXII, XXVIII, XXX, XXXI, XXXV, XXXVIII–XLIII.

This book in particular, *Diana of the Crossways*, though reasons might certainly be given for not placing it first among the author's achievements, and though for myself I very much prefer, for instance, the good parts of *Evan Harrington*, and should rank *The Egoist* immeasurably above it— as, indeed, in its own line, above anything which modern literature has to show—has nevertheless one noticeable advantage as a commencement of study. Here at least, there is no possibility of mistake or misunderstanding as to the primary importance which, among the elements of the artistic product, must be assigned to wit. The principal figure is notoriously and professedly a woman of wit, moves and has her being in wit, and simply because of her wit, attains the position and undergoes the experience in which we see her. The society in which she moves is consciously and professedly a witty society, could not live without wit any more than without food. Now, since wit always makes a part, and a very large part, of Mr Meredith's interest in his subject, whatever that subject may on the surface appear to be, and since—to repeat once more the only point on which I care to insist—the reader who does not appreciate linguistic dexterity, and does not rate it highly among human capacities, had much better let Mr Meredith alone, it is well that on this point our attention should be challenged at once. Doubtless there are many aspects in which *Diana of the Crossways* may be regarded. It is a study in the development of character; it exhibits many pleasant pictures ; it has scenes, two at least, of elaborate and nevertheless effective pathos ; its plot turns upon the deep problem of marriage. In these matters among others, and especially in the last mentioned, it is possible, it may just now be fashionable, to see the essential and most significant element. But none of these things are the essential —no, not the problem of marriage. If you want pathos, or pictures, or social problems, you can get them elsewhere, you will find them more easily elsewhere ; which is practically to say that you will find them better. What you have here is a touchstone which, were it not for other volumes from the same hand, would be in its kind unique among the products of England, to ascertain whether you have the faculty of enjoying dexterity in the manipulation of language ; this you have, and also an instrument with which to cultivate that faculty, if you happen to possess it. If we are Englishmen, it is probable, as Mr Meredith repeatedly hints to us[1], that by our nature we suspect wit with all the malice of honesty, and not unlikely that we hate it with all the vigour of sloth. The first is a grave and the second a grievous error. But a worse state yet would be the self-deception of supposing ourselves witty or capable of wit because in a witty author we have come to enjoy something else.

Manifestly, from the scope of the story, *Diana of the Crossways* could not have been attempted except by one who felt himself able to unfold the

[1] E.g. *Diana*, chaps. II, XI, XXXIX.

riches of clever speech. Of the luxuriance actually displayed no sampling can give a fair representation. There is scarcely perhaps any type of cleverness which is not exemplified copiously. There is the "sentence," "gnomé," or "epigram," scattered in dozens and hundreds. "The world is ruthless, because the world is hypocrite." "She was perforce the actress of her part....It is a terrible decree that all must act who would prevail." "Slumber...a paradoxical thing you must battle for, and can only win at last when utterly beaten." "She was delightful to hear, delightful to see; and her friends loved her and had faith in her. So clever a woman might be too clever for her friends." "Money is, of course, a rough test of virtue," said Redworth; "we have no other general test." "We are much influenced in youth by sleepless nights." "Men and women crossing the high seas of life he had found most readable under that illuminating inquiry—as to their means." Among such phrases some are in import simple, some profoundly penetrative; but their common quality is that they are rememberable, and this they are, because they are in turn and wording so scrupulously right. In the last cited, some of the merit lies in the felicity of the implied simile, which may be more fully seen in the context (chap. XXXIX): the power to find and to work out analogies has always been noted as a great branch of wit; indeed, where wit has been studied, the tendency has commonly been, as in the days of Queen Anne, to exaggerate the importance of this branch. At any rate it is through such power that wit most often attains to the form of eloquence. And in this kind also the mastery of our author is astounding : "With her, or rather with his thought of her soul, he understood the right union of women and men from the roots to the flowering heights of that rare graft. She gave him comprehension of the meaning of love—a word in many mouths, not often explained. With her, wound in his idea of her, he perceived it to signify a new start in our existence, a finer shoot of the tree stoutly planted in good gross earth ; the senses running their live sap, and the minds companioned, and the spirits made one by the whole-natured con-junction. In sooth, a happy prospect for the sons and daughters of Earth, divinely indicating more than happiness : the speeding of us, compact of what we are, between the ascetic rocks and the sensual whirlpools, to the creation of certain nobler races, now very dimly imagined." Could this possibly be better done ? Less brightness but more blaze is in the description of the scandal sometimes attending the publication of diaries and memoirs : "The Diarist ...howks the graves, and transforms the quiet worms, busy on a single poor peaceable body, into winged serpents that disorder sky and earth with a deadly flight of zig-zags, like military rockets, among the living." And there should be added here, if there were room, by way of a climax in this sort, the picture of jealousy from *The Egoist* (chap. xxiii), a thing to make one stupid with admiration—so perhaps one had best not dwell upon it.

Nearer to the popular notion of wit, because more heavily pointed, are such things as Diana's rebuke to her too presuming intimate : "You must come less often, even to not at all, if you are one of those idols with feet of clay which leave the print of their steps in a room, or fall and crush the silly idolizer." Or, again, the reflexions of Lady Dunstane, the "woman of brains," upon Diana's unfortunate husband : "Her first and her final impression likened him to a house locked up and empty ; a London house conventionally furnished and decorated by the upholsterer, and empty of inhabitants....*Empty of inhabitants even to the ghost!* Both human and spiritual were wanting. The mind contemplating him became reflectively stagnant." Or, again, Diana writing to Lady Dunstane on the political prospects of women : "The middle age of men is their time of delusion. It is no paradox. They may be publicly useful in a small way—I do not deny it at all. They must be near the gates of life—the opening or the closing—for their *minds* to be accessible to the urgency of the greater questions..." and so on, the whole passage (chap. xv) excellent, and enough in itself to establish Diana for a wit of the first rank.

As for the small change of wit, sallies, repartees, and so forth, the dialogue, everywhere and by the nature or necessity of the story, is starred with them. They cannot be overlooked, and it is not fair to take them from their setting; so we will not quote any, but will remark, however, that from *The Egoist,*

perhaps from *Beauchamp's Career*, we might cull
a score or so better than any of these. Over the
whole scale of smartness, from top to bottom, the
author ranges with justified assurance. He is not
afraid to tell us right out what was the particular
quip by which Diana repelled the malicious attack
of Mrs Cramborne Wathin (chap. XIV). Great
writers, the very greatest, have flinched at such a
trial. Scott does repeatedly; Thackeray does in
a famous crisis of *Vanity Fair*—and Thackeray
stands high among English wits. Mr Meredith,
amazing as it is to see, is perfectly ready, and hits
the mark exactly, giving just what is good enough
and not (an error scarcely less easy) too good.

The pursuit of wit has its dangers, and that Mr
Meredith always avoids or overcomes them, I at
least shall not for a moment maintain. It is the
way of wit, and it must be, to tread constantly on
the verge of darkness. To demand that wit shall
be always or often easy of understanding, would be
simply to expose our ignorance of its character and
conditions. But what we often use we may well
come to tolerate, or even to love, when there is no
use in it; and so may wit come to love darkness.
My own experience (each must speak for himself)
is that there is no noticeable work of wit which is
not sometimes sheerly incomprehensible. *Hamlet*
is an example, and to my mind, I confess, a very
black one. There are passages in *The Way of the
World* which to me are no better than headache.
No doubt in such a case we should be cautious in

decision; often it will appear in the end that what seemed wilful confusion has a purpose, and could hardly have been made simpler without some injury. But that it is always so we need not believe; and of Mr Meredith I will say frankly, though with the profoundest respect, that not very seldom (so far as with patient study I can judge) he is dark beyond or even without legitimate reason. Readers of *Diana* will find occasion to consider the question; only let them consider it long, and for each occasion afresh. Chapters I, IX, XIII (to go no further) should cost them some time.

And another danger is that the author may put wit in the wrong place, or too much of it, to the injury of dramatic truth. That Congreve did so, often and constantly, I think with Lord Macaulay; and notwithstanding well meant apologies. And here Mr Meredith especially might be put in a dilemma. Since the English, by temper, are so backward of wit as he says they are, how shall we allow, for pictures of English society, these scintillating clusters which he presents to us? Personally I do not find this a very serious matter, provided that the tone of the picture be consistent, be brightened or heightened throughout in proportion. Whether the result be historically true or not, we do not much care. Congreve, I hold, can scarcely be said to have satisfied the proviso; the dimensions of theatrical work constrained him. Whether Mr Meredith satisfies it is too complicated a matter for present discussion; I should say that, on the whole and with some lapses, he does.

I have not touched, and I do not mean to touch, on the ethical substance of *Diana of the Crossways*. There is no fear but that the reader will give to it all the attention that it deserves. The chief character is borrowed, in parts, with some of the chief incidents, as the first chapter informs us, from the career of an historic woman, whose conduct, nevertheless, differed from that of Diana essentially. Whether the author has triumphed perfectly over the immense difficulties of making from his historic model a true Diana, the reader must judge. Notable it is, and questionable, that her salvation, so to speak, is achieved, so far as appears, by the purest accident. After reading chapter xxv, one may be haunted by a certain weighty sentence (not in Johnsonese) of Dr Johnson's. Truly chapter xxvi may well drive that and everything else out of the mind. But—but—well, the reader must judge. I am not ashamed to say that I like Miss Asper, and am glad she married Dacier. So probably for my reasons or for others, is Mr Meredith. And I am sorry—is he?—for Mr Warwick.

# INDEX I

# INDEX II

*(Passages translated, quoted, or discussed)*